# The **APPLIQUE** Book

# The APPLIQUE Book

## by Charlotte Patera

⌂HL CREATIVE HOME LIBRARY®
In Association with Better Homes and Gardens®
Meredith Corporation

Patterns 32, 33, 49, 58, and 59 adapted from
*Design Motifs of Ancient Mexico* by Jorge Enciso,
Dover Publications, Inc., 1947.

 CREATIVE HOME LIBRARY®
© 1974 by Meredith Corporation, Des Moines, Iowa
All rights reserved
Printed in the United States of America
**Library of Congress Cataloging in Publication Data**
Patera, Charlotte, 1927–
    The appliqué book.
    Bibliography: p.
    1. Appliqué. I. Title.
TT779.P37 1974    746.4'4    73–19920
ISBN 0–696–11000–8

# About the Author

Before venturing into the world of needlecrafts eight years ago, Charlotte Patera enjoyed ten successful years as a package designer. It was in 1965 that she became inspired by the work of some of her contemporaries and discovered that her truly imaginative sense of design could be well expressed with fabrics, yarn, needle, and thread. In 1967 her work won the attention of one of the editors of *Better Homes and Gardens* magazine. Since then her designs have appeared in *Woman's Day, Ladies' Home Journal, Family Circle,* and *Good Housekeeping*. She now divides her time between designing projects for these magazines and preparing displays for art galleries. Her collection of Mexican, Central and South American, Indian, European, and early American folk art have had a great influence on her work. In addition to appliqué, and needlecrafts, Charlotte Patera enjoys bicycling, hiking, camping, skiing, exploring the West, experimenting with other crafts, and just being in the mountains. In fact, in earlier days she climbed the Grand Teton in Wyoming.

# Contents

# Introduction

Why have handcrafts, especially needlework, become so important in our present society? One theory is that throughout history, during times of abundance, needle decoration has always flourished. Refined ladies of wealth and royalty, having time on their hands, created richly encrusted tapestries, pillows, chair seats, and clothing. Is it our modern appliances and affluence that have given us leisure time for enriching our surroundings?

Pioneer women busily pieced together quilts from every scrap they could find to guard against the chill of a drafty log cabin. This work came from necessity, not from having idle hours to pursue a hobby. It was the way of life. Since they had to make them anyway, they chose to make them attractive. Our American Indians certainly prove that handcrafts do not result from luxury living.

Some of us prefer to believe that the present enthusiasm is a backlash of technology, a rebellion against the fast-paced, mass-produced, plastic world in which most of us find ourselves living. The current rate of technological progress is frightening! Spending long hours to create something beautiful, helps to slow the world down a bit. It also produces something that gives us back our individuality and assures us that our identity will not be lost forever in the form of a computer number. It keeps us from being victimized by the technology that we naïvely yearned for decades ago.

We are longing for the romance of the past. Antiquity, nostalgia, and old folkways have never seen such popularity. And so, needlework is flourishing again. The same technology and science that I speak of has also given us brilliant colors of fabric and yarn, which allow us to adapt needlecrafts to our contemporary environment.

This current trend began in the late 1950s and early 1960s. While Erica Wilson was leading embroiderers to new horizons, several celebrities were starting to bring new life to needlepoint. In California, Jean Ray Laury sat, quietly making her first quilt. Later she emerged as the leader of contemporary appliqué in the United States. Now quilt making is enjoying the latest, joyful renaissance.

Of the above-mentioned needlework techniques, appliqué has probably trailed behind embroidery and needlepoint. This is no doubt because of the fact that yarn shops are bursting with embroidery and needlepoint kits for those who want to feel the joy of creation but offer very few kits for

9

appliqué. Many people are therefore uncertain about it. It demands a little more effort and the proper fabrics and threads to assemble a design. Yet, many women sew clothing for their families and have already assembled many useful leftover scraps of fabric. They are already well equipped with the simple, necessary tools.

Appliqué is the process by which smaller pieces of cutout fabrics are secured to a larger background fabric. It is done with various methods of stitching. In this book, some of the designs depart from this basic definition. In reverse appliqué, cutouts are made in the background fabric and smaller pieces of the design are stitched behind the background and allowed to show through —just the reverse of traditional appliqué. Also included are designs that are glued for the "do-it-quick" projects.

I am probably drawn to appliqué because I've always loved simple, graphic forms rather than shaded painted effects. With appliqué, forms have to be kept to simple, solid shapes.

The intention of this book is to help you find the right project and open the door to appliqué for you. You may be a beginner with a pile of scraps or a seamstress, fully prepared. You may have become a "fabric addict," collecting more fabric in your closet than you could ever possibly use for the family clothing. Or you may be a needle expert with a strong desire to try the sophisticated reverse appliqué technique.

Enjoy the freedom of making changes in any design. If you need a different color scheme, go ahead and replace the colors given. If you want to use a different kind of fabric, do it. If you like one design but want to use a different technique for it, do whatever you wish. This book is meant to provide a starting place. You may follow the directions exactly, or you may prefer to experiment. You are encouraged to do anything to make the design your own. You may decide that a wall hanging idea would be nice on a skirt or a pocket. Take a pillow design and repeat it for draperies. If you like a design for a dress, try it on a pillow. Let your imagination whirl. If a design looks too intricate for you, omit some of the finer detail. If it is too simple, add whatever you like.

Do not feel compelled to plug away on one of the more tedious projects when your mind is on another one. Drop it as soon as it gets monotonous, and start a new one. You will find that you will have a fresh approach to the old project if you "take a vacation" from it. Work on several designs at once—two, three, or four. Some needlework jobs do get tiresome at times. Keeping several going at once will be more interesting.

Appliqué need not be a craft enjoyed by women only. Men should feel free to pick up a needle and try their hand at it. Long ago, Norman Laliberte put his whimsical designs into fabric. It is simply another medium to an artist, man or woman. Strong men from the African country of Dahomey appliquéd their bold designs without fretting about whether it would mar their masculine image. A brilliant young California teacher, Robert Gebhart, is, in his spare time, creating amazing appliquéd quilts with religious biblical themes. Why not? The desire to create with a specific medium should not be limited to one sex.

When Roosevelt Grier proudly displays his needlepoint on TV talk shows, he probably does much to liberate men from their reluctance to show an interest in the needle arts. No one is going to argue with him about what's masculine and what's feminine. Men find it just as relaxing as women do and are starting to join in on the fun. Children need less encouragement. They are eager to try anything creative. So how about some family projects?

# 1

# Facts on Fabrics, Tips on Tools, Hints on Techniques

## About Fabrics

The most important material in appliqué is the fabric. Experienced dressmakers are probably already very familiar with all the many kinds of fabric. Those who have not done much sewing will begin to acquire a "feel" for fabrics—what a certain fabric can and cannot do.

The background fabric should always be firm enough to support the fabrics applied to it. It can be either the same kind of fabric as that of the applied design or heavier. If, for some reason, a lighter fabric is desired for the background, it should be mounted to another fabric. Together they will support the design. This can be done by either basting them together around the edges or laminating one to the other with one of the iron-on bonding materials that is available by the yard.

Fabrics are made from either natural fibers, such as wool, cotton, flax, and silk, or from synthetic fibers, such as nylon, acetate, acrylic, and polyester. They fall into one of three categories—*woven, knit,* or *pressed*—depending upon which technique was used in manufacturing. You will be concerned primarily with these three categories.

*Woven:* Most of the fabrics we have been wearing all our lives fall into the woven category. Woven fabrics are those that are made through the interlacing of warp and woof—lengthwise and crosswise threads—on a loom. Different textures and patterns, such as checks, plaids, stripes, tweeds, twills, and jacquards, are achieved by varying the width or color of the threads and by the pattern of weaving.

These can also be printed with an almost endless variety of designs and colors. The list of woven fabrics with their descriptions could fill an entire book. Most of them are well suited for appliqué on a sewing machine. A fewer number can be used for hand appliqué. When you are choosing a woven fabric for appliqué, you should consider several factors. Is it too coarsely or loosely woven, so that it will ravel when cut into small pieces? Does it have enough body, or is it too flimsy? Is it too thick and heavy?

It is very frustrating to cut out pieces for appliqué only to find that they ravel before they can be sewn down permanently. If you have any doubts about how your chosen fabric will hold up, test a few scraps of it. Cut out a few shapes and sew them to a background scrap. All woven fabrics have raw edges when cut and are subject to some raveling. But, for a neat finish, these edges should not be visible.

The zigzag stitch on a sewing machine is one way to stitch and cover these edges. The more tightly woven the fabric is, the easier this is to do. Some very coarse, loosely woven fabrics are chopped up along the edges by the sewing machine action. Chiffon, crepe, China silk, and other light, flimsy fabrics are too difficult to work with. If a sheer effect is desired, use organdy, voile, dotted swiss, or batiste, all of which have enough body to be handled easily.

The range of woven fabrics that can be used for appliqué on the sewing machine is vast, indeed. Included are such contrasting textures as corduroy, peau de soie, homespun, brocade, velveteen, and seersucker. These are only a few of the fabrics that can be used to create the effect you wish. Very heavy fabrics, such as upholstery fabric, are well suited for backgrounds. And if the sewing machine can sew through them, they can also be used for the applied design.

In hand appliqué, the edges are turned under and whipped down with a needle and thread. Lightweight fabrics are preferred. Since thick, heavy fabrics usually end up having bulky edges, they should be avoided.

The best fabric for hand appliqué is inexpensive cotton broadcloth. It comes in a large variety of solid colors, stripes, prints, etc. I always keep a large supply of as many solid colors as I can find. I carry a swatch of each color in my purse so that when I am in a fabric store, I can check a color that I think is new against my samples to see whether I have this particular shade at home. I have about fifty colors. You may not find it necessary to collect that many, unless you want to continue doing a lot of appliqué by hand. Since it is quite inexpensive, it is easy to collect many colors, buying about one-third yard of each.

Other recommended fabrics are gingham, light sailcloth, Indian Head®, denim, or any fabric of a comparable weight. One of my favorites is KETTLE® CLOTH, a mixture of cotton and polyester. It is woven with threads that vary slightly in shade, giving it a "heather" look. This fabric is very well suited for hand appliqué and adapts to machine appliqué, as well. I find it convenient to keep a collection of assorted colors in KETTLE® CLOTH as well as in broadcloth.

*Knit:* If you visit a fabric shop today, you will notice that more and more space is being devoted to the display of knit fabrics. Because of their easy care and good looks, they are becoming more and more widely used for clothing, and there is no reason that they cannot also be used for appliqué.

Knits vary in their degree of stretchability. Those best suited for appliqué are the more stable knits, the ones with little stretchiness. Some knits, designed for clinging body wear, are quite stretchy and will not work for appliqué.

Very few knits have been used for the projects in this book. This is simply owing to the fact that I have not had many pieces leftover from dressmaking. Since they are generally more expensive, I hesitate to collect them as readily as I would the less expensive cotton weaves. I have also found that the result of using a knit for appliqué,

as opposed to a weave, is not interesting enough to warrant the larger cost. But, if you do have scraps left over from garments, by all means, use them.

In one of my experiments with knits, I made a discovery that will aid anyone who wishes to use them. I wanted to appliqué a decorative motif of woven fabric to the lower edge of a long knit skirt. When I first tested the idea, I was discouraged to find that because of the skirt's stretchiness, the applied design was very wavy. I then tried putting a thin piece of batiste behind the knit to give it more stability, and it worked. The motif lay evenly and flat. I then repeated this around the skirt. When it was completed, I trimmed away the excess batiste from the wrong side to eliminate as much weight as possible. This technique can be tried on any fabric that does not flatten well.

Knits are available in various weights. There are the supple jerseys, which are light single layers, and there are many kinds of double knits—fabric composed of two layers that have been locked together in the knitting process. These are available in many textures and can even have jacquard patterns knitted in. There are also bonded knits. These are knits that have been fused to another fabric to prevent stretching. Bonded knits can certainly be used for appliqué.

One advantage of working with knits is that their edges do not ravel as readily as woven edges do. They can all be used easily for machine appliqué, but very few of the lighter weights would be recommended for handwork when edges are to be turned under. In this case, they have no advantage over light woven fabrics. A further consideration is that some knits tend to roll along the edges, making them too difficult to use. If you have a good supply of knit scraps, you should experiment. And, since children seldom want to be bothered with turning edges under, knit scraps are made to order for teaching them how to appliqué.

*Pressed:* Pressed fabrics are made from mixed fibers, which, through the action of heat, moisture, and chemicals, are pressed flat. There are very few fabrics in this group, but it does include one of the most ideal for appliqué—felt. Felt is a favorite material for appliqué because once it has been cut, there are no rough edges to worry about. For this reason, it is especially good for beginners and children. Felt is fast to work with and is appreciated for its large range of available colors.

Another fabric in this group is pellon. Available in varied weights, it is like a very thin felt and is used primarily for interfacings and interlinings, which help give shape to garments. Because in dressmaking it is applied to the wrong side of the garment, it does not come in a range of colors—only black and white. It would be a wonderful appliqué fabric if colors were available. But, if you can use black or white in your design, you might find a place for it.

Most felts are made of 50 percent wool and 50 percent rayon. Sometimes you will find thinner types mixed in with the heavier ones, at the same price. These are suitable for the applied design but unless they are used double-strength, they tend to be too limp for the background.

One drawback of felt is that the colors may fade quickly if exposed to direct sunlight. Felt is very good for banners, seasonal decor, some clothing, and accessories as long as it does not get too much exposure to the sun. It can also be used for fine artwork, again provided that it will be hung in a place that doesn't receive too much sunlight. When felt is exposed to the rays of the sun, I have found that the range of yellows, golds, and oranges are the least affected, if at all, while strong blues and magentas are affected the most. In general, however, most colors will dull somewhat. The color that

fades the most is lavender. It will actually bleach almost to a white. I avoid it unless I am going to use it in an area that will receive no sunlight at all. Even then, I use only small accents of it. A new, synthetic felt is being developed, which will be washable. I hope this means that the colors will be sunfast also.

Felt is excellent for decorating children's rooms—wall ornaments, pillows, and stuffed animals—since children's items can be made quickly and have to last only until the child outgrows them. An active child's pillows or favorite stuffed toys may begin to show some wear, "fuzzing" or "pilling" on the surface, but new ones can be made quickly—that is, if you can coax him into parting with his toy.

In working with woven or knit fabrics, you come to learn about the grain of fabric. The lengthwise grain is called the *straight*. When you pull on the straight of a woven fabric, it will not "give"; in a stable knit it will give only slightly. However, the diagonal of both will stretch. This is called the *bias* of the fabric. As you cut out certain intricate shapes, you will have to cut across and sew on the bias of the fabric. Because of the stretching of the bias, you will find that it requires some practice and skill to sew these edges on a machine to avoid puckering and stretching. If you baste these edges first, it will be easier. As you sew, you can also use the point of a pin to ease the fabric in place. Actually, I do not mind a little puckering—it gives the piece a handmade look. This is not, however, to be confused with sloppy or careless work.

Since felt has no grain, this problem does not occur. When you have finished appliquéing a piece of felt, it may be rather wavy. When you press it, however, it will flatten beautifully. Since felt is a fabric that molds well—the reason it is used for hats—it also can be steam-pressed to lie flat.

It takes time, practice, and patience to

find the fabrics you enjoy using most. Certain fabrics, especially woolens, will flatten nicely when they are pressed. Others will stubbornly keep their puckers. Ultimately, you will discover the advantages or disadvantages of certain fabrics.

The width of most fabrics ranges from 42 to 45 inches. Cottons and linens sometimes come in 32- to 36-inch widths, and wools are usually 52 to 56 inches wide.

Felt is available in generous 72-inch widths, but is also sold in convenient smaller pieces—usually in rectangles measuring 9 by 12 inches. Some specialty shops sell larger and smaller sizes. If you are using only a small amount of a certain color of felt and are not planning to use that color in the future, it may be more economical to buy the small rectangles.

*Other materials:* There are a few other materials you may want to use in your appliqué. You may have on hand some scraps of leather or leatherlike fabrics. I have met with some difficulty using leather, but if you like it, you may want to use a few scraps or make a whole design of leather appliqué.

Some fabrics are manufactured to look as much like leather as possible. These include vinyls, in both shiny and dull finishes, Naugahyde®, and suedelike fabrics. These fabrics can add more texture to your work.

There are also many metallic fabrics that can add a dramatic touch to your work. Always test these fabrics before you plan your design. Try to appliqué them with the machine. If you have difficulty, you may find hand sewing is best.

You may want to use lace or net. If you have leftover trims, such as rickrack, lace edgings, ribbon, or braid, you may find the perfect place to use them as accents. Sometimes buttons, beads, sequins, or other trims can be added. Some designs in this book are based on needlework from India, which incorporates small mirrors in the designs. I substitute sequins, cut-up aluminum cooking tins, or a material from an art-supply store called metallic mylar. You may find other interesting materials to add to your work.

## About Tools

*Needles:* For hand appliqué, I suggest crewel needles. They are sold in packages of assorted sizes—from 1 to 5 for yarn and from 5 to 10 for thread. You can decide for yourself which size is best for you. I like crewel needles because they have large eyes.

For machine work, your sewing machine manual will specify sizes to use according to fabric to be sewn. If you are working with knits, you may want to use a ball-point needle. This is a needle that goes between the threads of the knit instead of through them. It should be used if you find that the thread keeps breaking with your regular needle. There is also a special needle for leatherwork, with a triangular, wedge-shaped point.

*Thread:* Mercerized cotton thread or polyester thread may be used for appliqué work. If the article is to be washed, a polyester thread is recommended. Cotton thread may shrink when washed, causing undesirable puckering of the fabric. Polyester thread, on the other hand, has great stretch and recovery qualities because it was originally intended for use with knits.

For machine felt appliqué, I like to use color-blending, nylon filament thread. It is such a thin thread—almost invisible—that it makes a very inconspicuous stitch. Although it works well with felt, it tends to pull on other fabrics, so that it requires a great deal of tension adjusting on your machine to use it successfully. Although many manufacturers use it for making clothing, it is not recommended for this because the exposed sharp ends irritate the skin. Another drawback is its stiff, wiry quality. It tends to "spring" and catch onto various parts of the threading and bobbin mechanism of your machine and can sometimes jam it. However, when it does run smoothly, there is nothing like the neat effect it gives to felt appliqué. You should experiment with it. I do not recommend it for handwork, but I've known people who do use it.

*Scissors:* Good, sharp scissors are essential for appliqué. When cutting large pieces of fabric, use dressmaker's shears. For handwork, small embroidery scissors are needed. To ensure a long life for your scissors, do not use them for cutting anything other than fabric, especially paper. In this way they will stay sharp longer. Pinking shears are handy for certain effects.

*Pins:* Straight pins are used to hold the design pieces in position until they are sewn.

*Thimble:* Some handworkers cannot sew without a thimble, while others cannot sew with one. I belong to the latter group. If you do use one, make sure it fits and is practical. Some of the more attractive ones are not. For those who do not feel mobile with one, try a piece of adhesive tape on the tip of the middle finger for protection.

*Ruler and yardstick:* It is important to be able to make accurate measurements. Metal tape measures are useful for work on items larger than 3 feet. An L-shaped ruler or a draftsman's triangle may be used for squaring corners, but these last two items are not essential.

*Paper:* You will need some kind of blank paper with which to enlarge the patterns from this book. Used wrapping paper, if unwrinkled, can be used, or it can be purchased in rolls. For patterns that exceed the width of the paper, tape several pieces together. For smaller patterns, pads of tracing paper or newsprint from art-supply shops are handy. They come in 9- by 12-, 11- by 14-, and 14- by 17-inch sizes.

*Tracing wheel and carbon:* Dressmaker's tracing carbon and wheel are sold at notions counters. Sometimes they are packaged together. The directions are simple. The pattern is taped to the fabric, with the carbon paper placed between them, carbon side facing the fabric. To trace, you roll a wheel, which has points evenly spaced along its edge, along the outline. These points transfer small carbon dots to the fabric for you to follow. (Drawing with a pencil would tear the paper.) Tiny details that cannot be done with the wheel can be traced by making a dotted line with a pencil point. Some dressmaker's carbon papers produce dots that can be washed out. These are barely visible, however, so I prefer the permanent type. The package will indicate whether it is washable or not.

A package of carbon contains both colored and white sheets. Select a color that will show up well against your fabric. Do not use typing carbon, since it may smudge.

*Chalk:* Notions counters sell tailor's chalk and chalk pencils. Tailor's chalk comes in a thin square, with two of its edges coming to points. It comes four pieces to a package, in white and two colors. It is handy for marking corners and edges for cutting. Chalk pencils, which have a brush on one end for erasing, are good for sharpening your traced design if it begins to rub off.

*Miscellaneous:* Other necessary items, which are probably part of your household already, are the following: steam iron, tape (cellophane or masking), felt-tipped pen, pencils, and white glue. Other supplies are listed with the design, as required.

## Collecting Fabric

I have mentioned various fabrics that I collect. You may not feel the necessity to "collect" fabrics, preferring to buy only what you need for a specific project. But if you find yourself getting really involved with appliqué, you will be collecting before you know it.

I have already mentioned that I collect broadcloth and KETTLE® CLOTH pieces. I also collect felt pieces—it is convenient to have a certain color at your fingertips when you need it. You may want to buy only fractions of a yard so that you can have a small amount of many colors. Generally, I do not collect expensive fabrics unless I find a good buy on a remnant that I know I will use. I also watch the remnant tables in fabric shops. Sometimes a nice background fabric can be found at a bargain. Occasionally, decorator shops will sell samples of upholstery fabrics. These can make excellent backgrounds for appliquéd pictures, hangings, pillows, etc.

Besides the previously mentioned fabrics, I also collect samples of certain patterns that appeal to me, such as geometrics, small provincial prints, and designs of an exotic or ethnic nature. Since certain designs pass in and out of fashion, I try to buy as many as I can when they are "in," to use when they are not. For instance, many years ago I tried to buy provincial prints, but they were impossible to find. When patchwork and country fashions became popular, however, provincial prints were plentiful. I have now bought many to use later on when they are not so popular.

Collecting fabric can be almost an addiction among women who sew. Having a variety of fabrics on hand will make your work less limited. A few collected fabrics from shops, along with a supply of leftover scraps from garment making, will probably be all you need. The one danger of buying fabric when you do not have a specific project in mind for it is that you don't know how much to buy. Often, long after a fabric is no longer available, I discover that I could have used more of it. Sometimes a print or geometric will become such a favorite of mine that as I use the last of it, I sadly regret not having bought more. I find myself trying to use every last bit of it, without any waste.

## Selecting Colors

The subject of color selection seems to be puzzling and sometimes frightening to many people. Some people seem to have natural feel for color while others are very unsure.

Ideas about color come and go with passing fashion trends. When some of us grew up, we learned that purple and red were never to be used together. Although a light shade of it called "peach" was accepted, orange was completely taboo. Nowadays purple, red, and orange are often used together, happily.

Many of us as children knew only of pastels. Bright colors were considered gaudy. Then, suddenly many colors entered our lives. Fabrics were being designed in "daring" new colors. Interior and fashion designers had a larger range to use. Now, any and all colors are taken for granted by the young. Along with the brilliant ones that are the result of advanced dyeing techniques, there is also a place for the muted, or "dusty," colors.

In selecting colors, I find it very helpful to place the available colors in an order, following the colors of the spectrum. I have done this with paints, pencils, chalks, yarns, fabrics, etc. This helps make clear just what you have to work with, and it reduces any confusion.

We have all learned about color in school. We have used the words *primary, secondary, tertiary, analagous,* and *monochromatic.* These are dull words for such an exciting subject as color. I suggest you forget them.

I find most of the color formulas written up in various books unsatisfactory. Although they may work for some groups of color, they do not work for others.

One safe way to deal with color, at this time, is to select colors that are near each other on the spectrum wheel. (See chart.)

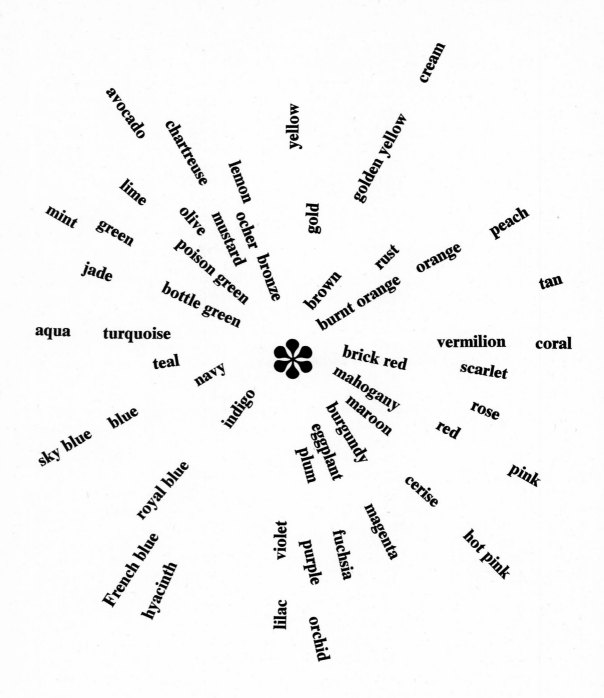

cream

avocado
chartreuse
yellow
golden yellow

lemon
lime
ocher
mustard
gold
peach

mint
green
olive
bronze
brown
orange

jade
poison green
rust
burnt orange
tan

bottle green
vermilion
coral

aqua
turquoise
brick red
scarlet

teal
mahogany
rose

navy
maroon
red

indigo
burgundy
cerise
pink

sky blue
blue
eggplant
plum
magenta
hot pink

royal blue
violet
fuchsia

French blue
hyacinth
lilac
purple
orchid

18

Point to red and you will find magenta, hot pink, brick red, and scarlet close by. This is an exciting color range. You can use this method all around the wheel. The colors selected this way are always related to each other. They have a common ingredient that holds them together. In this group the common ingredient is red.

If you sometimes want to get a little more dynamic with your colors to break up the monotony of a close-hued scheme, you can start with a series of these colors and then go across the wheel to one or more of their opposites.

If you have doubts about color, start a file of clippings of color schemes that excite you. Whenever you find a beautiful color scheme in a magazine, clip it out and save it. When you buy a print fabric you like in many colors, save a swatch of it for the file. Then, when you duplicate the color scheme, try to keep the same proportions of color as in the swatch, unless, of course, you want to experiment. When you start emphasizing one of the colors in the swatch over the other, however, you may get disappointing results.

I prefer to work with clear, bright color, but I also enjoy some schemes that are made from a blend of light pastels or dark, muted combinations. Besides the hue of each color, there are two other dimensions to consider —dullness and brightness; and lightness and darkness. These qualities of color can sometimes create chaos in a color scheme. You may have what you think is a very bright, clear color. But sometimes, when put next to another color, it may look very dull. Colors can enhance or kill each other. It is a matter of feeling out what looks good.

Dark, dingy colors may not be what you like. But if you love bright colors, you may find that one of those dull colors is just what you need to enhance the bright ones. A dull color, like mustard or olive, may be one you don't care to have around you. But when used with bits of clear, vivid color the results are often fascinating.

As exciting as bright colors are, they often are their own worst enemies when used as backgrounds for other bright colors. Black (the lack of color) has a way of enhancing rich color better than any color can. If you try to use bright colors with bright backgrounds, the result may be a gaudy or raw effect, hard to view calmly. When bright colors are desired for backgrounds, it is advisable to limit the appliqué to one or two colors. Bright colors seldom enhance other colors when used as backgrounds.

There are times when you want to observe certain traditions in color to retain some authenticity—red, white, and blue; the colors of a flag of a certain country, school, or family crests; etc. Sometimes certain colors are used symbolically, such as the liturgical colors of the church used for various seasons. Although Christmas designs are now done in many color schemes, you may prefer to stay with the traditional red and green. In the American Indian chair seat design, Pattern 44, colors were chosen in keeping with a type of inlay jewelry. This jewelry, which is made by the Indians of the Zuñi Pueblo, consists of coral, turquoise, shell, and jet.

Color is very important in a design. I have seen excellent examples of craftsmanship in various needlework pieces whose colors prevented them from lingering in one's mind. The colors chosen kept them within the realm of mediocrity. It takes time to shop for fabrics in the color you desire. It also takes years of selecting and collecting fabrics to have a full selection at your fingertips. Colors in fabrics come in and out of fashion. Sometimes the ones you want are not to be found and a good substitute must be chosen.

## Enlarging Designs

All the patterns shown in this book are

**Diagram 1**

marked off in squares. (See Diagram 1.) To enlarge a pattern, use a ruler or yardstick and paper (as suggested on page 16). The size of the paper needed will depend on the size of the pattern. Draw squares to the size indicated under step 1 of the pattern. Make the same number of squares across and down as shown in the pattern. Now, copy the design with a pencil, square by square. You may have to go over it several times to make the lines flow smoothly. For this reason, a pencil, not a pen, should be used at first. When the design is complete, make a permanent line with a felt-tipped pen. You may erase the pencil lines if you wish. The broken lines in the patterns indicate hidden edges that will be underlapped. Your pattern is now ready to be traced. (See Diagram 2.)

If you have confidence in your drawing ability, simply enlarge the design by eye if you wish. You may even want to make some slight changes.

The following are mechanical ways of enlarging patterns to be used. If you have access to one of these machines, use it as it will save time. In all these methods, the squares are ignored.

*Pantograph:* Art-supply stores sell an instrument called a pantograph. If you plan to enlarge or reduce many designs, it may be worth the investing in one. It comes with instructions for its use.

*Camera:* If you have a 35-millimeter camera, use it to take a close-up picture of the pattern in the book, using film that produces slides. Project the slide of the pattern on the wall, adjusting it as best you can to the proper size. Tape paper to the wall and trace the pattern. Any distortion to the pattern through this process can be corrected in tracing. Before you trace, mark off the perimeter of the design on the paper to the required size (as specified in step 1 for each design). Try to project the slide to the dimensions that you have marked.

*Photostat:* Another way of enlarging is to have the design blown up by a photostat company. If there is a photostat house nearby, find out the cost. It may be much too expensive, unless you share the design with a group, thus dividing the expense. Because of the limitations of a photostat machine, it may be necessary to have several enlargements made before it is the size you wish. Each step of enlarging adds to the total cost. The end result may be a white pattern on black but that need not make any difference.

*Luci:* If you happen to have a friend who is a commercial artist and who works in an art studio or large art department, ask him if he has access to a "luci" machine. Most commercial art studios have one. By placing the sketch or photograph in the machine and pressing the proper buttons, the artist

**Diagram 2**

can either enlarge or reduce the sketch to the size he needs. If you do have such a friend, perhaps he would take the time to make an enlarged tracing for you.

## Gluing Designs

Many of the projects in this book require gluing. There are several products on the market that may be used:

*Rubber cement* is an excellent adhesive for appliqué use. The cut fabric pieces are turned over and the cement is applied to the backs. The pieces are then pressed in place. Keep area well ventilated when using.

*White glue* is readily available in art-supply, craft, hardware, and dime stores. Dilute it with water and apply to backs of fabric with paintbrush for best results.

*Fabric glue* is different from a white glue only in that it does not stiffen quite as much when dry. It is brushed on the backs of the cut pieces. Both must be put on with care, though. If too much is used, it will show through to the front side. However, the piece should be completely covered. If the glue is just dabbed on, the dabbed spots will show, differing in appearance from the undabbed parts. This will give a very homemade, unprofessional appearance to your item. Fabric glue is sold in fabric, art-supply, and craft shops.

*Iron-on bonding material* is sold in fabric shops under various brand names, all of which come with directions for use. It is sold by the yard in various widths and in prepackaged lengths, as tapes. It is placed between the two fabrics to be adhered. The heat of an iron pressed over it adheres the fabrics together. Some must be cut to fit the appliquéd shape before ironing. Others are ironed on to the material to be appliquéd before the shape is cut. A backing paper is then removed and the shape is ironed on to the background fabric. Avoid getting any of it on the iron, as it is difficult to remove.

*Instant adhesive* comes in a tube, the size of a large lipstick. It is handy to work with because of its small size and the glue never touches your fingers.

## Framing and Finishing Designs

*Stretching:* Before a piece of appliqué work can be framed, it must be stretched over a backing. This can be done by using either artist's canvas stretcher bars or a ¼-inch-thick piece of plywood or pressed hardboard.

Stretcher bars are available at art-supply stores. They come in sizes ranging every inch, from 8 to 40 inches; and every 2 inches, from 40 to 72 inches. Their interlocking corners enable them to fit together. Since they are made standard, a set purchased at one store will fit a set purchased at another. They must, however, be purchased in pairs. Four bars are needed—two for the length and two for the width. The keys that come with the bars are hammered into slots inside the corners and are used to stretch out wrinkles for an extra taut fit.

The ¼-inch plywood or pressed hardboard is available at lumberyards. It must be cut to the size of the completed work. There is an extra charge if the lumberyard cuts it for you.

The bars are locked together by inserting corners into each other, as shown in Diagram 3. Place the design over the locked bars, matching the corner marks of the de-

**Diagram 3**

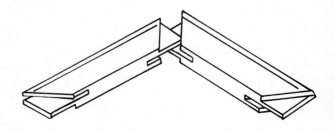

22

sign to the corners of the bars. Place a thumbtack or pushpin at each corner and in the middle of each long side to hold it in position. (See Diagram 4.)

Stand it on one end, bring fabric over to back, and using a heavy-duty staple tacker, staple it to middle of top bar. (See Diagram 5.) Repeat this for other sides. Remove tacks and lay face down. (See Diagram 6.)

Place staples all along the sides on back, stretching fabric as you staple. Make several folds, one over the other, on corners and staple securely. (See Diagram 7.) To remove some of the bulk, extra fabric may be trimmed away.

If any wrinkles remain on front, hammer keys into inside corner slots. This will expand the bars to make the fabric more taut. (See Diagram 8.)

Plywood or pressed hardboard is handled

**Diagram 4**

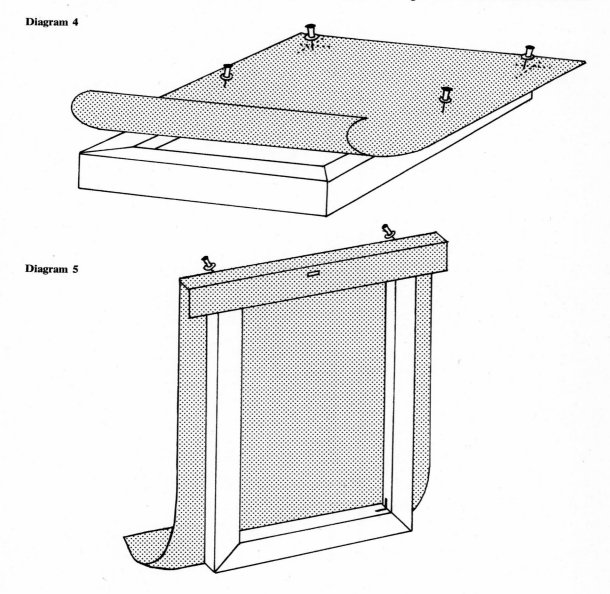

**Diagram 5**

23

**Diagram 6**

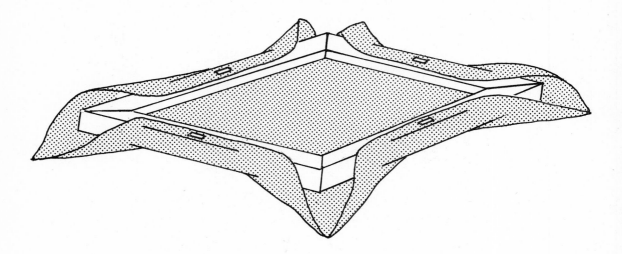

**Diagram 7**

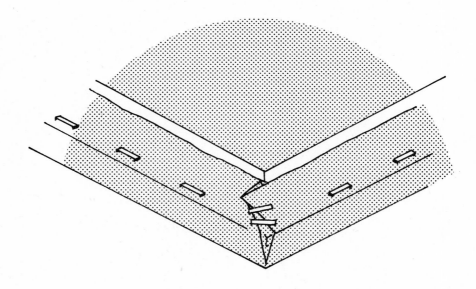

the same way as the stretcher bars. The only difference is that there is no way to make the fabric more taut after stapling other than by removing staples, stretching fabric tighter, and restapling. Whenever you are stretching, be careful not to pull the design out of shape.

The decision whether to use lumber or stretcher bars will depend on the frame. Since stretcher bars are ¾ inch thick, they can be used only if the frame is deep enough to accommodate them. If the frame is deep, either method may be used. But if the frame is shallow, you will have to use the ¼-inch

**Diagram 8**

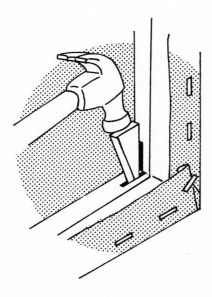

plywood or hardboard. Heavy cardboard is suitable if the completed work is quite small —12 by 16 inches or smaller. It is easier to cut than lumber. A mat knife or single-edged razor blade can be used instead of a saw.

Sometimes it is a good idea to place a sheet of white cardboard between the fabric

and the stretcher bars or plywood before you staple. This is recommended when the fabric is so thin that the color is dulled when placed directly on plywood or pressed board. The cardboard will also serve to hide the inside edge of the bars in case it shows through.

*Framing:* There are several ways to select a frame. The easiest, but most costly, way is to have one custom-made by a professional frame maker. If you decide to do this, it would be a good idea to discuss with him which frame molding would best suit your design. Then let him decide whether he would prefer the work stretched over bars or plywood.

Ready-made frames are available in standard sizes. If the work is a standard size, this is probably the easiest and most economical way to frame it. Frames are usually available in the following standard sizes: 5 by 7 inches, 8 by 10 inches, 9 by 12 inches, 11 by 14 inches, 12 by 16 inches, 12 by 24 inches, 16 by 20 inches, 18 by 24 inches, 20 by 24 inches, 24 by 30 inches, 24 by 36 inches, and 24 by 48 inches.

Another possibility is to make your own frame. Moldings are available at lumberyards and frame shops. There are books on the subject of frame making if you, or a friend, or relative are handy that way.

Still another alternative is to buy precut mitered moldings and assemble the frame yourself. Although the selection is somewhat limited, art-supply stores and frame shops usually carry a line. They come with easy directions for assembling.

*Matting:* A mat is a wide border that separates the work from the frame, usually 2 to 4 inches in width. You may want to add one to your work. It can help make a simple design look more impressive.

I usually add a mat if the design tends to be very busy, and especially if it comes to the edge. A mat helps to give the work breathing space. Pattern 29 illustrates this

25

point. If the design is centered, with a good area of background surrounding it, a mat may not be necessary. Pattern 4 is an example of this type of work. Whether you want to add a mat or not is purely a matter of personal taste.

For custom-made frames, the frame maker will have samples of neutral or white linens and possibly some subtle colors. If you want to use one of the fabrics from the design for the mat, simply provide the frame maker with the fabric. This must be done tastefully. Be careful not to overpower the design. It should enhance, not detract from, it.

Some ready-made frames come with mats already built into them.

If you prefer to make your own frame, a frame book will give instructions on how to construct and cover the mat.

*Finishing:* Once your work is stretched and your frame is ready, place the stretched work into the frame, using picture-frame nails to carefully hammer it in. Be sure not to pierce the front or sides of the frame.

I always like to staple a sheet of cardboard or corrugated board to the back of the framed work. This serves two purposes. If the work was stretched on bars, it will be better protected against damage if it is being transported. Cardboard also hides the back of the work or the staples and rough edges, giving it a more professional touch.

Place a screw eye on each side of the back of frame. (They can be purchased from a hardware store.) Place them at the same distance—from 2 to 4 inches—from top. Cut a length of picture-frame wire about 8 inches longer than the horizontal dimension of the frame. Insert this through the screw eyes and twist the ends securely so that the weight of the hanging work will not pull them apart. The ends of the wire should be covered with masking tape to prevent the sharp ends from scratching anyone.

## Cleaning and Caring for Appliqué

Spray-on fabric protector is recommended for all items that are not washable. This will help to retard soilage.

Wall hangings and other accessories for the home usually collect dust. These can be lightly vacuum dusted. If you live in an area where soot is part of your environment, you may want to put glass over your framed wall hanging. It is better, however, to avoid using the glass, since it detracts from the textural effect.

Covers for pillows should be removed and either dry-cleaned or washed. Whether an item should be washed or dry-cleaned is controversial. Today, people are inclined to put everything made of cotton into the washing machine. I am of the opinion that constant washing of most cotton and cotton mixtures gradually removes their original color and crispness. I certainly would suggest dry cleaning for clothing. I would not like to risk ruining a handmade dress that has taken hours to complete, by washing it. Unless it is a synthetic knit, with a simple design done by machine, I would not wash it. I often put soft items into the coin-operated dry-cleaning machines. This is again a matter of choice. Some items, such as table linens and children's wear, are made to withstand washing, but if the item is handmade, it should be gently hand-washed.

If felt hangings are to be stored, it is suggested that they be rolled with the design side out. This will avoid wrinkling of the applied pieces.

# Eight Basic Techniques

In this chapter, eight designs are presented to demonstrate the basic techniques used throughout the book. They are

**Technique 1:** Appliqué without stitching
**Technique 2:** Appliqué with felt by sewing machine
**Technique 3:** Appliqué with felt by hand
**Technique 4:** Appliqué with felt using French knots
**Technique 5:** Appliqué with woven fabric by sewing machine
**Technique 6:** Appliqué with woven fabric by hand
**Technique 7:** Reverse appliqué, method 1
**Technique 8:** Reverse appliqué, method 2

Each pattern in the following chapters will refer, by number, to the appropriate technique to be used. There are several variations of the above techniques.

The first projects involve the fastest and easiest methods and gradually advance into the more difficult and time-consuming techniques. You may choose one of the first designs to start with because it is fast or because you are a beginner. If you are already experienced with sewing and like the carved, dimensional look of reverse appliqué, you may want to start there. If you do each one step-by-step, you will have completed a course and become an adept appliqué craftsman, able to complete any design in this book. Some of the designs presented are very time-consuming, but if time is of an utmost concern, there should be a project for you, too.

# Castle in the Sky

*(Technique 7)*

*This castle design is for the child who is intrigued by stories of castles, knights, and chivalry. It is appliquéd with glue and can be hung in your child's room only a few hours after you have begun. No sewing is necessary. This is a design that a child might enjoy doing.*

### Materials
1 felt rectangle, 21 by 27 inches, in blue
1 felt square, 15 by 15 inches, in orange
1 felt rectangle, 5 by 14 inches, in hot pink
9- by 12-inch rectangles or scraps of felt in turquoise, light purple, magenta, and deep magenta
(If rectangles are purchased, buy 1 of each color.)

28

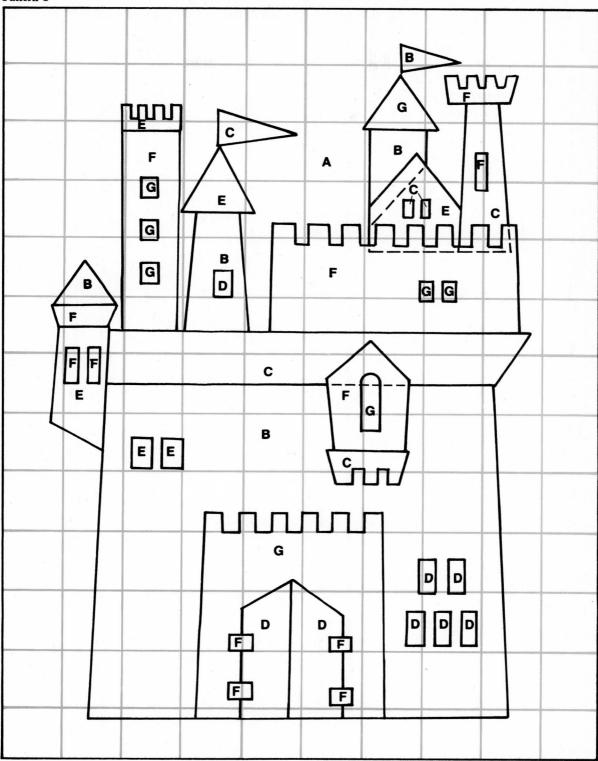

glue

20 inches buckram tape, 4-inch width (Sold where drapery hardware is sold, this is used for stiffening the tops of draperies.)

2 metal grommets (These are usually packaged with a small anvil for hammering them in place, although some require eyelet pliers, and are sold at notions counters.)

**Completed size:** 20 by 26 inches

**Color code:** A—blue, B—orange, C—hot pink, D—turquoise, E—light purple, F—magenta, G—deep magenta

Diagram 9

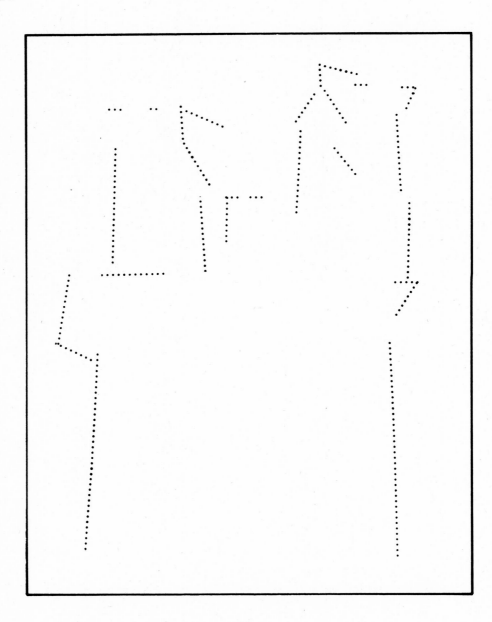

## Instructions

1. Enlarge pattern according to instructions given on page 19. Each square equals 2 inches. The enlarged pattern should measure 20 by 26 inches.

2. Press felt pieces with steam iron.

3. Tape enlarged pattern to blue felt background so that there is at least ½ inch of felt surrounding the design. (Extra allowance is given to compensate for any "drawing up" of fabric. It will be trimmed off when the hanging is completed.) Follow directions on page 16 for use of tracing wheel and carbon. Make marks on the blue felt to indicate placement of the castle pieces, as shown in Diagram 9. Untape pattern.

4. Tape orange felt to the back of pattern behind the main piece of the castle (marked B), and trace the outline. Make marks to indicate placement of smaller shapes within, as shown in Diagram 10. Remove the felt and cut out traced shape. Trace other orange shapes on remaining scrap of felt. This will mean that before tracing, the felt must be moved and taped to pattern behind each spot marked with a B.

5. In the same manner, trace all other shapes onto felt pieces as indicated on pattern. Cut out all pieces.

6. Lay out the design, placing all pieces in position.

7. Spread out some newspapers. Working with the underneath pieces first, such as the main section of the castle and the towers, transfer pieces from the design onto the newspaper, face down. Apply glue. Lift pieces one by one and press down firmly in proper position on blue background. Repeat this for each piece, making sure that the piece to go underneath it has already been placed into position.

8. Lift up design to see whether any pieces fall off. Reglue any loose pieces.

9. Place pattern over design and mark at corners on blue background. Remove pattern and connect the corner marks with a chalk line, using a yardstick for a guide. Cut carefully along the line.

10. Turn design over. Apply glue to buckram tape and press to upper edge of back of design. Turn back to front side, and place a grommet in each of the upper corners, following instructions that come with the grommets. The design is now ready for hanging.

**Diagram 10**

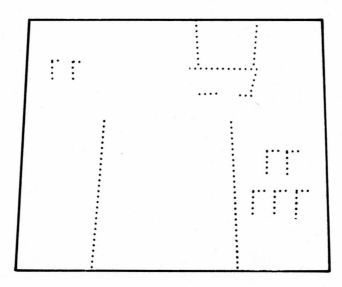

31

# Toby the Turtle

*(Technique 2)*

This happy little turtle waddles over a field of flowers to brighten a child's room. He is stitched together with two kinds of machine stitching, straight and zigzag. If your machine has only a straight stitch, ignore the zigzag stitching and use the straight stitch throughout. Stitching through, instead of around, the flowers gives them a dimensional look. This is also faster and easier.

### Materials

1 felt rectangle, 20 by 25 inches, in orange
1 felt rectangle, 10 by 18 inches, in turquoise
9- by 12-inch rectangles or scraps of felt in blue, hot pink, magenta, dark green, and white (If rectangles are purchased, buy 1 of each color.)
glue
thread in white, black, or orange or in clear nylon
23½ inches dowel rod, ¼ inch in diameter
yarn needle
30 inches yarn, in any compatible color
25 inches edging, up to ¾ inch wide, in any contrasting color (optional)

**Completed size:** 18 by 24 inches
**Color code:** H—orange, I—turquoise, J—blue, K—hot pink, L—magenta, M—dark green, N—white

### Instructions

1. Enlarge pattern according to instruc-

**Pattern 2**

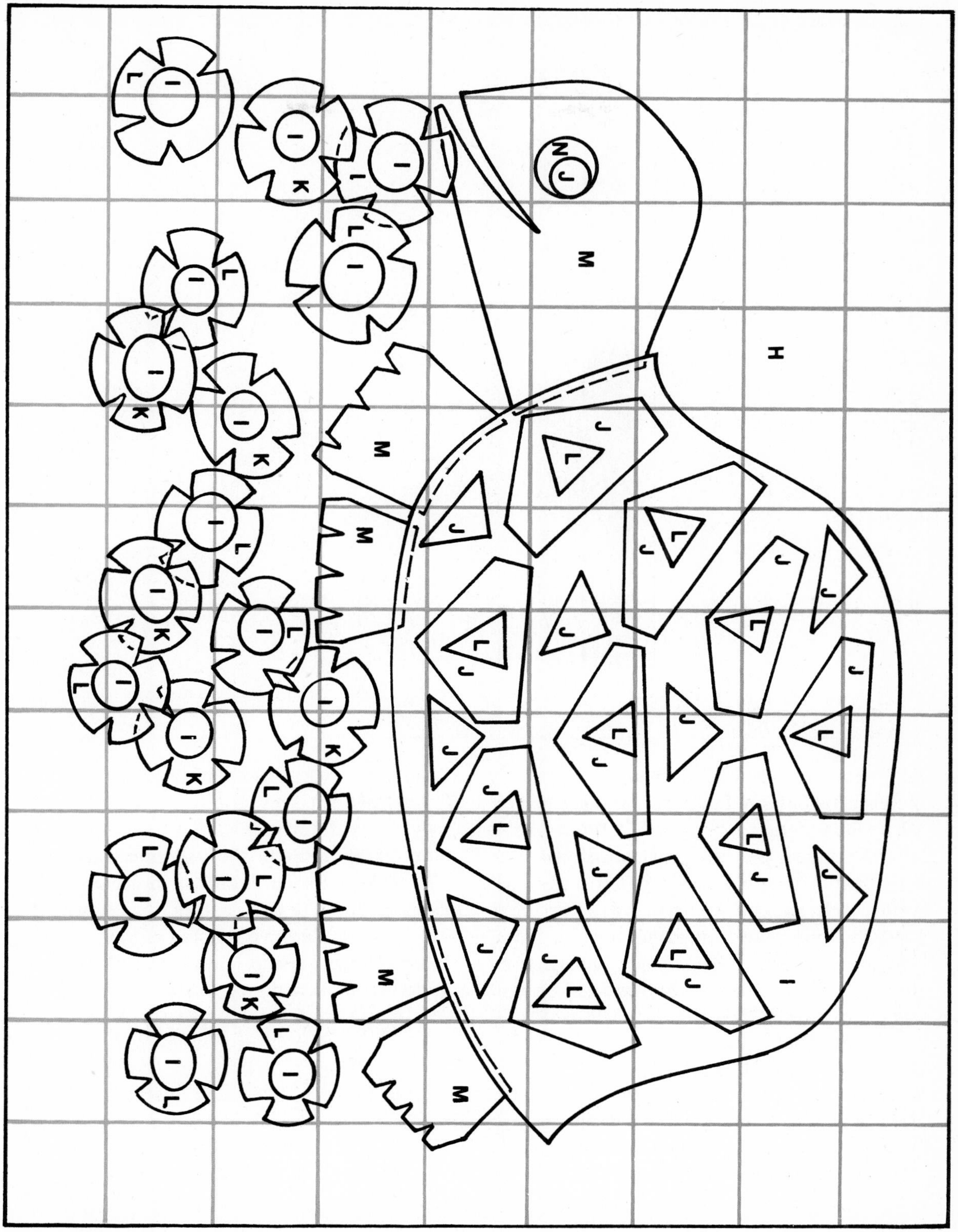

**Diagram 11**

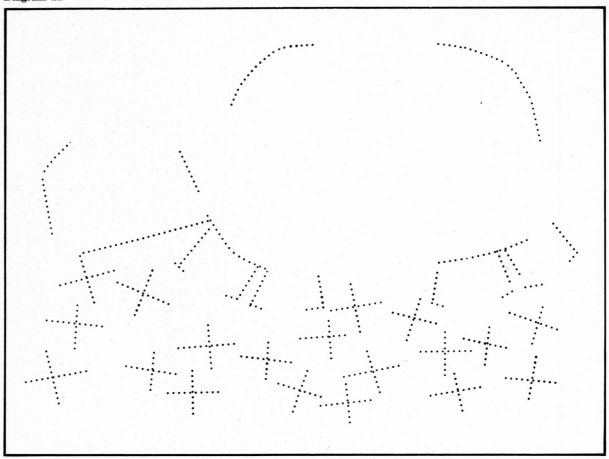

tions on page 19. Each square equals 2 inches. The enlarged pattern should measure 18 by 24 inches.

2. Press felt pieces with steam iron.

3. Tape the enlarged pattern to the orange felt background so that there is at least ½ inch of felt surrounding the sides and bottom and a 1½-inch allowance on the top. (Extra allowance is given to compensate for any "drawing up" of the fabric. It will be trimmed off when the hanging is completed. The allowance at the top is for underlapping and insertion of the dowel.) Follow directions on page 16 for use of tracing wheel and carbon. Make marks on the orange felt to indicate placement of the turtle and flowers, as shown in Diagram 11. Untape pattern.

4. Tape the turquoise felt to the back of pattern behind the turtle shell, and trace outline. Make sufficient marks to indicate placement of shell details within, as shown in Diagram 12. Remove felt and cut out traced shape. Without tracing first, cut out nineteen circles from remaining orange felt. Diameters may vary from ¾ inch to 1¼ inches. The amount in each size is immaterial.

5. To trace remaining shapes, tape appropriate colors to pattern back behind the pieces to be traced. Trace a few flower shapes on magenta and hot pink and cut out. The cut ones can now serve as models from

which to cut the remaining flowers. Trace and cut the blue wedge shapes, the blue and magenta triangles, and the dark green head and feet. Cut a white circle 1¼ inches in diameter and a blue one ¾ inch in diameter.

6. Lay out the design, placing all pieces in position. Glue the magenta triangles to the blue wedge shapes. Glue the white eye circle on the turtle's head and the blue circle within the white. Pin down all shapes. Allow ½ hour for glue to set thoroughly.

7. Using medium-width zigzag stitch set at 10 stitches to the inch, stitch the edge of the head and side edges of feet. Use straight stitch at any stitch length to sew on bottoms of feet, going straight across, above the toes. Sew around the edge of the shell with zigzag stitch and the wedge shapes with straight stitch. For the blue triangles, use a straight stitch and sew down the middle and the two sides. Sew two diagonals across the middle of the flowers, bisecting the petals.

8. Carefully steam press the design. Fold the top edge over 1½ inches and press the fold.

9. Place pattern over design and mark at the corners on orange background. Remove pattern and connect the corner marks with a chalk line, using yardstick for guide. Cut carefully along the line. If you are using edging, sew it along the bottom edge, turning its ends to the back side.

10. Sew along top, ½ inch from folded edge, to form a slot. Sew one end of slot closed. Insert dowel rod and sew the other end closed. Thread needle with yarn and knot the end. Attach to one corner of top. Bringing yarn over, attach to other top corner and knot. The wall hanging is complete.

**Diagram 12**

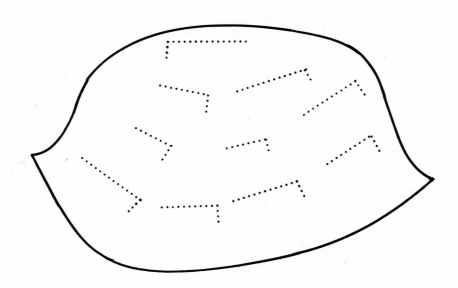

## Pattern 3: Wall Hanging

# Let the Sun Shine

*(Technique 3)*

*Your ecology-minded teen-ager might enjoy hanging this design in his room, or perhaps even making it himself. It would also go nicely in a family or recreation room.*

*The felt pieces of this design are secured in place with two kinds of stitches: the running stitch and whip stitch. Both are very simple. Diagram 13 shows the running stitch with variations. The needle is simply brought in and out of the fabric. The stitches may be tiny and far apart or long and close together. Diagram 14 shows the whip stitch. The stitch may be long or short and it may be spaced as far apart from the next one as you wish. It is used for the circles in the design.*

*A variation of the running stitch is shown in Diagram 15. It is made by lacing yarn through the stitches. It gives some variety and interest to the veins of the leaves on the left side.*

*Although these are very easy stitches to execute, it might be a good idea to practice them on some scraps so that you can arrive at a uniform stitch.*

*In this design, the felt is doubled by folding it in the middle. This is done to hide the knots made when the stitching is done on the front and to give the back a neat look. The thinner type of felt can be used for the background, but heavier felt will also work.*

**Diagram 13**

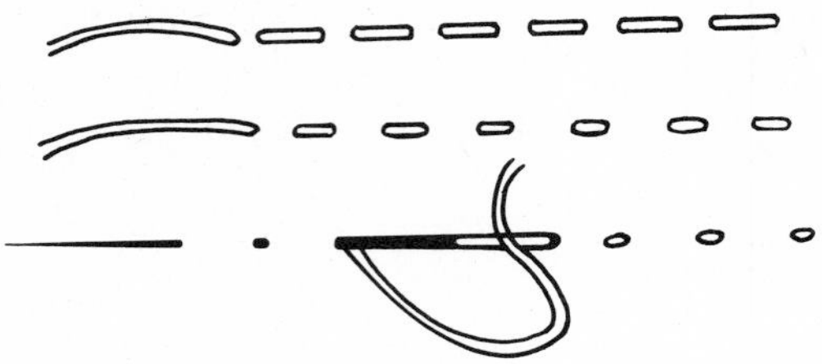

**Diagram 14**

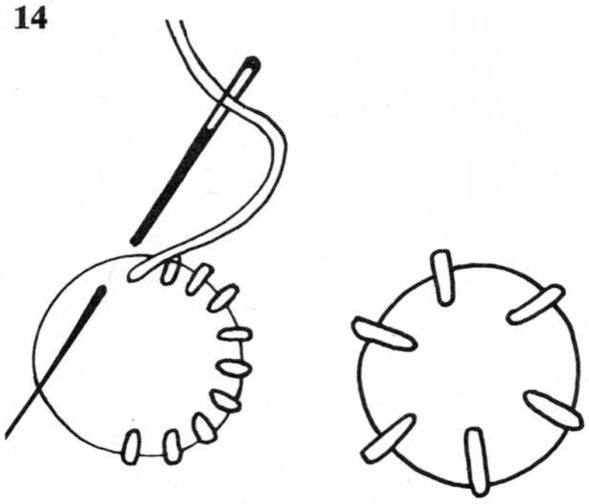

**Diagram 15**

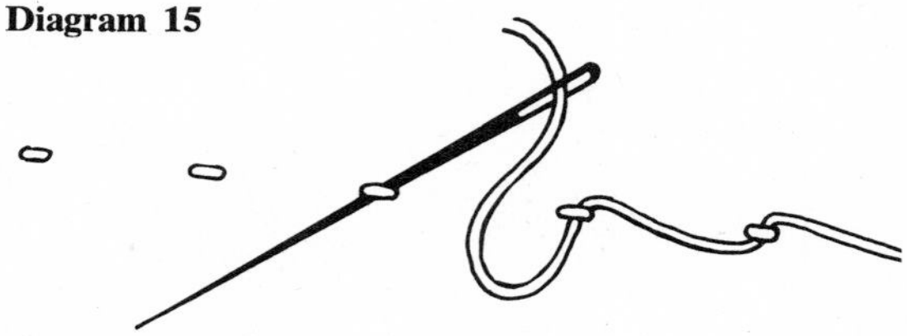

## Materials
**1 felt rectangle, 22 by 60 inches, in lime green**
**1 felt rectangle, 10 by 16 inches, in golden yellow**

36

LET THE SUN SHINE

9- by 12-inch rectangles or scraps of felt in kelly green, lemon yellow, white, magenta, orange, and brown (If rectangles are purchased, buy 1 of each color.)

pins

yarn needle

lightweight yarn, in green, yellow, or orange (This may be 3-ply sock yarn or single strands of crewel yarn. Buy smallest amounts available or use leftovers.)

thread in green

curtain rod, extending to 21 inches

**Diagram 16**

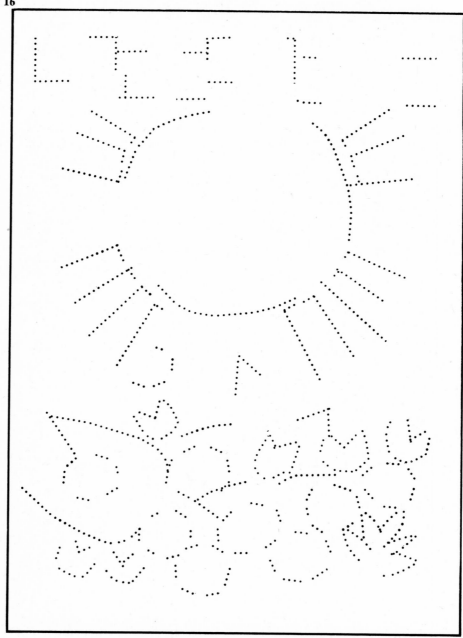

**Completed size:** 21 by 30 inches
**Color code:** O—lime green, P—golden yellow, Q—kelly green, R—lemon yellow, S—white, T—magenta, U—orange, V—brown

### Instructions

1. Enlarge pattern according to instructions on page 19. Each square equals 3 inches. The enlarged pattern should measure 21 by 30 inches.

2. Press felt pieces with steam iron.

3. Tape the enlarged pattern to the lime felt background so that there is ½ inch of felt edging on both sides and the bottom edges are flush. (Extra allowance is given to compensate for any "drawing up" of fabric. It will be trimmed off when the hanging is completed.) Follow directions on page 16 for use of tracing wheel and carbon. Make marks on fabric to indicate placement of sun, lettering, leaves, and flowers, as shown in Diagram 16. Untape pattern.

4. Tape golden yellow felt to the back of pattern behind the sun, and trace the outline. Trace marks to indicate placement of inner details, as shown in Diagram 17. Remove felt and cut out the sun. Trace the eight golden yellow sun rays and cut out. It will be necessary to move the felt around to the various positions and retape before tracing the parts. Now trace a few of the seven lemon yellow sun rays and cut out. The cut ones can serve as models for cutting the rest. Cut eleven circles from lemon yellow. Diameters may vary from about ¾ inch to 1 inch.

5. In the same manner, continue to trace and cut out all remaining shapes. Do not let the lettering frighten you. If it is a little uneven and wobbly, it will only add to the "individuality" of the design. A hint for making it more even is to cut an orange strip, 2⅛ by 8 inches, and a magenta strip, 2⅛ by 11 inches. Cut the strips into rectangles measuring 1¼ inches wide. Then snip out the letters as shown in Diagram 18.

**Diagram 17**

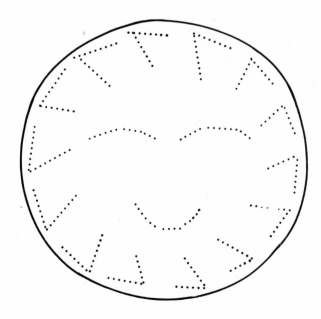

39

6. Lay out design, placing all pieces in position. Pin down all shapes.

7. Sew all pieces with running and whip stitches, varying length of running stitch as desired. The whip stitch is for flower centers, the running stitch for other pieces, and the lace variation for leaf veins, if desired.

8. Gently press out any wrinkles. Double the felt by folding it at top of design (30 inches above bottom edge). Press crease on this fold.

9. Place pattern over design and mark at the corners on lime background. Remove pattern and connect the corner marks with a chalk line, using yardstick for guide. Cut carefully along the line.

10. Using a zigzag stitch, sew the two layers of felt together along the two side edges. Start ¾ inch from the top and stop 2 inches from the bottom. Straight stitch along the lower edge, 2 inches from the bottom. Stitch the top edges together, ¾ inch from the fold, to form a slot.

11. To make fringe along the bottom edge, cut slits every ½ inch from the edge to the sewn line. Insert curtain rod through the slot at the top. The wall hanging is now complete. It may be hung with the hooks that came with the rod.

**Diagram 18**

# Fantasy Palace

*(Technique 4)*

This delightful technique was originated by Jean Ray Laury for her convinced-they-could-not-sew students. It is done by securing small bits of felt with French knots. The result is a very decorative texture. This design features an exotic palace from the Middle East. Except for a bit of machine sewing, it is done mostly by hand. Besides the French knot, it also calls for a few lazy daisy stitches. These stitches are worked with any lightweight yarn, such as a 3-ply sock yarn or a single strand of crewel yarn.

The most important stitch here is the French knot. (See Diagram 19.) The needle is brought up through the layers of felt and twisted around the yarn twice. Pulling the yarn taut with your free hand, insert the needle back through the felt, next to, but not through, the first hole.

The other stitch is the lazy daisy. It is used for a decorative effect. It consists of

**Diagram 19**

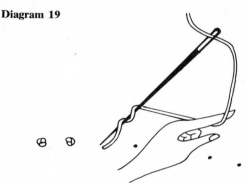

five identical stitches, worked so that they form a daisy. The needle is brought up through the felt and around to form a loop. Holding the loop down with thumb of free hand, bring the needle back down through the felt at almost the same spot it was brought up. Bring the needle up through fabric again, as shown in Diagram 20-A. To secure loop, bring needle down through felt, as shown in Diagram 20-B. This is repeated four more times to form a daisy.

If you have not done these stitches before, practice them on scrap felt before beginning.

**Diagram 20-A**  **Diagram 20-B**

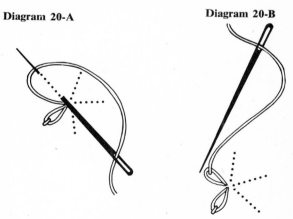

Pattern 4-A

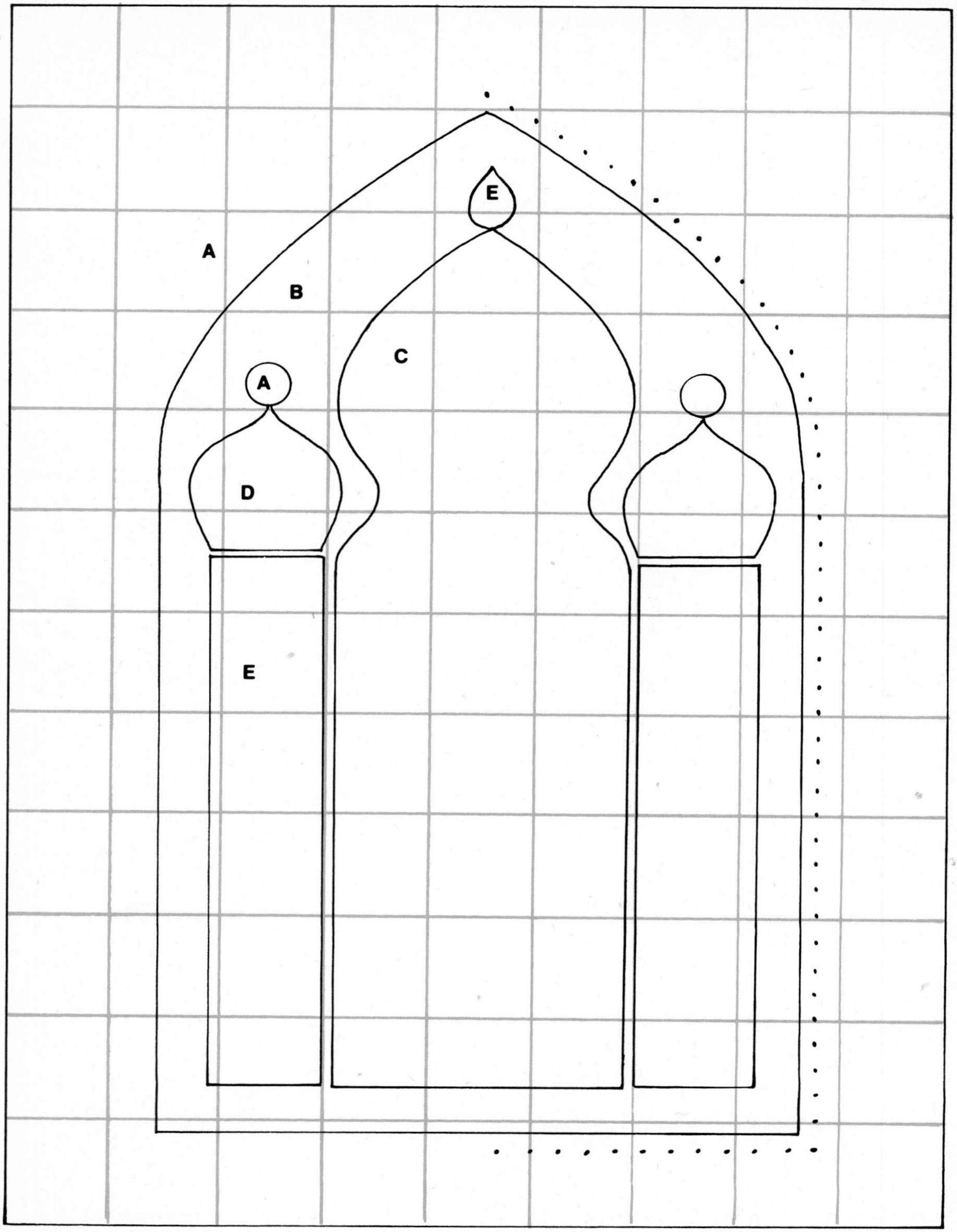

## Materials

1 felt rectangle, 22 by 28 inches, in magenta

1 felt rectangle, 13 by 21 inches, in green

1 felt rectangle, 6 by 17 inches, in orange

9- by 12-inch rectangles or scraps of felt in coral, hot pink, red, dark magenta, and dark green (If rectangles are purchased, buy 1 of each color.)

thread in green

yarn needle

lightweight yarn in orange, red, hot pink, green, or dark green. (Any or all of these colors may be used.)

glue

**Completed size:** 18 by 24 inches (excluding frame)

**Color code:** A—magenta, B—green, C—orange, D—coral, E—hot pink, F—red, G—dark magenta, H—dark green

## Instructions

1. Pattern 4-A shows overall layout of the design and Pattern 4-B shows the detail within. Enlarge both patterns according to directions on page 19, superimposing 4-B onto 4-A. Each square equals 2 inches. The enlarged pattern should measure 18 by 24 inches.

2. Press felt pieces with steam iron.

3. Tape enlarged pattern to magenta felt background so that there are 2 inches of felt surrounding the edge of the design. (This is allowed to compensate for stretching of design when completed.) Follow directions on page 16 for use of tracing wheel and carbon. Make marks for the upper point of the green arch shape and the two lower corners to indicate placement. Untape pattern.

4. Tape green felt to the back of pattern behind the arch shape, and trace outline. Make sufficient marks to indicate placement of building shapes, as shown in Diagram 21. Untape felt and cut out green arch shape.

5. Pin the green shape to the magenta background. Set your sewing machine for a medium-width zigzag stitch, 12 stitches to the inch, and sew around the edge. (If sewing machine is not available, then treat the green shape the same as the rest of the design, using French knots on the edge to secure it.)

6. Tape the orange felt to the back of pattern behind the center building, and trace the outline of the building. Trace marks, as shown in Diagram 22, to indicate placement of the major details within. Untape felt. Tape hot pink felt to pattern back behind one of the towers, and trace the outline. Trace marks to indicate placement of details, as shown in Diagram 22. Repeat for other tower. Cut out these three pieces.

Diagram 21

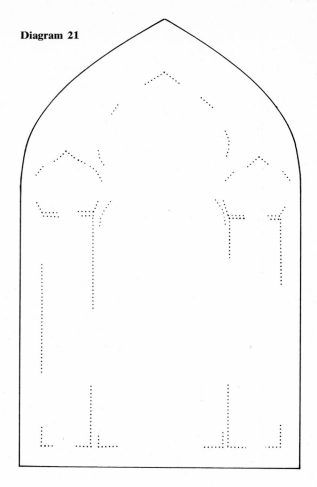

Diagram 22

7. Position the three pieces to the green arch shape, following the marks. Use tiny drops of glue to secure them in place. Use only enough glue to hold the design together while it is being worked. Too much glue will cause the felt to stiffen, making it difficult to push the needle through. Allow 1 hour for drying.

8. Trace all remaining pieces of the design that are 1 inch or larger, onto the specified colors. Colors are indicated on the left side of Patterns A and B. Repeated shapes need be traced only once, cut out, and then used as a model from which to cut the rest. Shapes that are 1 inch or smaller can be cut by eye without tracing. Cut out all shapes. It is wise to position them on the building as you cut them out to keep track of how many remain to be cut. Beginning with the major shapes, the positions of which are indicated on Pattern 4-B, position them and then place the others by eye.

9. Glue all these pieces in position, using a very small amount of glue. Allow 1 hour to dry thoroughly. When dry, pick up design to make sure nothing falls off. Reglue any loose pieces.

10. Using contrasting colors of yarn, make French knots throughout the design. Small dots on right side of Pattern 4-B indicate position for knots. Repeat for left side. Make French knots on the outside of the green shape as shown on Pattern 4-A, and twelve lazy daisies as shown on Pattern 4-B.

11. Tape the pattern to the design and trace the corner marks. Remove pattern. Design is now ready for stretching and framing. Directions for this begin on page 22.

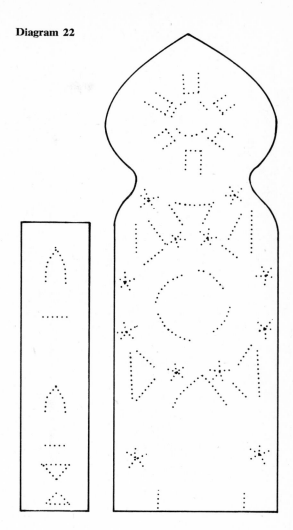

# The Artful Artichoke

*(Technique 5)*

This wall hanging is meant for a kitchen. It is ideal for a small wall space that needs something decorative. It calls for any left-over scraps you have, preferably in shades of green, gold, and yellow. Using the greener shades for the bottom of the artichoke, blend the colors so that the olive and goldish greens are next, and the gold and yellow pieces are at the top. The background for this design was made from a decorator's sample of orange upholstery fabric.

Stitch the artichoke by machine, using an even satin stitch. This is composed of wide zigzag stitches made close together. Each piece should be basted first, by hand or ma-

chine, to avoid puckering. If hand-basting is done, make running stitches close to the edge, as shown in Diagram 23-A. In Diagram 23-B, the machine-basting stitch is shown. The basting stitch in either case is covered by the satin stitch. (If you are using felt, basting is not essential. Felt does not "ride" out of place as easily as some other fabrics do.)

**Diagram 23-A**          **Diagram 23-B**

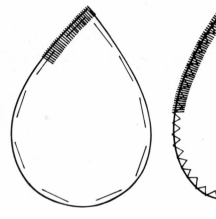

This is not necessarily a fast technique just because it is done on the sewing machine. A well-made satin stitch takes almost as much time to do as a handmade stitch. Some people snicker at machine-stitched appliqué, believing it to be an elementary and inferior way to work. However, it often requires more patience and time than handwork does. Depending on your attitude toward it, you will find it either fast and easy, or difficult. You should try this simple project to determine how you like the technique.

The lettering was done on the sewing machine, with a "free embroidery" attachment. This attachment enables the fabric to move freely while sewing because the foot goes up and down with the needle instead of holding it down constantly. It takes some practice to become proficient at this skill.

If you prefer to embroider by hand, use a

the artful artichoke

**Diagram 24**

*stem stitch. (See Diagram 24.) To make a stem stitch, bring the needle up on the left side of the line. In an upward direction, it then crosses over to the right side of the line, on an angle. This is then repeated, always with the needle brought up near the center of the previous stitch.*

*The hanging may be lined to give it a nice finish, but this is not necessary. I usually like the back of a wall hanging to look as neat and as finished as the front—especially if it is to be a gift or if it is to be displayed and handled by people who will notice a neatly finished back. This will set off the professional from the amateur. If it is for your own use, you may not feel this is essential.*

### Materials

1 fabric rectangle, 22 by 27 inches, in orange (for background)

scraps of green, gold, and yellow fabrics in 7, 8, or 9 different prints or textures

thread in gold, olive, and orange

yarn needle

30 inches 4-ply yarn (for hanging) (If lettering is hand-embroidered, use lightweight olive yarn.)

lightweight fabric, 22 by 26 inches (for lining) (optional)

curtain rod, extending to 20 inches

**Completed size:** 20 by 24 inches

### Instructions

1. Enlarge pattern according to directions given on page 19. Each square equals 2 inches. The enlarged pattern should measure 20 by 24 inches.

2. Press all fabric pieces.

3. Tape enlarged pattern to orange background fabric so that there is a 1-inch fabric border on both sides and bottom and a 2-inch border on top. Follow directions given on page 16 for use of tracing wheel and carbon. Trace the outline of the artichoke and the outlines of the individual pieces. Untape pattern.

4. One at a time, tape the scraps to the back of pattern behind the appropriate piece, and trace outlines. Cut out the pieces.

5. Place all pieces in position on orange background, overlapping where required. (If you want to make some changes in the color scheme, now is the time to do it.)

6. Once the color decision is final, pin down all pieces. Baste by hand or by machine, as shown in Diagrams 23-A or B.

7. Starting at top of artichoke and using olive thread for contrast, satin stitch edges of yellow and gold pieces. Underlapped edges need not be sewn. Moving downward, switch to gold thread and satin stitch edges of olive and green shapes.

8. Embroider lettering by hand or by machine. If you are embroidering by hand, stem stitch with lightweight olive yarn. For machine embroidery, use attachment and set stitch width to medium. Use olive thread.

9. Press hanging down flat. Turn bottom and side edges under 1 inch and press. Turn top edge under 2 inches and press. Clip corners to eliminate bulk.

10. About ½ inch from fold, hem the side and bottom edges with straight stitch, using orange thread. Sew top edge with straight stitch, ¾ inch from the fold, to form a slot. Insert curtain rod. (If you want to line the hanging, see step 11 before inserting rod.) Wall hanging is now complete. It may be hung with the hooks that accompany rod, or attach yarn.

11. (Optional) Before inserting curtain rod in step 10, turn under all edges of fabric lining 1 inch and press. Hem bottom edge, using straight stitch on machine. With turned-under edges against each other, pin lining to back of hanging. Line up top edge of lining to sewn line on hanging. Pin down all edges. Stitch by hand or machine along sides and top. Lower edge may hang free.

# Rosette

*(Technique 6)*

Diagram 25

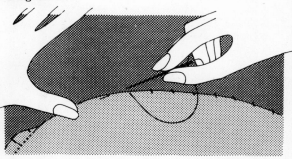

the fabric over your lap, use a kitchen tray or magazine to provide a flat surface.

See Diagram 19 and explanation on page 41 for a review on French knots. This time you will use thread instead of yarn to add a subtle accent.

### Materials

1 cotton rectangle, 26 by 34 inches, in vermilion
1 cotton rectangle, 18 by 28 inches, in gold
small scraps of cotton in royal blue and hot pink
thread in vermilion, gold, royal blue, and hot pink
embroidery scissors

**Completed size:** 22 by 30 inches (excluding frame)

**Color code:** I—vermilion, J—gold, K—royal blue, L—hot pink

### Instructions

1. Enlarge pattern according to directions on page 19. Each square equals 2 inches. Pattern should now measure 22 by 30 inches.

2. Press all fabric pieces with steam iron.

3. Tape pattern to vermilion fabric so that there are 2 inches of fabric surrounding the design. Follow directions on page 16 for use of dressmaker's carbon and tracing wheel. Trace outline of flower, stem, and leaves. Untape pattern.

4. Tape gold fabric to back of pattern behind flower. Using tracing wheel and carbon, trace outline of flower and all shapes within. Even though the stem, leaves, and

This simple but dramatic flower design will add a splash of color to that empty spot on your wall. I used Indian Head® cotton, but any other cotton of a similar weight will do nicely.

The design is sewn together with a whip stitch, similar to the stitch used for the Sunshine Hanging. (See Diagram 14.) This time, however, you will use thread instead of yarn and your stitches will be smaller. As shown in Diagram 25, the edges are turned under and held down with the thumb of your free hand. Make stitches ¼ or ½ inch apart. I have found that spreading out the fabric on a table keeps it flat. If you would rather hold

**Pattern 6**

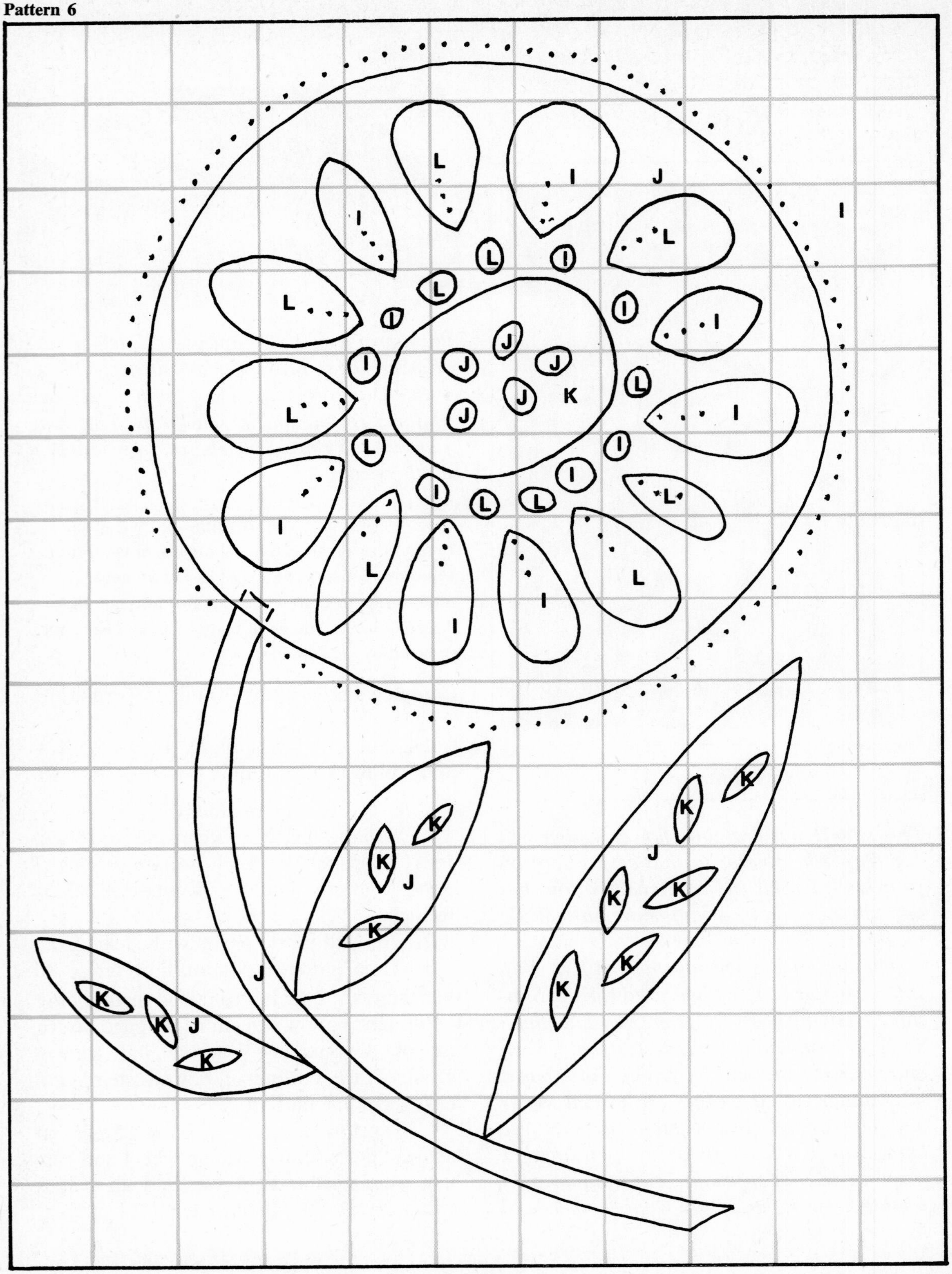

flower are connected in the pattern, trace them separately. Allow ¼ inch around each piece for turning under. Trace stem, leaves, and the blue shapes within the leaves. Remove the gold fabric from the pattern. Place the blue behind the inner circle of the flower. Tape it and trace the circle. Cut out all six pieces, remembering to allow ¼ inch around each piece.

5. Lay out the gold pieces on the vermilion background, and pin them in place.

6. Following Diagram 25, whip stitch all the edges of gold pieces with gold thread.

7. Seven of the petal shapes within the gold flower will be vermilion. These are simply holes that are cut out to reveal the vermilion background. With tip of embroidery scissors, pierce through one of these outlined shapes. Cut out the middle, leaving a ¼-inch allowance from the edge. Discard the cutaway part. Now clip curved edge almost up to the traced line, making clips closer together where curve is tighter. Turn edge under, with whip stitch, as shown in Diagram 26. Continue in this manner with all vermilion petals.

**Diagram 26**

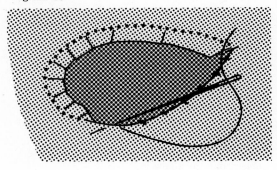

8. Pierce the small vermilion circles and clip almost to the traced line. Since some of these holes are very small, merely slit the fabric, instead of cutting it away and discarding it. Whip down all these edges, as shown in Diagram 27.

**Diagram 27**

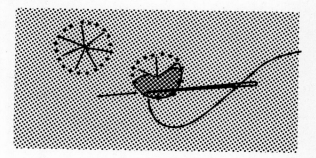

9. Almost the same technique is used for the pink petals and circles. This time, however, after you have cut and discarded the inner fabric parts and clipped the edges, insert a small piece of hot pink into each space. Make sure each piece is larger than the traced shape. You will now use the whip stitch to turn under the edges and to attach the pink petal. (See Diagram 28. Broken

**Diagram 28**

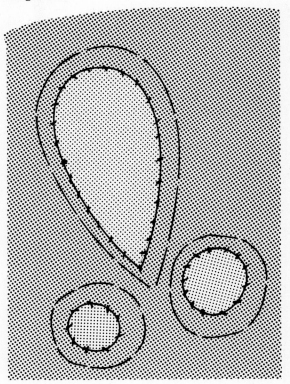

51

Diagram 29

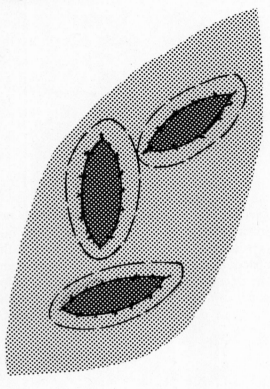

lines indicate hidden edge of pink fabric.)

10. Repeat this procedure for the blue shapes within leaves, using small pieces of royal blue. (See Diagram 29.)

11. Pin blue circle to center of flower. Using same procedure as for gold shapes, turn under and whip down edges with blue thread. The inner circles will be done the same way that the vermilion shapes were done in step 8. Slit, clip, turn under, and whip down edges to reveal gold.

12. The dots on the pattern indicate French knots. (If you have not done French knots before, practice on scraps.) Use vermilion thread to make French knots on hot pink and pink thread to make French knots on vermilion.

13. Tape pattern to design and trace corner marks. Remove pattern. Design is now ready for stretching and framing. See directions for stretching and framing on page 22.

## Patterns 7 and 8

The following two techniques are reverse appliqué. They are based on a technique practiced by the Cuna Indians of the San Blas Islands of Panama. These designs are outgrowths of former body-painting techniques. When fabrics, scissors, needles, and thread entered their culture, the Cuna Indians applied their body-painting technique to fabric designing. The rectangular designs are sewn to a yoke to make blouses. These blouses, called *molas,* are sewn with tiny stitches and involve intricate cutting and layering of fabrics. Many feature tiny vertical slits, called *tas-tas,* and narrow borders done layer upon layer. Some of them form a rickrack type of border, called *dientes.*

A well-made *mola* is considered to be one that has no raw edges, almost invisible stitches (thread has to be a perfect match), and no large, unfilled areas. *Tas-tas* are used to fill these spaces. The belief among the Cuna Indians is that Mu, mythical grandmother of unborn females, bestows the child with *kurgin*—the ability to do this craft—in varying degrees. Those that do not do a topnotch job have not been gifted with enough *kurgin,* and their designs are considered to be inferior.

The designs are usually based on native motifs. Sometimes, however, they are influenced by outside sources, such as magazine ads and television. The results are often delightful interpretations. The attempt has been made in this book not to duplicate the intricacy of their work but rather to incorporate their method. Their unique usage of fabric gives appliqué a new look.

# G.V.'s Flowers

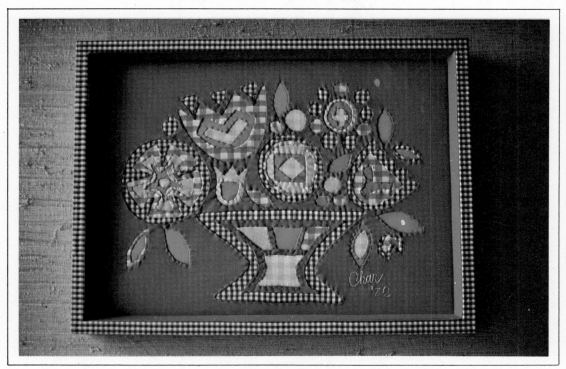

*(Technique 7)*

This design was inspired by Gloria Vanderbilt's famous collages. Miss Vanderbilt has an elegant way of using simple gingham to enhance her charming designs. I couldn't resist the temptation to enrich this reverse appliqué design by borrowing her idea. The design also features a matching gingham-covered frame. Usually, I prefer a simple natural wood frame but in this case the gingham frame adds a truly decorative touch.

The gingham fabrics used here are of two different-sized checks—⅛ inch and ¼ inch. Larger-sized checks come available in the stores, but I recommend smaller checks, such as these.

The design is made with six layers of fabric, basted together around the edges. The upper layer is cut through to reveal the next layer, and then that layer is cut to reveal the next one. This is continued until the bottom layer is exposed. To vary the sequence, more than one layer can be cut at one time. Since several layers of fabric are involved, it is important to use lightweight as opposed to heavy fabrics.

Reverse appliqué may seem like a very complicated technique to you now, but the more experienced you become at it, the more it will intrigue you. Your first attempt may be awkward, but it will get much easier as you go along.

## Materials

3 cotton rectangles, 16 by 20 inches, in orchid, pink, and turquoise

3 cotton gingham rectangles, 16 by 20 inches, in purple, orange, and pink

1 cotton rectangle, 19 by 23 inches, in purple gingham (for frame)

thread in orchid or pink

embroidery scissors

chalk pencil

unfinished picture frame, 12 by 16 inches, with straight, right-angle sides

glue

bias tape, ⅞-inch width, in turquoise

**Completed size:** 12 by 16 inches (excluding frame)

**Color code:** M—orchid, N—purple gingham, O—orange gingham, P—pink, Q—turquoise, R—pink gingham

### Instructions

1. Enlarge pattern according to directions on page 19. Each square equals 2 inches. The enlarged pattern should measure 12 by 16 inches.

2. Press fabric pieces.

3. Pin the six 16- by 20-inch pieces together, following sequence in color code above, with orchid piece on top. Baste pieces together by hand, about 1 inch from edge.

4. Tape pattern to orchid so that there are 2 inches of fabric surrounding the pattern. Follow directions on page 16 for use of tracing wheel and carbon. Trace outline of all shapes, but leave out the inner details. (They will be traced or drawn in later.) Untape pattern.

5. The two large flowers on the extreme left will serve as instructional models for the other parts. Pierce the inner circle of the flower on the left with tip of scissors. Cut out the circle, allowing ¼ inch from edge. Every ⅜ inch, make a clip from the edge almost to the traced line. Turn edge under with whip stitch, as shown in Diagram 30.

It is helpful to use the needle to push the fabric under as you work. Hold the fabric down with the thumb of your free hand while you stitch. (See Diagram 30.)

**Diagram 30**

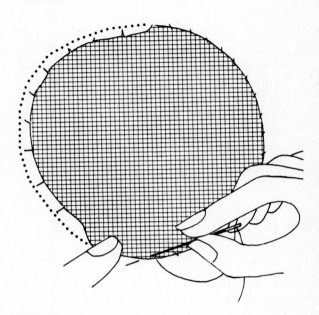

**Diagram 31**

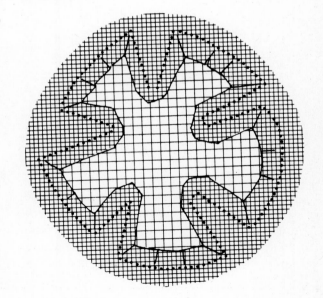

55

6. Retape pattern and trace the next detail (five-petaled flower shape) onto the purple gingham. After you have untaped the pattern, cut away the inside and clip, allowing ¼ inch from edge. (See Diagram 31.) Turn under and whip down the edge. Corners may prove to be a bit troublesome. Be sure to place a stitch in each one. The outward corners may tend to be bulky. Even though bulkiness adds to the dimensional quality of the work, trim some of the fabric away at these points. Dampening the corners with a drop of water will make them less stubborn. The inward corners are easier to do because they have no bulk. But if a raw edge is giving you trouble, a drop of water will help here too. (See Diagram 32.)

**Diagram 32**

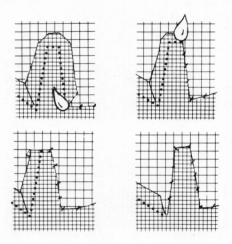

7. Retape pattern and trace next shape (smaller five-petaled flower) onto orange gingham. Repeat procedure mapped out in step 6 for this shape.

8. Retape pattern and trace next shape (five-pointed star) on pink. Untape pattern and cut away the center. Slit from the circle to the points, as shown in Diagram 33. Carefully whip the edge in the same manner as before.

**Diagram 33**

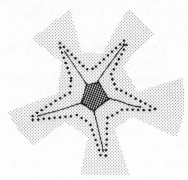

9. With chalk pencil draw the inner circle on the turquoise. Slit, as done for previous projects, clip, turn under, and whip, as shown in Diagram 27 for Pattern 6. The flower is now complete.

10. The large tulip next to the completed flower is done much the same way. Trim and clip the small triangles, as shown in Diagram 34. Turn under and whip down edges as before.

**Diagram 34**

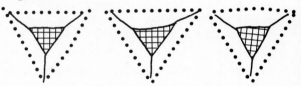

11. Cut and clip the tulip shape. This time, before whipping down the edges, the layer of purple gingham must be removed. Reach underneath it with scissors and carefully trim it away, trying to approximate the traced line as much as possible. (See Diagram 35.) Turn under and whip the orchid edges directly to the orange gingham.

12. Trace next inner shape (rounded V). Untape pattern. Cut and clip, as shown in Diagram 36. Remove the layer of pink with scissors to reveal the turquoise. Turn under edges and whip to the turquoise.

13. Trace the next shape (pointed V) or

draw freehand with chalk pencil. Slit and clip, as shown in Diagram 37. Turn under the edges and whip down.

14. Continue in this manner until all flowers and leaves are done. Diagram 38 shows how to do some of the other shapes. When necessary—according to designated colors on pattern—remove one, two, three,

**Diagram 37**

**Diagram 35**

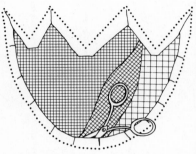

four, or five layers to reach the proper color for a given shape. Do not try to cut through more than one layer at a time. Each layer must be cut separately.

15. This design is a combination of both reverse and regular appliqué. Cutaway parts are re-placed and appliquéd on. You will notice that the inside of the pot has a layer of orchid. Trace the outline of the orchid pot shape and cut it out. Be careful not to damage it. After the outer orchid edge is whipped down, pin the inner orchid shape back to its original position. Turn edges under and whip it into place. (See Diagram 39.) Trace the inside shapes onto the orchid

**Diagram 38**

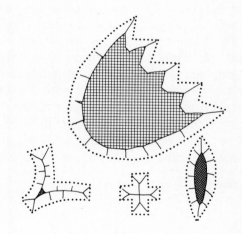

**Diagram 36**

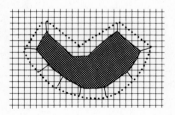

**Diagram 39**

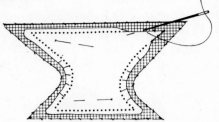

pot shape, cut through, and remove layers to reach the proper colors. Whip down the four inside shapes, turning edges under.

16. Remove the basting from outer edges of design. Trim 2-inch edge off all layers except the orchid. Tape the pattern to the design and trace corner marks. Untape pattern. Design is now ready for stretching, as described on page 22.

17. *Frame covering:* Place the 19- by 23-inch purple gingham piece on a tabletop. Put the frame, face up, on some old newspapers. Apply glue to top and sides of frame.

18. Place frame face down on the gingham, centering it so that there are 3 inches of gingham all around. Lift up two opposite ends of gingham and press to sides of frame. Carefully trim the corners flush with the corners of the frame. Apply glue to back of frame. Then press the fabric to the back of frame. Repeat this with the other two sides.

**Diagram 40**

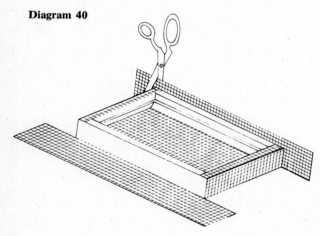

(See Diagram 40.) Press fabric firmly to the frame so that it is well adhered.

19. Turn frame over and cut away the inside of the gingham, leaving about ½ inch from the inside edge of the frame. Clip the corners. Apply glue to inside edge of frame. Press down this edge to the inside of frame. (See Diagram 41.)

**Diagram 41**

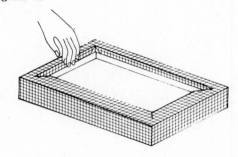

20. Cut bias tape to length of one inside edge of frame. If inside edge is beveled, cut end of tape to fit corner. Lay tape face down on newspaper and apply fabric glue to wrong side. Pick it up and apply it to inside of frame, covering edge of gingham. (See Diagram 42.) Repeat this for all four edges. Be sure tape meets at corners so that none of the bare wood shows.

**Diagram 42**

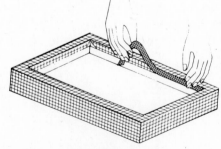

21. Place a fine line of glue on outside corners of frame to avoid any possibility of fabric lifting at corners. When dry, frame is ready to be placed on design. Instructions are on page 26.

## Pattern 8: Wall Hanging

# Mod Pods

*(Technique 8)*

In the preceding method, we started out by basting six layers of fabric together. This restricted us to using only those fabrics. Also, much of the fabric was wasted in that it was hidden beneath other layers. For these two reasons, I usually prefer to use the second method, which enables me to use as many colors as I wish, and cuts down on waste. Each part of the design is a separate piece. These pieces are cut and pinned to their appropriate positions, making it unnecessary to have a whole layer of color for only one or two spots. Method 2 conserves precious fabric and is more practical for a design of this type. If method 1 had been used for Mod Pods, there would have been many large layers of fabric, resulting in a very heavy workpiece. Also with method 2, you are able to use many more colors (Mod Pods uses ten) and you can scatter colors around more spontaneously.

Method 1 does have an advantage in that you are working with only a few pieces. If you plan to carry your work around with you, everything can be kept together in one compact unit.

When planning a design of your own, the method to use will depend on the design. If the design is small and the colors are distributed equally throughout, you will probably decide on method 1. You may feel more comfortable with this method anyway if the idea of constantly cutting up little pieces of fabric and pinning them in place does not appeal to you.

To make molas, the Cuna Indians combine both methods. They usually baste three layers of fabric together and then add small pieces throughout the design.

After exploring method 2, you will be in a better position to determine whether this is the method you prefer.

Mod Pods is a simple graphic display of the pods that appear in late summer. It is backed with sturdy upholstery fabric and brightened with a mitered yellow border, which contrasts well with the autumn color arrangement of the design.

### Materials
1 broadcloth or KETTLE® CLOTH rectangle, 21 by 25 inches, in mahogany

small scraps of cotton in white, gold, light brown, bronze, olive, lime, green, brick red, and burnt orange

1 upholstery fabric rectangle, 28 by 33 inches, in olive

1 upholstery fabric rectangle, 13½ by 48 inches, in yellow

**3 cotton rectangles, 5 by 6½ inches, in olive**
**embroidery scissors**
**thread in mahogany and gold**
**chalk pencil**
**25 inches lath, ¼ by 1 inch (This is available at a**
**lumberyard.)**
**curtain rod, extending to 26 inches**

**Completed size:** 26 by 30 inches (excluding loops and rod)

Completed size of inner design without yellow border: 20 by 24 inches

**Color code:** A—mahogany, B—white, C—gold, D—light brown, E—bronze, F—olive, G—lime, H—green, I—brick red, J—burnt orange

### Instructions

1. Enlarge pattern according to directions on page 19. Each square equals 2 inches. Pattern should measure 20 by 24 inches.

2. Press cotton pieces.

3. Tape pattern to mahogany with 1 inch of fabric surrounding design. Follow directions on page 16 for use of tracing wheel and carbon. Trace outlines of all shapes, leaving out inner details. (They will be traced or drawn in later.) Untape pattern.

4. Begin at the middle of the design with the coil-centered pod. Cut a piece of gold fabric, large enough to cover the five upper point shapes. Pin the gold to back of mahogany fabric behind these shapes. One by one cut on traced line of mahogany, allowing ¼ inch from edge, clip edges, turn under, and whip down to gold fabric. (See Diagram 43-A. Broken lines indicate edge of gold fabric underneath.) Refer to Diagram 25 for review on whip stitch. Turn design over and trim away excess gold fabric, as shown in Diagram 43-B.

5. Trace or draw by hand the white circles within the gold shapes on the gold fabric. Cut out circles of white fabric, about 1½ inches in diameter. Pin these behind the traced circles on the gold. Cut, clip, and turn under the edges of gold. This time, however, use a running stitch to sew edges down, as shown in Diagram 13. (Also see Diagram 44.)

6. Cut a piece of bronze fabric, large enough to cover lower part of pod below

**Diagram 43-A**

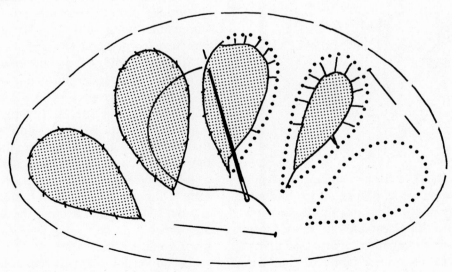

Diagram 43-B

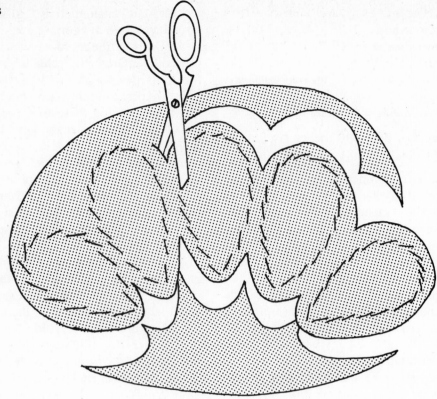

Diagram 44

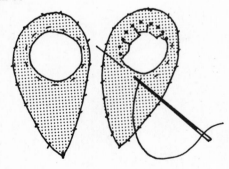

coil. Pin fabric to back of mahogany behind this traced shape, clip, turn under, and whip mahogany edges to bronze fabric, as shown in Diagram 45. Complete one side of shape before doing the other. Turn design over and trim excess bronze fabric ¼ inch from stitching.

7. From burnt orange fabric, cut a circle about 5 inches in diameter. Pin this behind the traced coil. Sewing this coil may look impossible but is actually a lot of fun once you have learned how to do it.

Starting at end of coil, slit about 2 inches at a time. Turn under and whip down inner edge. (See Diagram 46-A.) Continue slitting, clipping, turning, and whipping down inner edge, a little at a time, until you get to the middle. As the coil gets smaller toward the middle, clips should be closer together, enabling the edges to be turned under easily. (See Diagram 46-B.) Continue in same manner back up and around the coil, whipping down the outer edge, as shown in Diagram 46-C.

An important point to remember is that whenever a large or awkward shape is attempted—such as this coil—it is always best to cut a little at a time. Otherwise the result in this case would be a long, ungainly "noodle" of fabric, difficult to position. Make sure also that the outline is traced accurately before beginning to sew.

8. Cut a piece of olive fabric, large enough to cover stem and leaves. Pin it to the back of mahogany, underneath these traced shapes. Slit the stem, clip, and whip down the turned-under edges. Cut away the leaves to reveal olive. Clip, turn under, and whip down the edges. Trace the inner leaf shapes onto the olive leaves or draw freehand with a chalk pencil. Cut two pieces from lime to cover these shapes. Pin behind the olive leaves. Cut, clip, turn, and with a running stitch, whip the olive edges to the lime.

9. Turn design over. With scissors, trim away all excess fabric. This is to keep bits of fabric from overlapping each other. It is a good idea to do this after sewing each detail, especially those that are close.

10. Work the rest of design in this manner, following pattern for color. Use running or whip stitch, as desired. Alternate between gold and mahogany thread, if you wish, to provide more contrast. Diagram 47 shows further cutting and slitting details.

11. Tape pattern over the design and mark the corners with chalk. Using a yardstick, connect the corners with a straight chalk line and cut along this line.

12. Press olive upholstery fabric. Pin design to it, leaving a 4-inch border on top and sides and a 5-inch border on bottom. Sew the mahogany edges to the olive on sewing machine.

13. Turn under edges of olive fabric, 1 inch on top and sides and 2 inches at bottom. Press edges flat and clip off corners to remove bulk.

14. Stitch top and side edges, about ¼ inch from crease, and bottom edge, 1⅛ inches from crease.

15. Cut three 4½-inch-width strips from yellow upholstery fabric. Make two of the

**Diagram 45**

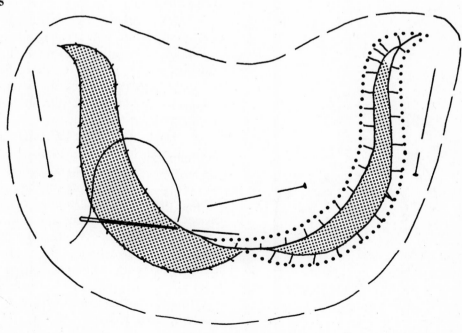

strips 27½ inches in length and cut the remaining strip into two 24-inch strips.

16. Turn under edges of all four strips ⅝ inch, and press flat. These strips will form the yellow frame between the design and the olive backing. To miter the corners, press under the ends of the two 24-inch strips at a 45-degree angle. Trim off folded-under por-

**Diagram 46-C**

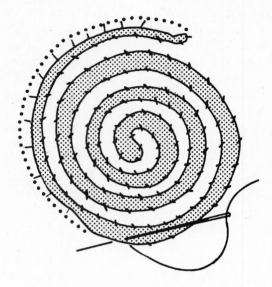

**Diagram 46-A**

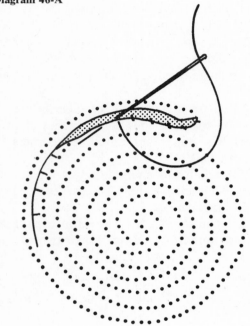

**Diagram 46-B**

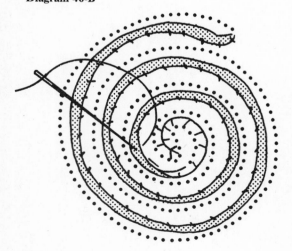

tion of corners, about ½ inch from the pressed angled edge, and clip excess fabric from corners. All four strips are to be pinned to the olive backing, 1¼ inches from the edge. Pin the two 27½-inch strips onto vertical edges, and then the two mitered 24-inch strips onto horizontal edges.

17. Baste these strips, neatly tacking their corners into place. Using a wide zigzag stitch, set at 10 stitches to the inch, sew the outer edges of yellow to olive. Stitch the mitered corners down and the inner edges of yellow to design. Insert lath into the 1⅛-inch slot on bottom.

18. Fold the three rectangular olive pieces in half to measure 2½ by 6½ inches. Make seam, ¼ inch from edge, on long edge and one end. Turn inside out and press. By hand or machine, turn in edge of other end on each rectangular piece. Fold these three strips to form loops over the top and sew to edge of hanging. Space them about 6½ inches apart, with the two end strips 3 inches from side. Insert curtain rod through loops. Use the hooks that come with rod to hang the completed design.

Diagram 47

65

# 3

# Gifts for Giving, Bazaars, and Boutiques

There are times when you want to give someone a special gift—one that just can't be bought in any store. Often, a purchased, manufactured item just doesn't express the same feeling that a gift on which you spent time rather than money does. Gifts you make yourself should have both the sophisticated look of a store-bought item and that unique, personal quality only homemade items have.

This is the same quality that people are looking for in items sold at fund-raising bazaars. These people are also looking for low prices. Consequently, an item produced for a bazaar should be able to be made quickly so that the price can be low, but it should also be attractive and useful. Large items, such as quilts and afghans, will not sell rapidly. It is the small item that brings in the money. Make items that look irresistible and that can be made in quantity.

This chapter contains a few suggestions for such items. Some take more time than others. The ones that can be produced in quantity, by a sewing group, are ideal for selling at bazaars. You may want to use the ones that require more time for gift giving. Some of the ideas in the other chapters will also serve as fine gifts.

If there are boutiques in your town that are looking for unique items to sell, you might try to make some extra money by selling your gift items to them. It is, however, difficult to produce a handmade item that will sell at a reasonable price, and still make money for you. Be aware of the percentage to be made by the shop when you set your price. Keep your price low enough so that the item will still sell when the store's percentage is added on. Ask yourself whether you would pay that much for this item if you saw it in a shop. In these days of handcraft enthusiasm, if an item is too simple and easy to make, a customer will surely realize that she could make it herself. She will pay only

a small price for such an item. Do not be misled into thinking that there is a class of people "who have money" and who will pay high prices without a thought. Even if there are such people, don't count on their finding their way to this particular shop when they can jet to the marketplaces of the world.

*Pattern 9: Covered Hangers*

# Happy Geometrics

*(Technique 1)*

*These hangers can be produced in quantity for a bazaar or boutique. Every household has extra wire hangers. Simple felt coverings on those hangers make them a well-received addition to any closet. The felt covers prevent sweaters from getting lumpy, stretched*

**Pattern 9**

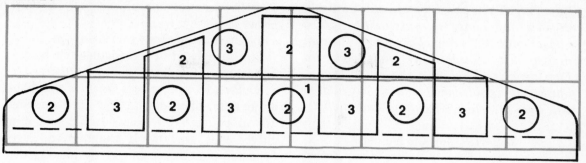

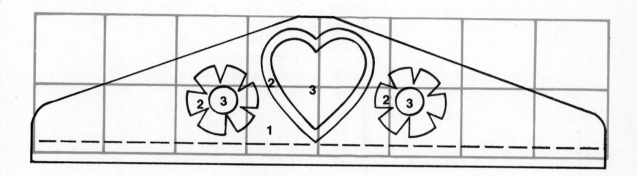

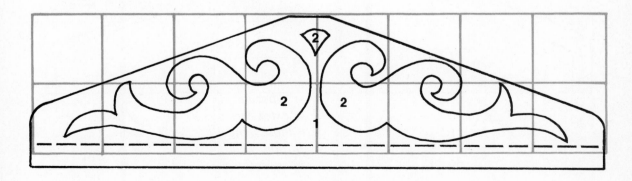

69

shoulders. *They also keep sweaters, low-cut dresses, and jumpers from sliding off the hanger onto the floor. The quick, stick-on designs add a bright, gay look to closets. For a man's closet, use shades of brown, black, navy, gold, russet, and olive. Children will love to help with cutting and sticking.*

### Materials (for one hanger)

**2 felt rectangles, 6 by 18 inches, in any desired color**

**9- by 12-inch rectangles or scraps of felt, in many colors**

**wire hangers**

**glue**

**edgings or fringe, any type, cut in 17-inch lengths (optional)**

**Completed size:** 16 inches in length (standard hanger size)

**Color code:** Any desired color schemes (numbers on pattern indicate color distribution)

### Instructions

1. Enlarge pattern according to instructions on page 19. Each square equals 2 inches. Pattern should now measure 4 by 16 inches. Trace outline of hanger, and add a ⅝ inch border all around except for bottom. Draw the design within.

2. Press felt pieces with steam iron.

3. Pin pattern to rectangular felt pieces. Cut two for each hanger.

4. Pin these two pieces together and seam along seam line, leaving a ½-inch opening at top point. Trim excess fabric and clip curved ends, as shown in Diagram 48. Turn to inside out. Insert hanger by placing the hook through the upper point opening. Using zipper foot on sewing machine, sew along bottom edge, very close to hanger.

5. One by one tape fabric scraps to back of pattern. Follow directions on page 16 for use of tracing wheel and carbon. Trace appliqué shapes on desired colors. Repeated shapes need be traced only once, cut out, and then used as a model for the rest.

6. Cut out all shapes. Use pinking shears for cutting where desired.

7. Place the cut shapes on some newspaper. Apply glue to backs, position by eye, press shapes into place on hangers, and allow 1 hour to dry.

8. Edgings or fringe are sewn along bottom edge. Edge can also be trimmed with pinking shears if desired.

**Diagram 48**

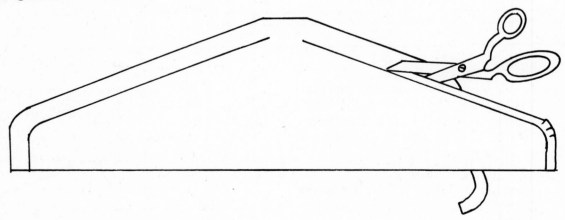

# Tulips and a Daisy

*(Technique 1)*

*Gifts often come in boxes that are too nice to be thrown away. It seems as though everyone has a supply of cardboard boxes at home. These boxes can be useful containers, holding all sorts of treasures, and in themselves make a fine gift. They are lined carefully with gift wrapping paper and then covered with felt. Felt cutouts give them a boutique look. Children will enjoy working on this project, with some help from you.*

### Materials (for one box)
**2 felt pieces, large enough to cover box and lid, in any desired color**
**scraps of felt, in compatible colors**
**box, any size or proportion**
**gift wrapping paper, enough to line box**
**glue**

### Instructions
1. Measure inside lid of box. Draw a square or rectangle on the wrong side of gift wrap, following these measurements. Add the dimension for depth of lid and draw lines. Cut out rectangle and slit at each corner, as shown by heavy lines in Diagram 49. (Broken lines indicate fold line.) Fold and slip into box lid to check fit.

2. Remove the gift wrap and apply glue to its back. Place it in the lid, pressing it down all over. Let the corners underlap, as shown in Diagram 50.

**Diagram 49**

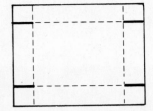

**Diagram 52-A**

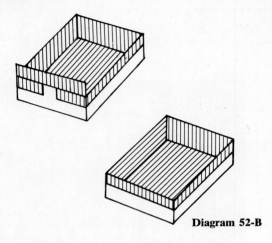

**Diagram 52-B**

3. Measure inside of box. Draw a square or rectangle on the wrong side of gift .wrap, following measurements. Add the dimension for depth of box and depth of lid. Draw lines. (The part of the box that fits into the lid will be covered with gift wrap. If felt was used, it would be too thick for the lid to fit over it.) Cut out and slit, as shown by heavy lines in Diagram 51. Fold and slip into the box to check fit.

**Diagram 50**

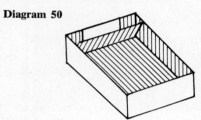

**Diagram 51**

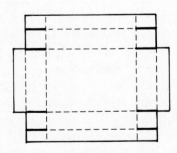

ing the depth, the corners can be cut without allowing for underlap. Repeat same for lid. (See Diagram 53.)

6. Apply glue to backs of these pieces and press onto the box and lid, pressing down all over.

7. In freehand, draw on back of felt the five shapes shown in pattern. Size is up to you. Cut out. Repeated shapes need be cut only once and then used as a model for the rest.

8. Arrange the cut shapes on the box lids, as shown in Pattern 10, or experiment with your own shapes and designs. Place the pieces on newspaper and apply glue to the backs. Press the pieces into place on the lid and sides of the box.

**Diagram 53**

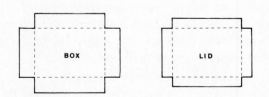

4. Remove and apply glue to back. Place it in the box, pressing down all over. Let the corners underlap on the outside of the box, as shown in Diagrams 52-A and B.

5. Measure the bottom of box and depth up to lid edge. Draw a square or rectangle on felt, following measurements. When add-

72

# Contemporary Geometrics

*(Techniques 2, 3, or 4)*

No bazaar would be complete without a *selection of pot holders. Since these pot holders are made of felt, which is a nonwashable fabric, I recommend that they be saved for special-occasion dinners. In the meantime let them hang decoratively in your kitchen, and use good old supermarket pot holders for everyday meals. Children can surprise mommy, aunt, or big sister with a few of these colorful helpers.*

*The designs are simple geometric shapes. The dimensional quality comes from a layer of Dacron batting that is sandwiched between two layers of felt for protection against heat. The pot holders may be sewn by hand or by machine.*

## Materials

(for one pot holder and mitt)

**2 felt squares, 8 by 8 inches, in any desired color (for pot holder)**

**4 felt rectangles, 8 by 10 inches, in any desired color (for mitt)**

**9- by 12-inch rectangles or scraps of felt, in compatible colors**

**1 layer bonded Dacron batting for pot holder**

**2 layers bonded Dacron batting for mitts**

**thread in any desired color**

**yarn needle (if hand-appliquéd)**

**yarn (if hand-appliquéd)**

**Completed size:** 8- by 8-inch pot holder; 6- by 9½-inch mitt

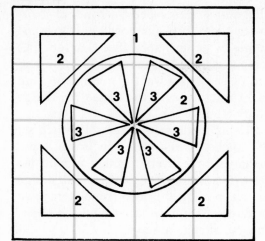

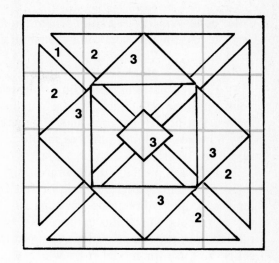

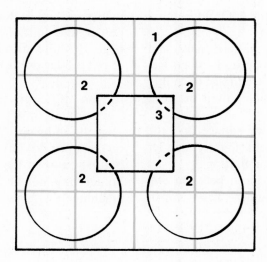

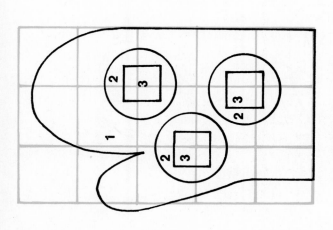

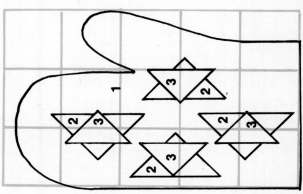

75

**Color code:** Any desired color scheme (numbers on pattern indicate color distribution)

### Instructions

1. Enlarge patterns according to instructions on page 19. Each square equals 2 inches. Pot-holder patterns should measure 8 by 8 inches, and mitt patterns should measure 6 by 10 inches.

2. Press felt pieces with steam iron.

3. Tape mitt pattern to one of felt rectangles. Follow directions on page 16 for use of tracing wheel and carbon, and trace outline of mitt. Untape pattern. Cut out mitt shape and use for model from which to cut three more mitt shapes. Since you already have two 8-inch squares for pot holder, there is no need to trace outline.

4. Tape felt scraps to pattern back, and trace geometric shapes to desired colors. Repeated shapes need be traced only once and used as models from which to cut the rest. Cut out all shapes.

5. Using the pot-holder square and the mitt shape as patterns, cut slightly smaller shape from bonded Dacron batting.

6. Place a layer of Dacron between two felt squares and pin together. Take two of the felt mitt shapes, place Dacron mitt shape between them, and pin together. Do same for other two mitt shapes. (See Diagram 54.) Place cut geometric shapes in position and pin in place. If you want the design on both sides of mitt, be sure to reverse the design for the bottom side.

7. Using medium-width zigzag stitch set at 10 stitches to the inch, sew down appliqué shapes. Sew layers together around the edges with a wider zigzag stitch. With design sides out, pin together two completely sewn mitt shapes. Sew together around the edges, leaving wrist edge unsewn.

8. Steam press if necessary.

9. Cut two lengths of felt, ¾ inch by 3 inches, in any matching color, for each pot holder and mitt. Sew together around the edge. Fold this strip over and sew to a corner of pot holder or mitt.

*Note:* If designs are stitched by hand, use Technique 3 or 4, as described in step 7 on page 40 and step 10 on page 45. Sew appliqué shapes to only one layer. Place the batting between the felt layers. Edges of pot holder may then be sewn together on sewing machine or with a whip stitch by hand.

**Diagram 54**

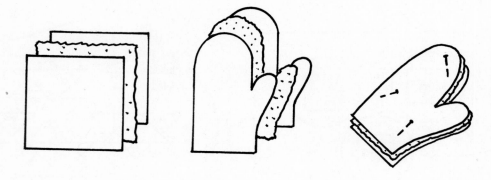

# Beads and More Beads

*(Variation of Technique 3)*

*These easy-to-make accessories will be appreciated by little girls, teen-agers, and all those who are young at heart. Each design can be used for either belt, headband, or hatband. They are appliquéd by hand. The beads add an interesting variation in texture.*

**Materials** (width of fabric and colors vary according to motif)

**Belt:**

3 felt strips, length of waist or hip measurement (depending upon where belt is to be worn) plus 6 inches

scraps of felt

glue

thread

beads

buckle to fit width of belt

5 eyelets

eyelet pliers

**Headband:**

2 felt strips, length of head measurement minus 1½ inches

scraps of felt

glue

thread

beads

3 inches elastic, 1 inch wide

**Hatband:**

1 felt strip, length of hat crown measurement plus 1 inch

scraps of felt

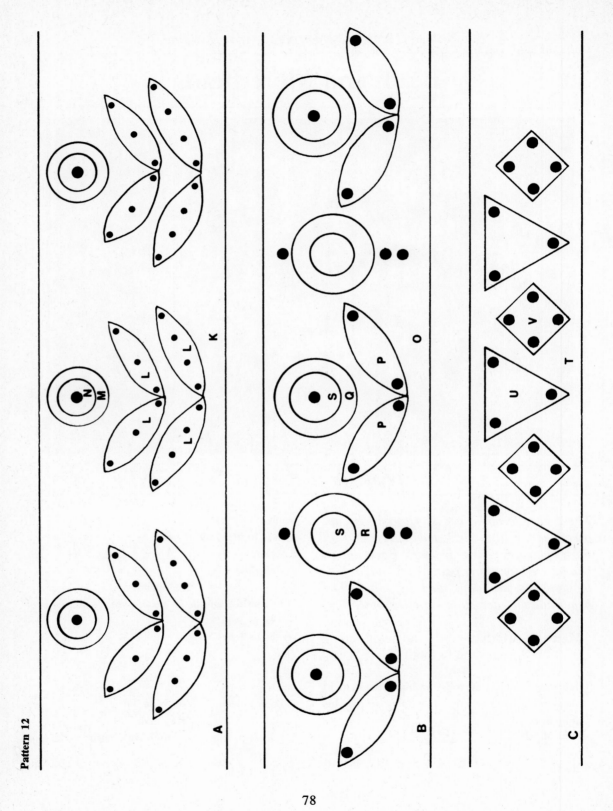

78

pellon for lining (same size as band)
glue
thread
beads

**Motif A (shown here on belt)**

1 felt strip, length as required, 2¼ inches wide, in turquoise

scraps of felt, in green, royal blue, and medium blue

1 package 11-millimeter beads, in royal blue

1 package ⅛-inch-diameter beads, in green

**Motif B (shown here on headband)**

1 felt strip, length as required, 2 inches wide, in red

scraps of felt, in green, orange, cerise, and hot pink

1 package ⅛-inch-diameter beads, in green

**Motif C (shown here on hatband)**

1 felt strip, length as required, 1⅜ inches wide, in navy blue

scraps of felt, in orange and turquoise

1 package ⅛-inch-diameter beads, in orange and turquoise

**Completed sizes:** As required
**Color codes:**
  *Motif A* K—turquoise, L—green, M—royal blue, N—medium blue
  *Motif B* O—red, P—green, Q—orange, R—cerise, S—hot pink
  *Motif C* T—navy blue, U—orange, V—turquoise

### Instructions

**Belt**

1. Measure waistline or hipline where belt is to be worn and add 6 inches to this. If you want a curved, contour belt for a better fit on the hips, cut pattern from a favorite belt or experiment with lengths cut to various curves, using paper or muslin until you find one that fits. If you plan to sell these belts, make them in several waistline measurements.

2. Cut three pieces of felt to this length (each belt has three layers of felt) and to

width of desired motif. Make one end pointed. Lay one of the felt pieces out on table.

3. By eye, cut the motif shapes from paper, to use as patterns. Pin patterns to appropriate colors of felt, and cut out. Arrange one motif on belt. Continue to cut and position motifs on belt, spacing evenly. The motifs should begin about 6 inches from pointed end and extend to 3 inches from other end.

4. Apply a minimum amount of glue to motif backs, and press each into place. Allow 1 hour for glue to dry.

5. Sew down each motif, attaching beads as you sew. The black dots on the patterns indicate where to position beads. If you wish, you may use running stitch and whip stitch as shown in Diagrams 13 and 14.

6. Pin three layers of felt together. Using medium-width zigzag stitch on machine, sew edges of three layers together. If sewing by hand, use whip stitch.

7. In the center of belt, make a ¾-inch, horizontal buttonhole 1 inch from buckle end. Place buckle on this end, inserting prong of buckle through buttonhole. Fold end of belt over center bar of buckle and stitch it down in place.

8. Place five eyelets ¾ inch apart, starting 2½ inches from tip of pointed end.

**Headband**

1. Measure head at position where headband is to be worn, and subtract 1½ inches from this measurement.

2. Cut two strips of felt to this length and wide enough to accommodate the motif you want to use. Lay one strip out on the table.

3. By eye, cut the motif shapes from paper, to use as patterns. Pin parts to appropriate colors of felt, and cut out. Find exact center of headband and insert pin to mark the spot. Measure 6 inches on either side of pin. Motif will extend across these 12

inches. Form one motif on headband. Continue to cut and position motifs on headband as you cut, spacing evenly.

4. Apply a minimum amount of glue to motif backs, and press into place. Allow 1 hour to dry.

5. Sew down each motif, attaching beads as you sew. Dots on patterns indicate where to position beads.

6. Pin the two layers of felt together. Taper the ends of headband to 1 inch in width, as shown in Diagram 55.

**Diagram 55**

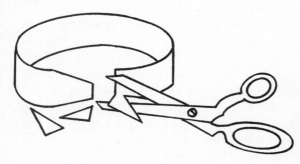

7. Sew edges of two layers together with medium-width zigzag stitch. If sewing by hand, you may use the whip stitch.

8. Sew elastic ends to ends of headband.

### Hatband

1. Measure crown of hat and add 1 inch to this measurement.

2. Cut one strip of felt to this length and wide enough to accommodate desired motif. Lay it out on a table.

3. By eye, cut the motifs from paper, to use as patterns. Pin parts to appropriate colors of felt and cut out. Form one motif on hatband. Continue to cut and position motifs on hatband as you cut, spacing evenly. Try to space motifs so that there will not be a noticeable space at the back seam. If necessary, place motif over seam after it is sewn.

4. Apply a minimum amount of glue to motif backs, and press in place. Allow 1 hour to dry.

5. Sew down each motif, attaching beads as you sew. Dots on patterns indicate where to position beads.

6. Pin the band to strip of pellon.

7. Sew edges of felt and pellon bands together, with a medium-width zigzag stitch. If sewing by hand, you may want to use the whip stitch.

8. Sew two ends together, making a ½-inch seam. If necessary, sew last motif over seam.

*Pattern 13: Suspenders*

# Alpine Art

*(Technique 2)*

*These colorful suspenders can be worn by girls of all ages. Just as the men in Bavaria*

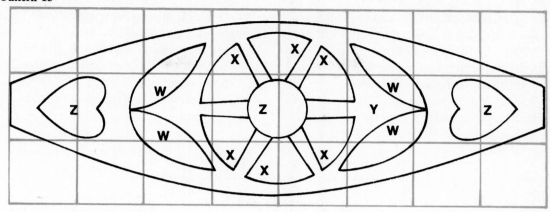

*or the Tyrol wear them with lederhosen, free-spirited men might enjoy wearing them around a ski resort or for holiday festivities. They might, however, prefer a more subtle color scheme.*

### Materials

**1 felt strip, length required to fit, 4 inches in width, in orange**

**1 felt strip, length required to fit, 4 inches in width, in green**

**9- by 12-inch rectangles or scraps of felt, in magenta and red**

**thread in green**

**pinking shears (optional)**

**Completed size:** As required

**Color code:** W—green, X—orange, Y—magenta, Z—red

### Instructions

1. Measure from front of waistline at spot where suspenders would be attached, across shoulder, to back of waistline, making allowance for suspenders to cross in the back. Also allow an extra 1½ inches on each end for buttoning.

2. Press felt pieces with steam iron.

3. Cut two strips from orange felt to measured length, 1¼ inches wide, using pinking shears if available. Cut two green strips to same length, 1¾ inches wide.

4. Pin orange strips to green strips, centering the orange so that there is an equal amount of green showing on each side. Stitch along edge of orange with a straight stitch. Make buttonholes at ends of each strip. Sew corresponding buttons inside waistline of the garment to be worn with suspenders.

5. Try the suspenders on. Measure space on chest between outer edges of suspenders and subtract ½ inch. Cut a piece of paper to this width and fold it into halves, three times. You now have eight segments. Draw three rows of squares on these eight measurements, as shown in the pattern. Enlarge crosspiece pattern, according to instructions on page 19.

6. Tape pattern to magenta felt. Follow directions on page 16 for use of tracing wheel and carbon. Trace outline of crosspiece and a few marks to show placement of the appliqué shapes. Untape pattern.

7. Cut out magenta crosspiece and pin to orange felt. Cut orange felt around the magenta, about ⅛ inch from edge. If pinking shears are available, use them for top and bottom edge.

8. With these pieces still pinned together, pin them to green felt. Cut green felt around the orange, ⅛ inch from edge.

9. Tape pattern to appropriate colors of felt and trace the appliqué shapes.

10. Cut out these pieces. Lay them out on the crosspiece and pin in place.

11. Sew all pieces into place, stitching through the three layers of felt. Use zigzag stitch set at medium width, 10 stitches to the inch. Straight stitch around the magenta, close to the edge.

12. Sew ends of crosspiece to suspenders on outside edges.

*Pattern 14: Pillow*

# Katy the Cat

*(Technique 2)*

*This stuffed cat and her pal, Peggy the Pig, in the next pattern, make great pillows for children's rooms or nursery shelves. Your little ones will love them. They can be made quickly and replaced easily when wear and tear begins to show.*

### Materials
2 felt squares, 16 by 16 inches, in turquoise

9- by 12-inch rectangles or scraps of felt, in blue, navy, and chartreuse (If rectangles are purchased, buy 1 of each color.)

thread

**Pattern 14**

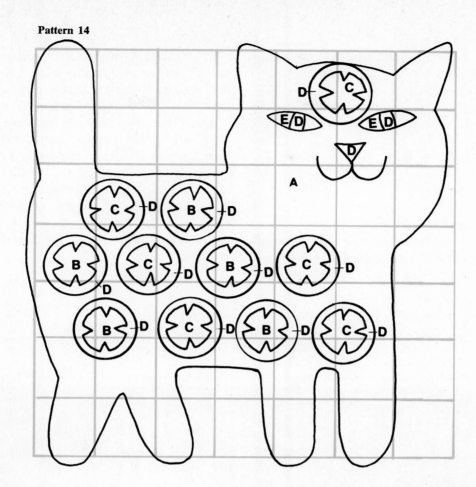

5 inches yarn, in white
½ pound polyester fiberfill

**Completed size:** 12½ by 13½ inches (at longest dimension)

**Color code:** A—turquoise, B—green, C—blue, D—navy, E—chartreuse

### Instructions

1. Enlarge pattern according to instructions on page 19. Each square equals 2 inches. Pattern should measure 14 by 15 inches.

2. Press all felt pieces with steam iron.

3. Tape pattern to turquoise felt so that there is enough felt all around for ½-inch seams. Follow directions on page 16 for use of tracing wheel and carbon. Trace outline of cat and line for mouth. Make marks for placement of eyes, snoot, and circles. Untape pattern. Place carbon paper underneath traced cat so that carbon side is up and touching wrong side of felt. With tracing wheel, press hard over the outline of cat. You will now have the outline of cat on both sides of felt.

4. Tape pieces of felt to back of pattern and trace shapes to appropriate colors. Repeated flowers and circles need be traced only once and then used as models from which to cut the rest. Cut out all pieces.

5. Lay out design on cat and pin all pieces into place.

6. Sew around circles, snoot, and eyes using medium-width zigzag stitch, set for 10 stitches to the inch. Stitch across through middle of flowers, bisecting the petals.

7. On sewing machine, using a wide zig-zag stitch, set for 8 stitches to the inch, couch yarn onto mouth line of the cat. (See Diagram 56.)

**Diagram 56**

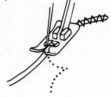

8. Carefully steam press.

9. Place cat face down on other piece of turquoise felt and pin together.

10. Stitch the two pieces together along traced outline on wrong side. Leave an opening below the tail that is large enough through which to insert your hand.

11. Trim around cat, ⅜ inch away from sewn edge. Clip corners and curves and trim ear points close to the seam. Turn cat inside out. Push out ears, legs, and tail with eraser of pencil or other blunt, pointed tool.

12. Insert fiberfill, beginning with legs, ears, body, and ending with tail. Close up the back seam opening by hand, stuffing as you sew.

---

*Pattern 15: Pillow*

# Peggy the Pig

*(Technique 2)*

---

*Peggy the Pig and her friend, Katy the Cat, make quite a team. They belong together.*

**Pattern 15**

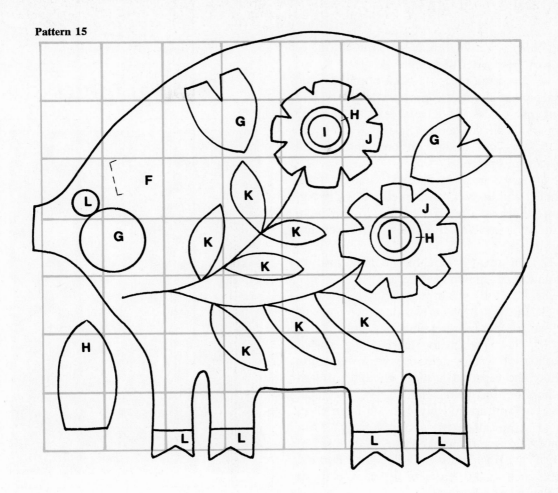

## Materials

2 felt rectangles, 15 by 17 inches, in cerise

9- by 12-inch rectangles or scraps of felt, in hot pink, orange, golden yellow, lemon yellow, green, and olive (If rectangles are purchased, buy 1 of each color.)

15 inches yarn, in green

thread

¾ pound polyester fiberfill

1 pipe cleaner

**Completed size:** 12½ by 14 inches (at largest dimension)

**Color code:** F—cerise, G—hot pink, H—orange, I—golden yellow, J—lemon yellow, K—green, L—olive

## Instructions

1. Enlarge pattern according to instructions on page 19. Each square equals 2 inches. Pattern should measure 15 by 17 inches.

2. Press felt pieces with steam iron.

3. Tape pattern to cerise felt so that there is enough felt all around to allow for seams. Follow directions on page 16 for use of tracing wheel and carbon. Trace outline of pig. Make marks for placement of flowers, leaves, eye, and cheek. Untape pattern. Place carbon paper underneath traced pig, with carbon side up, touching wrong side of felt. With tracing wheel, press hard over out-

line of pig. You will now have the outline of pig on both sides of felt.

4. Tape felt pieces to back of pattern and trace other shapes to appropriate colors. Cut out all pieces. If available, use pinking shears for flower centers.

5. Lay out design on pig, and pin all pieces into place.

6. Sew around flowers, leaves, eye, cheek, and hooves, using medium-width zig-zag stitch, set for 10 stitches to the inch. Stitch across flower centers with straight stitch.

7. On sewing machine, couch yarn to stem line, as shown in Diagram 56.

8. Carefully steam press.

9. Place pig face down on other piece of cerise felt, and pin together.

10. Sew pieces together, along traced outline of wrong side. Leave an opening along the top that is large enough through which to insert your hand.

11. Trim around pig ⅜ inch from sewn edge. Clip all corners and curves. Trim hoof and snout points close to the seam. Turn pig inside out. Use blunt, pointed tool, such as the eraser of a pencil, to push out snout and hooves.

12. Beginning with hooves and snout and ending with body, insert fiberfill. Close up seam opening by hand, stuffing as you sew.

13. By eye, cut two ear pieces from orange felt. Sew pieces together around the edge, using zigzag stitch. Dotted line on pattern indicates where ear should be placed. Crease ear down the middle, and sew blunt end to this spot. Tack down underside of ear and underlayer of top side with a stitch.

14. Curl pipe cleaner. Turn back tips to prevent their scratching a child. Sew one end to appropriate place on back of pig.

# Supergraphics

*(Technique 2)*

*This pattern and the one following, are for extra large tote bags. They come in handy especially at Christmastime for shopping expeditions and for delivering gifts to family holiday celebrations. They perform all the duties of other tote bags and many more. This super tote can be made quickly on the sewing machine. Young people will like the graphic, geometric design.*

## Materials

1⅛ yards felt, in magenta

9- by 12-inch rectangles or scraps of felt, in orange, yellow, green, and turquoise (If rectangles are purchased, buy 2 of each color.)

thread
1¼ yards buckram
½ yard #300 cable cord

**Completed size:** 18 by 19 inches, 7-inch gusset

**Color code:** M—magenta, N—orange, O—yellow, P—green, Q—turquoise

### Instructions

1. Enlarge pattern according to instructions on page 19. Each square equals 2 inches. Pattern should measure 18 by 19 inches.

2. Press felt pieces with steam iron.

3. Cut a piece of magenta felt to measure 19 by 20 inches. Tape the pattern to the magenta so that there is ½ inch of felt surrounding pattern edge. Follow directions on page 16 for use of tracing wheel and carbon. Make marks to show positioning of the main circles and triangles. Untape pattern.

4. Tape the remaining pieces of felt to the back of pattern and trace the other parts of the design to appropriate colors. Cut out all shapes.

5. Lay out design, placing all pieces in position. Pin in place.

6. Using medium-width zigzag stitch, set for 10 stitches to the inch, sew down all shapes.

7. Carefully steam press the design.

8. Place the pattern over the design and mark corners. Remove pattern. Using yardstick for guide, connect corner marks with chalk line. Cut carefully along marked edge.

9. Cut three more pieces of magenta felt the same size as the design. One will be the back and the other two will be linings. Cut four 7- by 19-inch pieces for gussets and linings and two 7- by 18-inch pieces for bottom and lining.

10. From buckram cut two rectangles, 17½ by 18½ inches, and one rectangle, 6½ by 17½ inches. These pieces will be used to stiffen the front, back, and bottom. The gussets will not be stiffened.

11. From any remaining color of felt, cut two 2- by 11-inch rectangles for the handles. Cut the cable cord into two 9-inch lengths. Put cable cord on each rectangle and fold felt in half, over cord. Pin side edges together. Using zipper foot of machine, stitch along edges, very close to cord. Trim edges, allowing ⅛ inch from seam.

12. Place one of the large pieces of buckram between design and front lining. Bend and center one handle to the front top edge. Pin ends 6 inches apart, between lining and buckram. Stitch around the edges attaching felt, lining, and buckram with a wide zigzag stitch. Make sure that stitches at handle go over cable cord. Repeat this procedure for back of bag. With buckram between, stitch bottom to bottom lining. Sew gussets to linings.

13. Sew inside of front to inside of bottom, using a wide zigzag stitch. In the same way, sew bottom of bag to back. Stitch gussets to front and back to form the bag.

## Pattern 17: Tote Bag

# Americana

*(Technique 4)*

*This super tote features the decorative French knot texture. The black background highlights the bright colors of the hearts-and-flowers design.*

### Materials
⅝ yard of felt, in black
½ yard of felt, in turquoise
¼ yard of felt, in green
¼ yard of felt, in magenta
9- by 12-inch rectangles or scraps of felt, in orange and yellow (If rectangles are purchased, buy 1 for each color.)
glue
lightweight yarn, in several matching colors
yarn needle
thread
1¼ yards buckram
½ yard #300 cable cord

**Completed size:** 18 by 19 inches, 7-inch gusset
**Color code:** R—black, S—turquoise, T—green, U—magenta, V—orange, W—yellow

### Instructions
1. Enlarge pattern according to instructions on page 19. Each square equals 2 inches. Pattern should measure 18 by 19 inches.
2. Press felt pieces with steam iron.
3. Cut a piece of black felt to measure 19 by 20 inches. Tape the pattern to felt so that there is a ½-inch border of felt surrounding pattern. Follow directions on page 16 for use of tracing wheel and carbon. Make marks to show positioning of parts of design. Untape pattern.
4. Tape remaining pieces of felt to back of pattern and trace shapes to appropriate colors. Cut out all pieces.
5. Lay out the design, placing all pieces in position. Glue in place, using minimum amount of glue. Allow 1 hour to dry.
6. Using yarns of contrasting colors, make French knots throughout the design following small dots on pattern. Refer to page 41 and Diagram 19 for a review on French knots.
7. Place the pattern over design and mark corners. Remove pattern. Using yardstick for guide, connect the corner marks with a chalk line. Cut carefully along marked edge.
8. Cut another piece of black felt that is the same size as the front design for back of bag and two pieces of the same size from turquoise for linings. Cut four 7- by 19-inch pieces of felt—two of magenta for gussets

89

and two of green for gusset linings. Cut a 7- by 18-inch rectangle of black for bottom and another of turquoise for bottom lining.

9. Cut two rectangles from buckram, 17½ by 18½ inches, to stiffen front and back of bag. For bottom, cut one more measuring 6½ by 17½ inches. The gussets will not be stiffened.

10. From any remaining color, cut two 11- by 2-inch rectangles for the handles. Cut cable cord into two 9-inch lengths. Put cable cord on felt and fold felt over cable cord, pinning edges together. Using zipper foot of machine, stitch sides together very close to the cord. Trim edges ⅛ inch from seam.

11. Place one of the large cut pieces of buckram between design and front lining. Bend and center one handle to front top edge and pin it between lining and buckram. Make ends 6 inches apart. Stitch around the edges, attaching front, buckram, and lining, making sure that stitches go over cable cord. Repeat procedure for back of bag. Stitch bottom to bottom lining with buckram between, and stitch gussets to linings.

12. Sew inside of front to inside of bottom, using a wide zigzag stitch, set for 8 stitches to the inch. In the same way, stitch bottom to back. Stitch the gussets in place to form the bag.

# In the Country

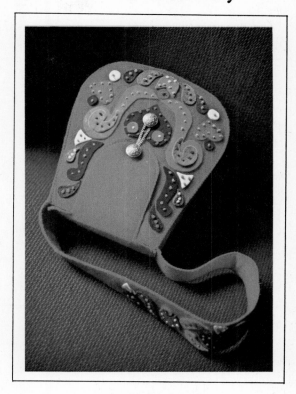

*(Technique 4)*

*This shoulder bag is roomy inside and its construction is easy. It was designed to be worn with peasant-type dresses but will go just as well with jeans.*

### Materials

½ yard felt, in red

9- by 12-inch rectangles or scraps of felt, in white, orange, hot pink, royal blue, turquoise, green, and dark green (If rectangles are purchased, buy 1 for each color.)

glue

yarn needle

lightweight yarn in several matching colors

⅞ yard buckram

91

**Pattern 18**

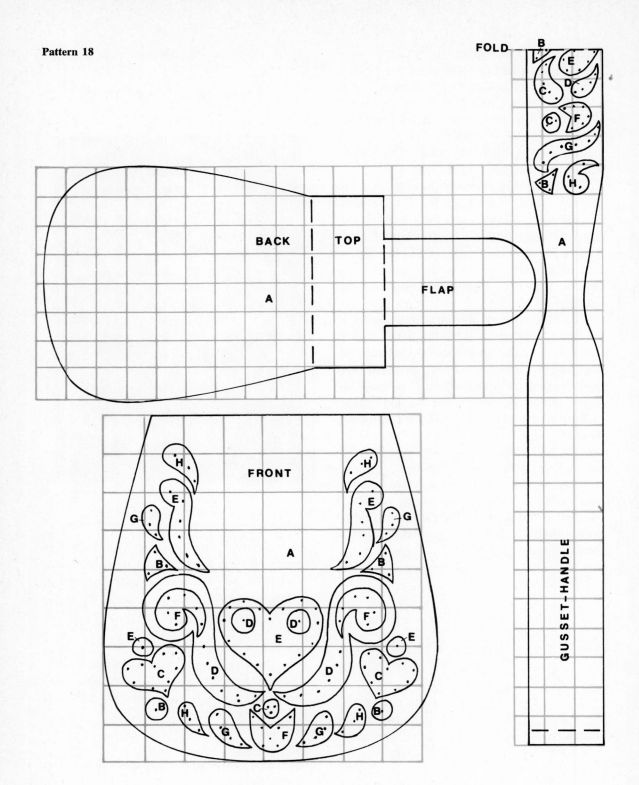

FOLD

BACK TOP

A FLAP

A

FRONT

A

GUSSET–HANDLE

92

thread in red
9 inches iron-on mending tape
set of 2 buttons with chain loop

**Completed size:** 8 by 9¼ inches at widest point, 2½-inch gusset
**Color code:** A—red, B—white, C—orange, D—hot pink, E—royal blue, F—turquoise, G—green, H—dark green

### Instructions

1. Enlarge patterns according to directions on page 19. Each square equals 1 inch. Cut out the three pattern pieces.

2. Press felt pieces with steam iron.

3. Fold the red felt in half and pin corners together. Pin the three pattern pieces to red felt, with gusset handle placed on fold, as marked. Cut two gusset handles. Cut two back pieces and two front pieces — the front should have an extra inch allowance all around. Duplicate pieces will be used for linings. (An extra inch is not needed for the handle since "drawing up" of the fabric will be minimal.)

4. Tape front pattern to the larger front piece so that there is 1 inch of felt surrounding edge. Follow directions on page 16 for use of tracing wheel and carbon. Make marks to indicate placement of design pieces. Untape pattern. Repeat this procedure on one of the gusset-handle pieces.

5. Tape pieces of felt to back of pattern and trace shapes to appropriate colors. Repeated shapes need be traced only once and then used as models from which to cut the rest. Cut out all pieces.

6. Lay out design on bag front and handle. Using a minimum amount of glue, secure all pieces. Allow 1 hour to dry.

7. Using yarns of contrasting colors and following small dots on pattern, make French knots throughout design. For a review on French knots, refer to page 41 and Diagram 19.

8. Tape the front pattern over front piece

and trace outline. Cut out on traced line.

9. Cut buckram piece to match the three pattern pieces. Buckram for gusset handle will have to be cut in two pieces. Allow ½ inch on ends of each piece for overlapping. Overlap and sew these two pieces together, as shown in Diagram 57. Trim away ⅛ inch from all edges of buckram pieces.

10. Place front buckram piece between front and front lining. Using medium-width zigzag stitch, set at 8 stitches to the inch, sew all around the edge. Seam ends of gusset-handle piece together on seam line (folded line on pattern). Do same for lining. Place gusset-handle buckram piece between the gusset handle and its lining. Stitch around edges, using same zigzag stitch as above. Following the broken lines on pattern, cut across the remaining piece of buckram. Place the pieces on ironing board, in their original position. Cut mending tape into one 3-inch and one 6-inch piece. Iron mending tape over the cuts, as shown in Diagram 58.

**Diagram 57**

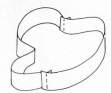

**Diagram 58**

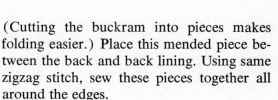

(Cutting the buckram into pieces makes folding easier.) Place this mended piece between the back and back lining. Using same zigzag stitch, sew these pieces together all around the edges.

11. Match seam of gusset handle to center of front bottom edge. Using a wide zigzag stitch, sew front to gusset handle. Sew back to gusset handle in the same way.

12. Bring flap over to front of bag. Creases will bend easily. Sew one button to center of heart shape. Sew button with chain loop to center of flap so that it lines up with button on heart.

# The Clean Scene

*(Technique 6)*

*Start your own antilitter campaign by carrying these colorful, plastic-lined litter bags in your car. They will discourage highway littering and are great for taking along on picnics. The handles, which unsnap quickly so that the bag can be emptied easily, enable the bag to be hung conveniently over parts of the car interior. Make one for dad or any other car owner you know.*

## Materials (for 1 bag)

**4 felt rectangles, 9 by 12 inches, in any desired color**

**1 felt rectangle, 8 by 14 inches, in black**

**small scraps of felt, in any desired color (for the lettering)**

**2 scraps fabric, in any color**

**fabric glue**

**thread in contrasting color**

**1 large plastic garbage bag**

**1 heavy-duty snap**

**snap pliers**

**Completed size:** 8 by 10 inches, 4-inch gusset

**Color code:** Any desired color scheme (numbers on pattern indicate color distribution)

## Instructions

1. Enlarge pattern according to directions on page 19. Each square equals 1 inch. Pattern should measure 8 by 10 inches.

2. Press all fabric pieces with steam iron.

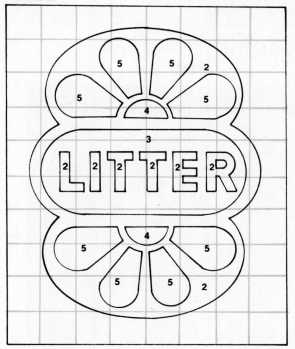

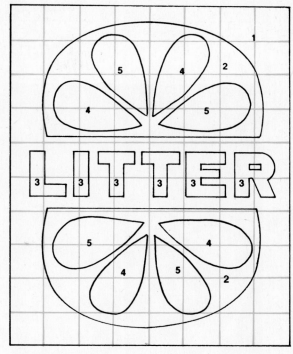

3. Tape pattern to 9- by 12-inch square of felt so that there is ½ inch or more surrounding edge of pattern. Follow instructions on page 16 for use of tracing wheel and carbon. Make marks to indicate placement of design parts.

4. Tape black felt and other fabric pieces to back of pattern and trace other parts of design to colors. (Black felt is for area behind leaf shapes.) Cut out all pieces. See page 40 and Diagram 18 for an easy way to cut out letters.

5. Lay design parts out on front of bag and pin in place.

6. Using medium-width zigzag stitch, set at 20 stitches to the inch, sew around all pieces of design. Gently steam press.

7. Place pattern over design and mark corners. Remove pattern. Connect corner marks with chalk line and cut along line.

8. Cut one piece of felt for back, making it the same size as front. Cut two 4- by 10-inch pieces for gussets, one 4- by 8-inch piece for bottom, and two 1½- by 10-inch pieces for handle.

9. Cut out plastic pieces from plastic garbage bag to match all pieces of bag except handle.

10. Place all bag parts other than handle face down on newspaper. Apply glue.

11. Adhere plastic lining pieces to matching felt pieces, pressing well all over.

12. Using a wide zigzag stitch, set at 10 stitches to the inch, with plastic linings facing each other, sew along the edges to attach front to gussets, gussets to back, and bottom to front and back.

13. Place two pieces for handle together. Pin and sew together around the edges. Following directions that come with snaps and using pliers, place snap top on one end. Place snap bottom to back of bag, at the center of top edge. Sew other end of handle to front of bag, at the center of top edge.

# Evening Out

*(Technique 6)*

These two envelope bags are for evening use—one in jewel-toned silk for formal evenings and one in gingham and calico for more casual evenings. Use leftover scraps from a patchwork dress or skirt. The silk bag is enhanced with sequins for an added touch of glamor, and the gingham bag features edging and beads.

### Materials (for silk bag)
2 silk rectangles, 8¾ by 20½ inches, in any desired color
4 silk scraps, 3 by 4 inches, in contrasting color
embroidery scissors
thread in matching colors
24 sequins, in matching colors or in 1 color
24 glass beads, 11-millimeter size
2 inches elastic cord
1 buckram rectangle, 7⅝ by 18¾ inches
14 inches iron-on mending tape
1 metal or jeweled button

**Completed size:** 6½ by 7⅝ inches

### Materials (for gingham bag)
2 gingham rectangles, 10¼ by 14¾ inches, in any desired color
3 calico scraps, 3 by 4 inches, in contrasting color
embroidery scissors
thread in matching colors
12 beads, ⅛ inch in diameter
2 inches elastic cord
1 buckram rectangle, 9 by 13¼ inches

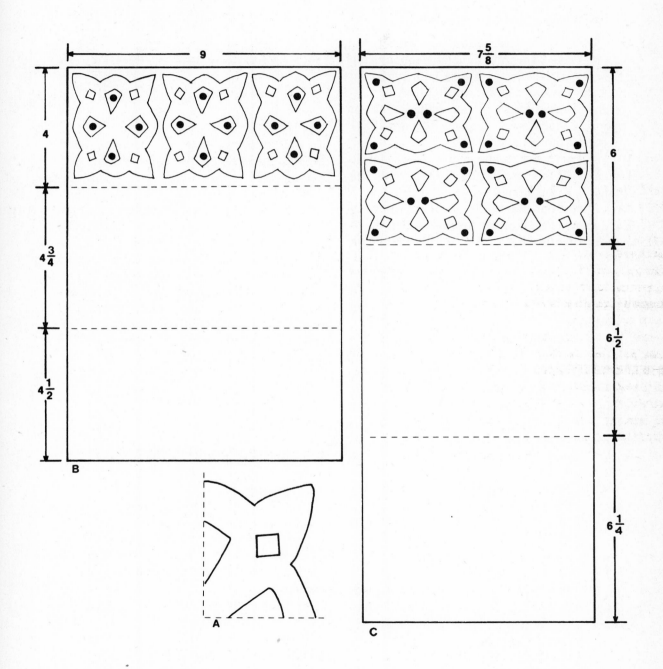

**18 inches iron-on mending tape**

**20 inches edging, ¼ inch wide, in two 10-inch strips in same or different colors to blend with calico**

**1 button**

## Completed size: 4¾ by 9 inches

### Instructions

1. From paper, cut a rectangle measuring 2¾ by 3½ inches. Fold in half twice and cut out the shape shown in Figure A on pattern. (Dotted lines indicate folded edges of paper.) Open up the paper. You now have a cutout motif pattern.

2. Pin motif pattern to small fabric scraps. With sharp pencil, trace around the edge and the shapes within.

3. Cut out the motifs of fabric, allowing ¼ inch from edge for turning under.

4. Lightly chalk mark the fold lines on the bag fabric (silk or gingham), as indicated by broken lines on patterns. Mark the edges of bag. With penciled sides up, pin motifs in place on front flap, as shown on patterns.

5. Appliqué the motifs to the bag fabric using whip stitch, as shown in Diagram 25. Refer to page 51, steps 7 and 8, for review, and Diagram 59 for slitting detail.

**Diagram 59**

6. Following dots on patterns, sew sequins and beads on silk bag and beads on gingham bag. Sew sequins by bringing needle up through fabric, sequin, and bead and back down through sequin and fabric.

7. Pin the second piece of fabric (lining) face to face with appliquéd piece. Tack two ends of elastic cord to top center of front flap. (See Diagram 60.) Mark seams, fol-

**Diagram 60**

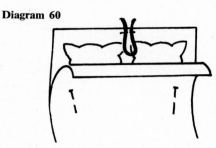

lowing measurements of pattern. Seam around marks on the two sides and flap end, making sure to sew over elastic. Clip corners and turn inside out.

8. Mark fold lines on buckram and cut across them. Place the cut pieces on ironing board in their original positions. Cut mending tape into two equal-length strips and iron on over the cuts. (See Diagram 58.)

9. Insert into bag, making sure each section is in its proper place. Close open end of bag along the edge with wide zigzag stitch. Fold two creased lines to form front and back. (See Diagram 61.)

**Diagram 61**

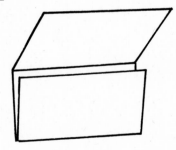

10. Leaving front flap free, sew wide zigzag stitch along edges to attach bag front to back.

11. Sew edgings in place by hand on gingham bag, neatly tacking ends under. Sew button to front of bag at center of bottom edge to meet elastic loop.

# Starflower

*(Techniques 7 or 8)*

*This decorative typewriter cover makes a nice gift for someone who types at home or in an office. It adds a bright and cheery note to any desk.*

## Materials

**1 piece fabric large enough to make loose-fitting typewriter cover and lining, in olive**
scraps of fabric squares, 11 by 11 inches, in white, lime, yellow, and pale lime
old typewriter cover
embroidery scissors
thread in olive

**Completed size:** May be adapted to fit any typewriter

**Color code:** I—olive, J—white, K—lime, L—yellow, M—pale lime

## Instructions

1. Cut apart seams of cover of typewriter and use it as a pattern from which to cut cover and lining.

If typewriter cover is not available, take measurements of typewriter, as shown in Diagram 62. Draw pattern on paper to fit these measurements, as shown in Diagrams 63-A and B, allowing an extra ½ inch in all width dimensions for a loose fit. It is a good idea to make the first cover from some old fabric or muslin to make sure the fit is right.

2. Measure width at measurement B.

This is the area where design is to be placed. Subtract 4 inches from this width to determine width of the design. Divide the width into five equal parts. Enlarge pattern according to directions on page 19. Each square equals size of one of the five parts.

3. Pin pattern to fabric, and cut out the top and two sides. Allow ⅝ inch all around for seams and hem and an extra inch around top piece, to be trimmed off later.

4. Tape design pattern to top of cover in proper place. Follow directions on page 16 for use of tracing wheel and carbon. Trace outline of shapes. Omit inner circles within flower and large center circle shapes.

**Diagram 62**

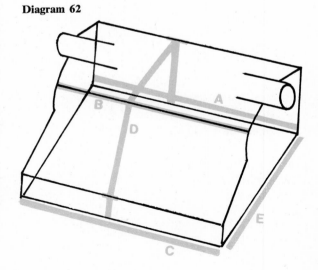

5. Use either Technique 7 or 8 to work design. To use Technique 7, first arrange the fabrics so that white is on the top, followed by lime, yellow, and pale lime. Now cut these pieces into circles. Then place them underneath the olive fabric. Baste them together around the edges and attach to olive.

6. Pin pattern top to finished design top. Trim edges, leaving a ⅝-inch seam allowance. Make notches, as shown in Diagrams 63-A and B. Remove pattern.

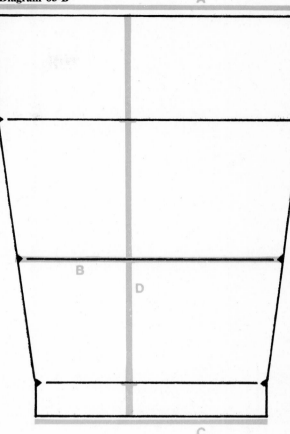

**Diagram 63-B**

**Diagram 63-A**

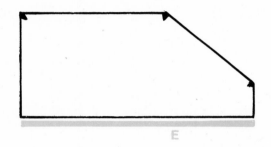

**Diagram 64**

7. With notches matching, seam top to sides. Pin pattern to remaining olive fabric and cut top and two side pieces for lining. Seam with ⅝-inch allowance.

8. Do not press seams open. Press them down toward center and topstitch over them, ⅛ inch from seam line. (See Diagram 64.) This need not be done on lining.

9. Turn under bottom edge of cover and lining ⅝ inch. Hem and press. Pin lining to cover around the edges, with wrong sides facing. Stitch together with straight stitch, ⅛ inch from edge.

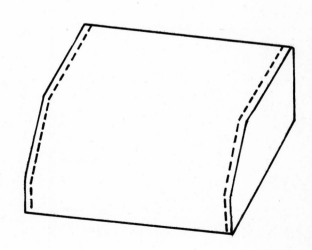

101

# Appliqué as an Art Form

Appliqué, as well as other kinds of needle art, can certainly be classified as one of the fine arts. There is no reason that painting, graphics, and sculpture should have this exclusive claim. Because so much of the needlework seen today is mass produced, needlework has come to be regarded by some as merely a "hobby craft." Nevertheless, many talented designers are producing prominent needlework designs. The time has come for needlework to take its rightful place as a respected art form.

This chapter will help get you started in this joyful endeavor. The projects in Chapter 2 demonstrate eight techniques. This chapter will show you how to create more artwork for your walls with appliqué. The projects here are intended not to make you the subject of lofty critical acclaim or to provide you with space in a museum but simply to enable you to experience the pleasure and joy of creating your own artwork.

Perhaps you have walls that need decorating. A framed or unframed appliqué design adds texture and a pleasant contrast to your home. Walls that feature only paintings tend to look humdrum. A mixture of paintings, appliqué art, and other personal treasures on your walls creates a much more interesting effect.

The instructions for wall hangings in this chapter include directions for mounting and finishing. New methods for this are offered, in addition to those already discussed. In some designs, buckram tape is suggested for stiffening the upper edge of a hanging. Buckram tape helps overcome such problems as drooping upper corners, sagging across the top, and wrinkling. For bottom edges that are too limp, use a strip of wood lath or dowel, inserted into a slot across the bottom, or glue a strip of lath to the back edge.

Although optional, lining the back of a wall hanging gives it a nice finishing touch. A lining helps to keep the edges from curling or hanging limp. Your wall hanging should hang freely without looking stiff, but sometimes, firming it just a little will give it a more professional look.

*Pattern 22: Framed Design*

# Bouquet Collage

*(Technique 1)*

*Doing this quick and easy design may help you develop an interest in collages. Children usually enjoy making collages, as well.*

*A collage is made by cutting and gluing paper shapes to a background piece. It can also be done with fabric and is a marvelous way to use leftover scraps. After cutting the few simple shapes in this design, you will probably want to go on and experiment with*

**Pattern 22**

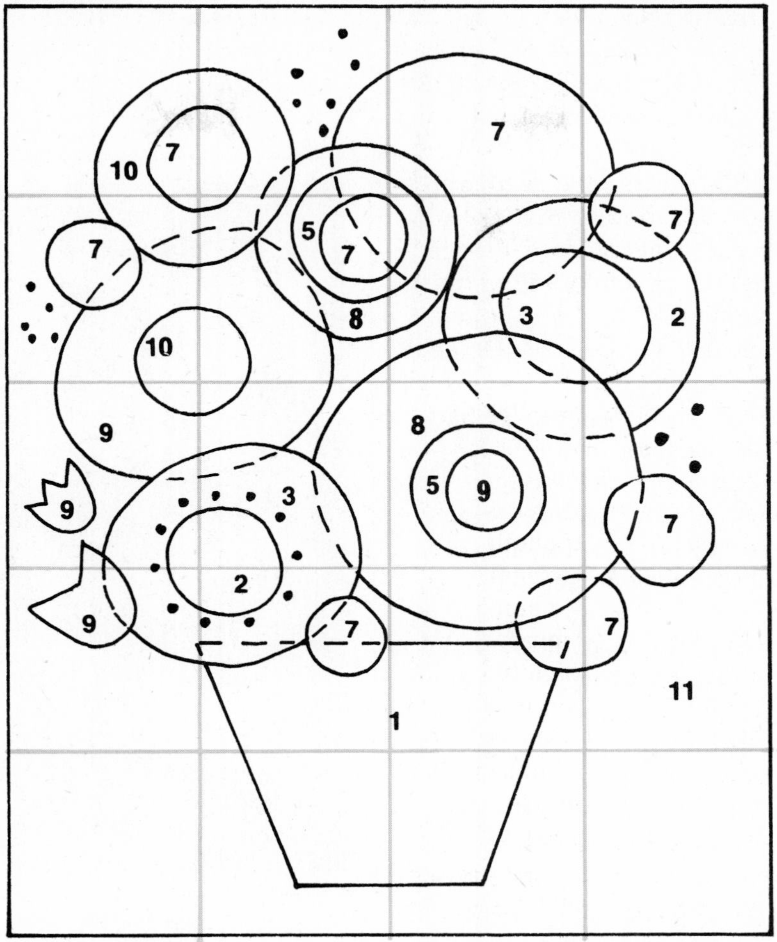

your own ideas. It is far more enjoyable to pick up the scissors and start cutting and snipping pieces for your own arrangements than it is to follow a precise design. Children prefer this method to the bother of following a pattern. Follow their example and have some fun.

By using just this one pattern, you can achieve many different collage variations simply by varying the fabric. The yellow bouquet has a few French knots. You may want to add them after gluing.

## Materials

1 fabric rectangle, 10 by 12 inches, in any desired color

scraps in 8 varieties of fabrics—prints, solids, dots, stripes, or checks

glue

leftover yarn for French knots

**Completed size:** 8 by 10 inches (excluding frame)

**Color code:** Any desired color scheme (numbers on pattern indicate color distribution)

## Instructions

1. Enlarge pattern according to instructions on page 19. Each square equals 2 inches. Pattern should measure 8 by 10 inches.

2. Press all fabric pieces with steam iron.

3. Tape pattern to fabric so that at least 1 inch of fabric surrounds edge of design. Follow directions on page 16 for use of tracing wheel and carbon. Make marks to indicate placement of flowers and pot. Untape pattern.

4. One by one, tape fabric pieces to back of pattern and trace shapes.

5. Cut out all pieces.

6. Lay out the shapes on the background to see how the arrangement looks. You may want to make substitutions in fabric. Simply recut and reposition.

7. Remove center circles of flowers and place them face down on newspaper. Apply glue and place them in their original position. Do same for all pieces, gluing and positioning the underlapped ones first. Press down firmly.

8. When design is completely glued together, French knots may be added. Dots in pattern indicate placement. See Diagram 19 and directions on page 41 for review on French knots.

9. Pin pattern to design, and mark the four corners. Remove pattern. Design is now ready for stretching and framing, as discussed on page 22.

# Stained Glass

*(Technique 2)*

*If you love the look of old stained-glass windows or if a touch of Art Nouveau appeals to you, you will enjoy working on this design. It may be that you could not afford to buy a stained-glass window even if you found one. This fake one is not nearly as expensive and will hold you over until you can have a real one. Stretching it and placing it over a door panel creates a coloful, glass window effect. The one shown here was used to add a turn-of-the-century look to a very special wall.*

*The colorful pieces of felt are placed on a black background. The black showing in between creates the look of leaded glass.*

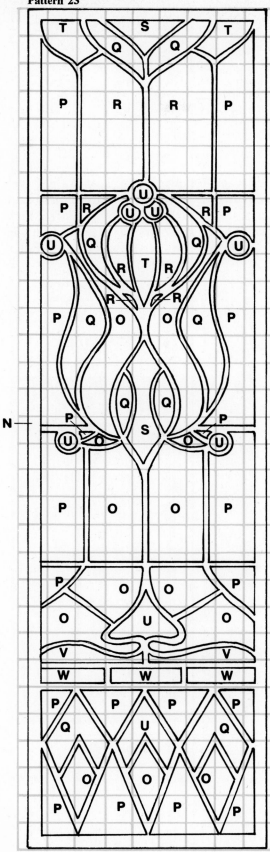

## Materials

⅝ yard felt, in black
½ yard felt, in bronze
½ yard felt, in tan
¼ yard felt, in violet
9- by 12-inch rectangles or scraps of felt, in gold, lemon yellow, golden yellow, turquoise, aqua, and dark green (If rectangles are purchased, buy two 9- by 12-inch pieces in gold and 1 in each of other colors.)
thread in black or clear nylon
17 inches buckram tape, 4 inches wide, cut in half to 2-inch widths
2 curtain rings

**Completed size:** 17 by 62 inches
**Color code:** N—black, O—bronze, P—tan, Q—violet, R—gold, S—lemon yellow, T—golden yellow, U—turquoise, V—aqua, W—dark green

### Instructions

1. Enlarge pattern according to instructions on page 19. Each square equals 2 inches. Pattern should measure 17 by 62 inches.

2. Press felt pieces with steam iron.

3. Cut a piece of black felt to measure 19 by 64 inches. Tape pattern to it so that there is 1 inch of black felt surrounding edge. (If you are making a panel instead of a wall hanging, see *Note* following step 16.) Follow directions on page 16 for use of tracing wheel and carbon. Make marks to indicate placement of all pieces. Untape pattern.

4. One by one, tape appropriate colors of felt to the back of pattern. Trace outline of all shapes and cut out.

5. Place black background on a large table or space on floor. Lay out pieces on black background and pin in place.

6. Baste the pieces in place by hand.

7. Using medium-width zigzag stitch, set at 10 stitches to the inch, sew around edges of all pieces. Remove basting.

8. Carefully steam press design.

107

9. Tape pattern over the design and mark corners. Untape pattern and connect corner marks with a chalk line. Use a yardstick to help you connect top and bottom corners and a tape measure for sides. (If you have decided to make this project into a panel instead of a wall hanging, see *Note* following step 16.)

10. Carefully cut along marked line.

11. From remaining black felt, cut two strips measuring 1¼ by 62 inches and two more measuring 1¼ by 17 inches.

12. Fold strips lengthwise, ½ inch from edge, so that the width of the other side of fold is ¾ inch.

13. Pin the two 62-inch lengths to sides of design and one 17-inch length to bottom, with the ½-inch strip on front of design. (See Diagram 65.) The top edge will be done later.

14. Sew strips in place on front side of

**Diagram 65**

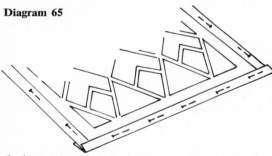

design, close to inside edge, as shown in Diagram 66.

15. Pin the ½-inch part of remaining strip across top edge. Place two buckram strips on the underside of top edge, one on top of the other. Fold the ¾-inch part of strip over the buckram. With thumb of free hand, hold all three in place, while stitching them down. Make sure buckram strips are secured.

16. Sew a curtain ring to each upper corner of hanging.

*Note:* Perhaps, instead of a wall hanging, you would prefer a panel for your door. If

**Diagram 66**

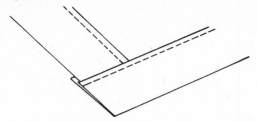

so, when following step 3, make a 2-inch, instead of a 1-inch, border around the edges of design. Ignore steps 10 through 16. Panel is ready for stretching, as described on page 22. It may be left unframed, if desired.

*Pattern 24: Wall Hanging*

# Four Seasons

*(Technique 3)*

*Seasonal changes were inspirations for this*

**Pattern 24**

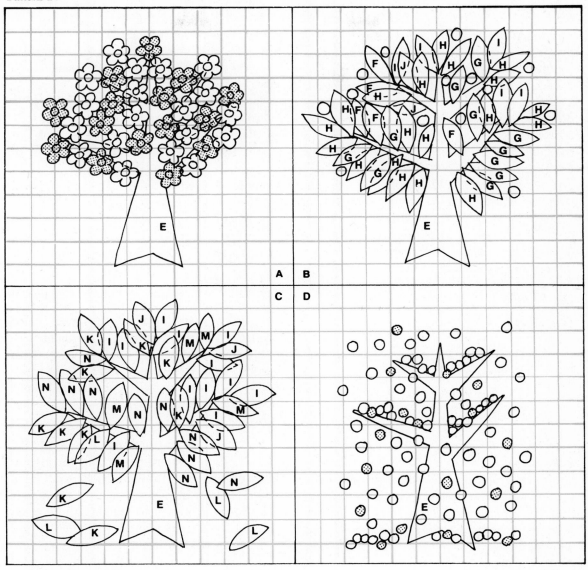

109

*wall hanging. It is made from four decorator's upholstery fabric samples. They are usually found in 27- by 27-inch squares. Sometimes fabric shops or wholesale showrooms sell discontinued samples at very low prices to close them out. These particular samples were priced at only 25 cents each.*

*Each square has the same basic tree trunk shape and its own seasonal treatment—the blossoms of new life in the spring, the fruits of summer, the last splash of color in the fall, and the dormant tree, surrounded by the swirling snow of winter.*

*The winter segment introduces the star stitch. It is used here to suggest snowflakes. The needle is brought up through the center of the circle, down near the edge, up again through the center, and then down again, directly across from the first one. Repeat this two more times for a six-pointed star. (See Diagram 67.)*

**Diagram 67**

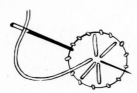

*After each square is done separately by hand, they are seamed together on the machine. Its dramatic size makes it perfect for a high wall or stairway. Instead of a long, narrow hanging, it could also be pieced together to form a square, as shown in the arrangement in the pattern. The shape you choose will depend on your individual decorating needs.*

### Materials

4 upholstery sample squares, 27 by 27 inches, in gold, olive, turquoise, and royal blue

⅜ yard felt, in black

9- by 12-inch rectangles or scraps of felt, in white, pale apricot, lemon yellow, golden yellow, chartreuse, lime, bright green, light olive, olive, gold, bronze, aqua, and turquoise (If rectangles are purchased, buy 2 of white, bright green, and light olive and 1 each of others.)

thread in gold, olive, turquoise, and royal blue

2¾ yards lining fabric, any width for long version or 1⅜ yards in 48-inch width for square version

glue

24 inches lath, ¼ by 1 inch for long version or 48 inches for square version

curtain rod, extending to 24 inches for long version, 48 inches for square version

**Completed size:** 24 by 96 inches (long), 48 by 48 inches (square). Each panel is 24 by 24 inches.

**Color code:** (UF indicates upholstery fabric) A—gold UF, B—olive UF, C—turquoise UF, D—royal blue UF, E—black, F—chartreuse, G—lime, H—bright green, I—light olive, J—olive, K—gold, L—bronze, M—lemon yellow, N—golden yellow, shaded blossoms—pale apricot with golden yellow centers, other blossoms—white with lemon yellow centers, fruit—turquoise, shaded snowflakes—aqua, other snowflakes—white

### Instructions

1. Enlarge pattern according to instructions on page 19, drawing each panel on a separate sheet of paper. Each square equals 2 inches. Each enlarged panel should measure 24 by 24 inches.

2. Press all fabric pieces.

3. Tape each pattern to appropriate color of upholstery fabric. Leave an equal margin all around edge of design on olive, turquoise, and royal blue. On the gold panel, however, leave a margin of at least 2 inches from top edge of design. If you are making the square version, leave 2 inches across top edge of olive, as well. Follow directions on page 16 for use of tracing wheel and carbon. Make

marks to indicate placement of tree trunks, leaves, flowers, and circles. Untape pattern.

4. Tape appropriate colors of felt to the back of patterns and trace a few of the flower, leaf, and circle shapes. Cut them out and use them as models from which to cut the rest. If you wish, cut the leaf shapes and circles by eye. Trace the tree trunk to the black felt, cut it out and use it as model to cut three more.

5. Lay out the individual panels, placing pieces on appropriate backgrounds.

6. Baste all pieces in place.

7. Using whip stitch, as shown in Diagram 14, sew around edges of shapes in each panel. Use thread to match background. Make running stitches, as shown in Diagram 13, up and down tree trunk. (See Diagram 68.) This will give texture to the tree. Make running stitches through centers of as many leaves as you wish, to suggest veins.

Make a six-pointed star stitch on some circles in winter section. See page 110 and Diagram 67 for instructions.

**Diagram 68**

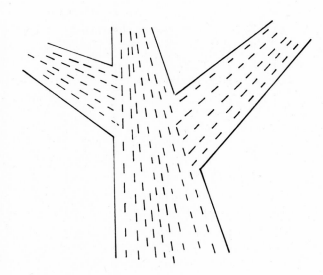

8. Press each panel with steam iron.

9. Tape patterns to back of individual panels and mark corners. Untape patterns. Using yardstick for guide, connect corners of each panel with chalk line.

10. For the long version, pin bottom edge of gold to the top edge of olive. Seam across chalk line on sewing machine. Repeat same procedure, attaching olive to turquoise, and turquoise to royal blue. For the square version, seam the right edge of gold to the left edge of olive. Next, seam the right edge of turquoise to left edge of royal blue. Trim the seams to ½ inch and press open. Seam these two pieces together, with the gold and olive piece above the turquoise and royal blue. Make sure that all four corners meet. Trim seams to ½ inch and press open.

11. Turn border of hanging under on chalk line and press flat. Trim sides and bottom edges to ½ inch.

12. Topstitch the hanging along top edge, 1 inch from fold, to form a slot.

13. For the long version, cut lining fabric to measure 25 by 97 inches. For the square version, cut lining to measure 48 inches wide and 49 inches long.

14. Turn edges of lining under to match size of hanging so that top edge lines up with stitched line under top fold. The two selvaged edges of the fabric need not be turned under for the square version. Press the turned-under edges flat.

15. By hand or machine, hem lower edge of hanging and lining. Press flat. Pin or baste lining to back of hanging around the edges, with turned-under edges against each other. For the square version, pin selvaged edges of lining to side edges of hanging. Stitch edges together by hand or machine. Press hanging flat.

16. Glue lath to back of lower edge of hanging, between back and lining. Insert the curtain rod through upper slot. Use the hooks that came with the rod for hanging.

## Pattern 25: Framed Design

# Kantha

*(Technique 4)*

This design is based on a traditional textile art of Eastern Bengal, called a kantha. It was done mostly by women of the nineteenth century. They patched together old pieces of rags and delicately embroidered them with a design. The old, useless tatters were given a fresh, new life. Today this is commonly referred to as "recycling."

The kantha *always featured a lotus flower in the center and a tree in each corner to symbolize the four directions. Each woman embellished her design with motifs, meaningful to her at that point in her life. She also designed her own border. No two* kanthas *were ever alike.*

This kantha *is quite a departure from the traditional version. Originally, only the colors of red and blue on a white background were used. Green and yellow were introduced later. I have made another change in that I have used felt and the French knot technique for this design. I have also incorporated another idea from India—the tiny mirrorlike bits found in many Indian embroideries. These mirrors are used to ward off evil demons. In authentic Indian works, the mirrors are made from mica, but this effect can also be achieved by using a material called metallic mylar. It can be found in art-supply stores, but if you have trouble finding it, cut-up aluminum foil tins will do nicely. Use a pair of old scissors to cut these materials.*

### Materials
1 felt rectangle, 24 by 28 inches, in orange
1 felt rectangle, 16½ by 21 inches, in green
1 felt rectangle, 16 by 20 inches, in magenta
9- by 12-inch rectangles or scraps of felt, in yellow, gold, and hot pink (If rectangles are purchased, buy 1 of each color.)
thread in violet and orange
glue
metallic mylar, the smallest amount your shop will sell (If too expensive, use an aluminum foil pie tin.)
yarn needle
lightweight yarn in matching colors

**Completed size:** 20 by 24 inches (excluding frame)
**Color code:** S—orange, T—green, U—magenta, V—yellow, W—gold, X—hot pink, Y—metallic mylar

### Instructions
1. Enlarge pattern according to instructions on page 19. Each square equals 2 inches. This is half of the design. Broken line indicates the vertical center line. Other half of design repeats this half. Pattern half

112

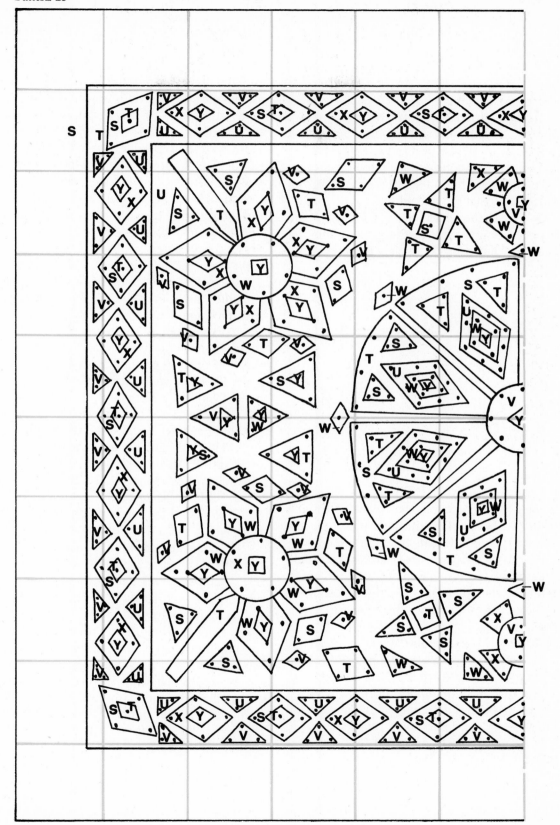

should measure 12 by 20 inches.

2. Press all felt pieces with steam iron.

3. Pin green felt to orange background so that 4 inches of orange surround the edge of the green.

4. Sew around edge of green with violet thread. If your sewing machine has such a selection, choose a decorative zigzag stitch. I used the diamond stitch, but if your machine does not have a selection, use a zigzag stitch of any length and width.

5. Turn the work over. Cut away the layer of orange behind the green panel, as shown in Diagram 69. This will prevent the

**Diagram 69**

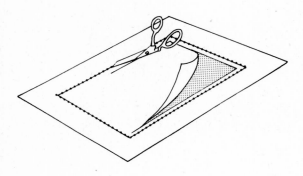

design from becoming too thick for French knots to be worked through. Save the removed piece, however, for later use.

6. From magenta felt, cut a rectangle measuring 13½ by 18 inches. Pin it to green panel so that there is a 1½-inch margin of green all around. Save the magenta scrap for later use.

7. Stitch around the edge of magenta with orange thread. Use the same stitch as in step 4 or a satin stitch if you prefer.

8. Turn the work over and cut away layer of green behind the magenta. Save it for later use.

9. Tape pattern over left half of this background piece, lining up pattern edges

with border edge. Use tracing wheel, pencil point, and carbon, as directed on page 16. Make marks to indicate placement of all pieces. Trace the broken vertical line. Untape pattern and turn it upside down. Tape it to right side of background, lining up broken line of pattern to traced line and pattern edges to border edges. Trace shapes.

10. Tape appropriate colors of felt to back of pattern. One by one, trace shapes of design. Repeated shapes need be traced only once and then used as models from which to cut the rest. You may want to reverse the position of some colors on the right side. See photograph. Shapes that are 1 inch or less may be cut by eye. Trace the metallic shapes onto the felt shapes that will contain them. This traced shape will be cut out to reveal metallic material underneath.

11. Cut out all pieces. Place them in position on background as you cut to keep account of how many you have cut.

12. Cut the designated metallic shape out. Be careful not to damage felt surrounding it. First, pierce the felt with tip of scissors, and then cut out the diamond, circle, or square. Cut the metallic bits from either mylar or aluminum foil, so that they are about ⅛ inch larger than hole on design.

13. Place these underneath felt shapes from which holes were cut.

14. Glue all pieces in position, using a minimum amount of glue. Allow 1 hour to dry. When dry, pick design up to make sure nothing falls off. Reglue any loose pieces.

15. Using yarns in colors to contrast, make French knots throughout design. Follow small dots on pattern for placement. See Diagram 19 and directions on page 41 for review on French knots.

16. Tape pattern to design and mark corners. Untape pattern. Design is now ready for stretching and framing as described on page 22.

# Circus Elephant

*(Technique 5)*

*Here is a pink elephant your child can add to his own art collection. This design was machine-stitched on* KETTLE® CLOTH, *but any fabric may be used. Sequins on the elephant's cover, spangles on his headband, and soft sparkles with shiny silver buttons in the background add a touch of circus glitter and glamor to this design.*

## Materials

1 fabric rectangle, 20 by 24 inches, in rose
1 fabric rectangle, 13 by 18 inches, in pink
1 fabric rectangle, 8 by 9 inches, in violet
1 fabric rectangle, 8 by 9 inches, in magenta
1 fabric rectangle, 6 by 7 inches, in green

9- by 12-inch rectangles or scraps of felt, in brick red
thread in gold
8 inches fringe, ¾ inch wide
33 sequins, 19 in green, 8 in pink, and 6 in magenta, or all in same color
33 glass beads, 11-millimeter size
8 silver buttons

**Completed size:** 16 by 20 inches (excluding frame)
**Color code:** A—rose, B—pink, C—violet, D—magenta, E—green, F—brick red

## Instructions

1. Enlarge pattern according to instruc-

115

tions on page 19. Each square equals 2 inches. Pattern should measure 16 by 20 inches.

2. Press all fabric pieces with steam iron.

3. Tape pattern to the rose fabric so that there are 2 inches of fabric surrounding edge of pattern. Follow directions on page 16 for use of tracing wheel and carbon. Make marks to indicate placement of elephant and sparkles.

4. One by one, tape appropriate pieces of fabric to pattern back and trace all shapes. Cut out.

5. Pin pink shapes to green shapes where indicated. Sew around edges with satin stitch. Sew green shapes to magenta in same way, and then sew magenta to violet piece. These pieces may be basted before stitching either by hand, as shown in Diagram 23-A, or by machine, as shown in Diagram 23-B. Sew fringe to elephant's cover. Gently press.

6. Position elephant's cover, eye, and ear in place on the elephant and pin them down. Baste and sew with satin stitch.

7. Position elephant and sparkles to background and pin in place. Baste and sew down elephant and sparkles with satin stitch. Stitch over lines for tail.

8. Following dots on pattern, sew sequins and beads in place. Match colors if you have bought an assortment. (Beads are to be placed on sequins.) To sew on, line up holes of sequins and beads, bring needle up through the fabric and holes, and back down again through sequin and fabric. Knot thread.

9. Sew a silver button to center of each background sparkle. They may be glued with white glue if they droop after being sewn.

10. Tape pattern to design and mark corners. Untape pattern. Design is now ready for stretching and framing, as described on page 22.

# Dove of Peace

*(Technique 5)*

*Probably the most popular symbol of peace is the dove with an olive branch. This design was made mostly from swatches of upholstery fabric. (See Pattern 24.) These samples sometimes have swatches of the other colors available in that fabric attached to them. This provides you with an interesting blend of colors in matching textures. This design uses two sets of such swatches and two scraps of leftover fabric. Any fabric may be used, however. The colorful tassels enhance the colors in the design. They are secured through eyelets.*

**Materials**

**1 felt square, large enough for a 21-inch-diameter**

117

circle, in any desired color

1 upholstery fabric rectangle, 28 by 38 inches, in compatible color

1 fabric rectangle, 8 by 12 inches, in any desired color (for dove's body)

1 fabric square, 6 by 6 inches, in any desired color (for dove's head)

assorted swatches or scraps of fabric

thread in white

1 fabric rectangle, 28 by 38 inches (for lining)

26 white eyelets

eyelet pliers

1½ yards buckram tape, 4 inches wide

yarn in blending colors

curtain rod, extending to 28 inches

**Completed size:** 27 by 28½ inches (excluding loops, rod, and tassels). Circle is 21 inches in diameter.

### Instructions

1. On paper, draw a circle with a 10½-inch radius. To do this, place a thumbtack with a string knotted to it in exact center of paper. (Work on a surface that will not be damaged by thumbtack.) Tie a pencil to other end of the string so that it is 10½ inches from thumbtack. Draw the circle, using string as a compass. Enlarge pattern onto circle, following instructions on page 19. Each square equals 2 inches. Circle should be 21 inches in diameter.

2. Press fabric pieces with steam iron.

3. Tape pattern to felt square. Follow directions on page 16 for use of tracing wheel and carbon. Make marks to indicate placement of main parts of dove and lettering. Untape pattern.

4. One by one, tape pieces of fabric to pattern back, and trace all shapes. Cut out pieces.

5. Lay out body of dove, olive branch, and head on felt background and pin in position.

6. Baste around edges of pieces by hand or machine. Using a wide satin stitch, stitch around these pieces, skipping over parts that will be covered by wings, tail, or neck feathers. (See Diagrams 23-A for hand basting and 23-B for machine basting and stitching.) Make a line of stitches over stem of olive branch.

7. Position the tail section in place, baste, and sew. Do same for neck feathers, wings, eye, and lettering. (See page 40 for easy way to do lettering.) Gently press.

8. Retape pattern to felt, and trace edge of circle. Untape pattern. Cut out circle on this line.

9. Position circle on upholstery fabric so that it is centered 3½ inches from either side and 5½ inches from bottom.

10. Stitch around the edge of circle with medium-width zigzag stitch.

11. Make loops for top of hanging by cutting, as shown in Diagram 70. Measure carefully and mark lines with chalk before cutting.

12. Cut lining fabric to match hanging.

13. Pin hanging face to face with lining. Seam ½ inch from edge around sides, top, and loops. Clip inward corners and trim outward corners. Turn inside out. Use blunt, pointed tool, such as a pencil eraser, to push out corners.

14. Press edges of hanging flat.

**Diagram 70**

15. Cut buckram tape into two pieces, each measuring 27 inches in length. Place them on top of each other along back of top edge. Fold loops over to back, overlapping the edge about 1 inch. (See Diagram 71.

**Diagram 71**

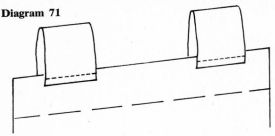

Broken line indicates lower edge of buckram tape.) Hold tape in place and sew down the two ends of loops. Make sure that the stitching goes over the inside tape to hold it in position.

16. Turn under lower edge of hanging and lining 1½ inches. By hand or by machine, stitch 1 inch from edge. Press flat. Topstitch sides and top edge of hanging ¼ inch from edge. Be sure stitching goes over tape at top edge.

17. With eyelet pliers, place eyelets, starting and ending 1 inch from sides. Centers should be ¾ inch from lower edge and 1 inch apart from each other. Follow directions that came with eyelet pliers.

18. To make tassels, cut a 12-inch length of yarn and draw it through an eyelet. Find a flat object 4 or 5 inches wide, such as a

**Diagram 72-A**

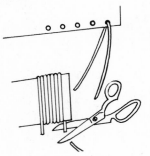

thin notebook or a piece of cardboard. Wind a piece of yarn around it six or seven times and cut off the end. (See Diagram 72-A.)

**Diagram 72-B**  **Diagram 72-C**

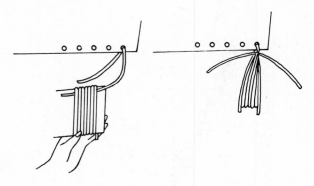

Hold ends at bottom and draw yarn from eyelet through top side of cardboard, catching all loops. (See Diagram 72-B.) Slip the yarn off cardboard and knot yarn from the eyelet to secure loops, as shown in Diagram 72-C. Let the ends become part of the tassel. Cut another 12-inch length of yarn and tie it around top of tassel, about ½ inch from the knot. (See Diagram 72-D.) Let these ends join the others. Cut ends of tassel and trim evenly, as shown in Diagram 72-E. Continue making tassels across bottom edge, randomly varying colors.

19. Slip curtain rod through the loops at top and use accompanying hooks to hang.

**Diagram 72-D**  **Diagram 72-E**

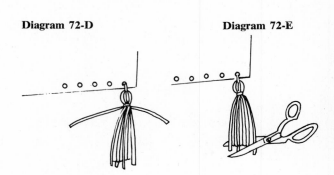

# Pressed Flower

*(Variation of Technique 5)*

*This small flower design demonstrates how you can use the zigzag stitch on your sewing machine to create an interesting texture. This technique breaks all the rules. Wrinkles and puckering are used to create a unique effect and even some raw edges are left uncovered. The stitches are widened and narrowed as you sew and the stitch length is also varied at will. This is for the rebel who likes to play freely, without restrictions—the uninhibited soul who hates to follow precise instructions. Such a person would probably rather create his own design. This one is presented to show you how. It is fun and free— sort of like doodling on the sewing machine.*

*Different fabrics create different effects. Though broadcloth was used here, try velveteen or silk. Remember to laugh at the mistakes you are allowed to make. They add to the design.*

## Materials

1 broadcloth rectangle, 10 by 12 inches, in vermilion

1 broadcloth square, 6 by 6 inches, in burnt orange

1 broadcloth rectangle, 4½ by 5 inches, in gold

scraps of broadcloth, in yellow, orange, turquoise, aqua, and olive

thread in navy or black

**Completed size:** 8 by 10 inches (excluding frame)

**Color code:** G—vermilion, H—burnt orange, I—gold, J—yellow, K—orange, L—turquoise, M—aqua, N—olive

## Instructions

1. Enlarge pattern according to instructions on page 19. Each square equals 2 inches. Pattern should measure 8 by 10 inches.

2. Press fabric pieces.

3. Tape pattern to vermilion background so that there is a 1-inch border of fabric surrounding edge of pattern.

4. Follow directions on page 16 for use of tracing wheel and carbon. Make marks to indicate placement of flower, leaves, and stem.

5. Tape fabric scraps, one by one, to back of pattern and trace shape outlines. Cut out.

6. Lay out pieces on vermilion and pin in place.

7. Using various stitch widths and lengths, sew around edges of all pieces. Sew right on the edge for some and a little away from the edge for others. Adjust stitch lengths and widths as you sew. Be free and work quickly, without worrying about puck-

**Pattern 28**

[Pattern diagram of a flower with petals labeled J and K, center labeled M, and surrounding areas labeled G, H, I, L, N]

ering. This will result in a loose outline similar to some pen-and-ink artworks. (See Diagram 73.) Stitch down the center of leaves to indicate veins.

8. Once pieces are stitched in place, start outlining the flower and leaves with more rows of stitching. Vary the stitch on each row, alternating between increasing the length of stitch while keeping the width narrow and widening the stitch while maintaining the same length. Vary the space between rows. Experiment!

9. Tape pattern to design and mark corners. Untape pattern. Design is now ready for stretching and framing, as described on page 22.

**Diagram 73**

# Moscow Monument

## (Technique 6)

*This design is a simplified version of the famous church on Red Square in Russia. I have used striped and dotted fabric, scraps of lacy edgings, piping, and rickrack for this design. What you choose from your scrap bag will make the design truly your own.*

## Materials

1 fabric rectangle, 24 by 30 inches, in any neutral color (for background)

scraps of dotted, striped, and other geometrically patterned fabrics (Use lightweight fabrics with easy-to-turn-under edges.)

assorted edgings, ½ to ¾ inches wide

embroidery needles

embroidery floss

thread in any color

**Completed size:** 20 by 26 inches (excluding frame)

## Instructions

1. Enlarge pattern according to instructions on page 19. Each square equals 2 inches. Pattern should measure 20 by 26 inches.

2. Press all fabric pieces with steam iron.

3. Tape pattern to the background fabric so that there are 2 inches of fabric surrounding edge of design. Follow directions on page 16 for use of tracing wheel and carbon. Make marks to indicate placement of pieces.

4. Tape fabric scraps, one by one, to back of fabric and trace all building parts. Cut out as you trace, allowing at least ¼ inch around edges for turning under.

5. Lay the pieces out on background in proper positions and pin in place. (You may prefer to baste them in place.)

6. Using whip stitch, as shown in Diagram 25, whip down all edges, beginning with underneath pieces.

7. By hand, sew down assorted braids and edgings to represent ledges and parapets and to accent the design. Turn ends under and tack them down neatly.

8. French knots may be used to add texture to dotted or striped fabric. See Diagram 19 and page 41 for review on French knots. They may be made with either thread or floss. Place them inside dots, center them between dots, or work rows of them between stripes. (See Diagram 74 for suggestions.)

9. Floss may be couched on, as shown in Diagram 75. This is a stitch in which floss is secured by using thread to sew it on. This is also used to make the circles at the tops of the buildings. The stitch forms a spiral. Start in the middle and sew the floss in a circle. (See Diagram 76 for enlarged de-

Diagram 74

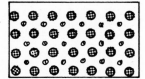

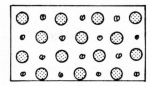

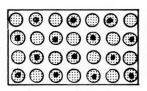

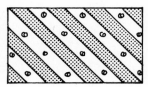

# Butterfly

*(Technique 6)*

tail.) Use the couching stitch for accenting stripes, defining edges, making the points on tops of buildings, and other details. You may embellish this design as much as you want, to re-create the ornate detail of the Moscow church.

10. Tape pattern to design and mark corners. Untape pattern. Design is now ready for stretching and framing, as described on page 22.

*This light, airy design will cheer up your kitchen, bathroom, or any other room in the house. By the way, don't forget the laundry room! Its walls can be decorated too. A butterfly is a symbol of beauty and will be a welcome addition, wherever you put it.*

### Materials

1 fabric rectangle, 21 by 26½ inches, in solid yellow, stripes, checks, dots, or any pattern desired (for background)

1 cotton square, 17 by 17 inches, in lemon yellow

1 cotton rectangle, 15½ by 18 inches, in yellow orange

**Diagram 75**

**Diagram 76**

Pattern 30

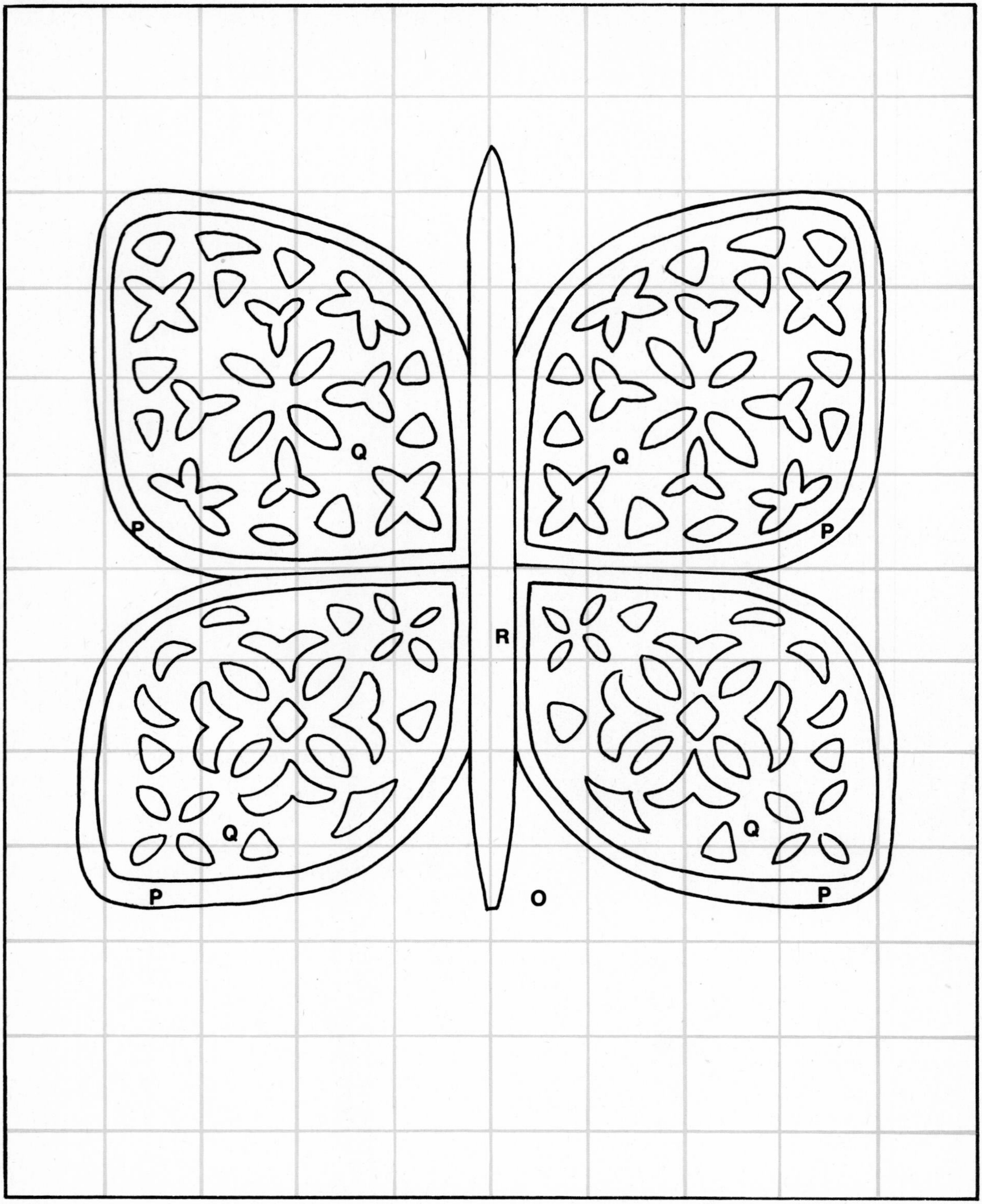

1 **fabric strip, 2 by 17½ inches, in burnt orange**
**embroidery scissors**
**thread in yellow**
1 **package bias tape, ½ inch wide, in copper**
1 **cotton rectangle, 21 by 26 inches (for lining)**
20 **inches buckram tape, 4 inches wide**
**curtain rod, extending to 20 inches**

**Completed size:** 20 by 25½ inches
**Color code:** O—yellow background, P—lemon yellow, Q—yellow orange, R—burnt orange

### Instructions

1. Enlarge pattern according to instructions on page 19. Each square equals 2 inches. Pattern should measure 20 by 25½ inches.

2. Press fabric pieces with steam iron.

3. Tape pattern to background fabric so that there is ½ inch of fabric surrounding edge of pattern. Follow directions on page 16 for use of tracing wheel and carbon. Make marks to indicate placement of the butterfly.

4. One by one, tape appropriate colors of fabric to back of pattern, and trace wings, body, and wing pieces. Small designs on wings will be cut out from yellow orange panels to reveal lemon yellow underneath. Trace these shapes onto the yellow orange pieces. Cut out all pieces, allowing at least ¼ inch all around for turning under. Leave the small cutouts for later.

5. Pin the lemon yellow wings in position on the background. Use whip stitch, as shown in Diagram 25, to whip down all edges. Do same for burnt orange body piece.

6. Pin yellow orange panels in position and whip down edges. Refer to Patterns 7 and 8 for technique used to work the cutout designs on wings. This is similar, of course, to the reverse appliqué technique. The difference is only that the cutouts are not made in the background but rather in an appliquéd panel. (Refer to Diagrams 26, 27, 34, and 38 for slitting and whipping techniques.) The inside portions of the cutouts are slit to the corners, and the edges are turned under and whipped down. Practice on some scraps first.

7. Since bias tape is narrow and easy to bend around curves, it is used to accent the edge of the butterfly. Start at the corner where upper wing joins body. Whip the inner edge of tape to edge of lemon yellow. It will curve easily along the rounded corner. When you reach the corner where the two wings meet, cut the tape diagonally to fit. (See Diagram 77.) Whip down.

**Diagram 77**

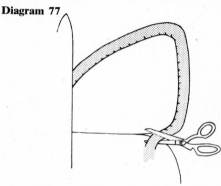

Recut end of remaining tape and fold it to fit, over already-sewn end in the corner. (See Diagram 78.) Work the raw edge under the tape with tip of needle so that it is

**Diagram 78**

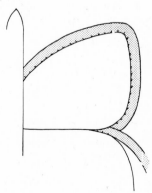

hidden, and continue to whip the edge around the lower part of wing. Repeat this same procedure at corner where lower wing meets the body. Continue whipping down bias tape.

When you reach the tip of the body, fold corners so that they are mitered, as shown in Diagram 79. Continue whipping down

**Diagram 79**

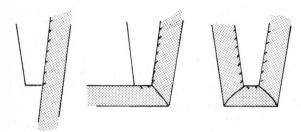

inner edge of tape in this manner until butterfly is edged completely. Trim end of tape at the starting point to fit. Trim and fold the final end over it, and whip it into place.

Whip down the outer edge of tape. Pressing at the corners with an iron will make it lie flat. Gently press entire hanging.

8. Tape pattern to hanging and mark corners. Untape pattern. Connect corner marks with chalk line.

9. Turn edges under on chalk line and press flat. Press edges of the lining fabric under to match size of hanging.

10. Hem bottom edges of hanging and lining. If fabric is coarse enough, you may want to fringe edge. If so, instead of hemming it, pull out the horizontal threads of fabric. Make sure, however, that edge is cut evenly before pulling out threads.

11. Pin lining to hanging, face to face, and seam at top edge. Turn lining over to back of hanging and press seam flat. Cut buckram tape so that there are two 20-inch strips, 2 inches wide. Place these one on top of the other along the top edge, between

hanging and lining. Hold in place with thumb of free hand while stitching 1 inch from folded top edge to form a slot.

12. Pin side edges of lining to hanging and sew together by hand or machine. Gently press.

13. Slip curtain rod through slot at top of design. Use hooks that accompany rod for hanging.

*Pattern 31: Framed Design*

# East Meets West

*(Technique 6)*

*This design combines an adapted Middle Eastern appliqué technique with the Western motifs of American quilts and European folk art. In this design I have substituted large colored sequins, trimmed down in size, for*

**Pattern 31**

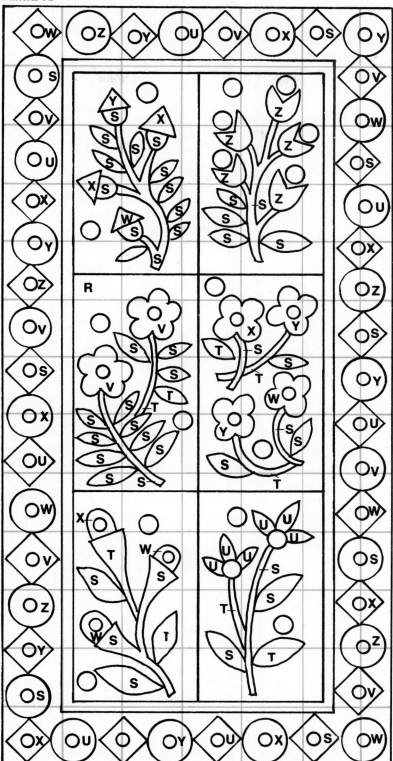

129

*the shiny metallic bits found in Middle Eastern needlework. They are glued in place and then edged with an embroidery stitch called the chain stitch. The same stitch is used to define the edge between the border and central part of the design.*

*To do the chain stitch, bring the needle through the fabric and back down again, right next to the same point. It is then brought up again to secure a loop, as shown in Diagram 80. This is repeated to form a chain. It is made in a circular chain to edge the sequins. (See Diagram 81.)*

**Diagram 80**                    **Diagram 81**

*The sequins used here are called paillettes. They are 13/16 inch in diameter and have a large hole. To get the right effect trim them down to ½ inch in diameter and ignore the hole. (See Diagram 82.) Middle Eastern needleworkers would probably titter at this unconventional adaptation of their stitchery, but it does give the result we want!*

**Diagram 82**

## Materials

1 linen-type fabric rectangle, 17 by 30 inches, in medium blue (for background)

scraps of broadcloth, in light olive, darker olive, turquoise, aqua, orange, red, hot pink, and hyacinth blue

embroidery scissors

thread in medium blue

embroidery needle

embroidery floss in olive, aqua, red, and blue

4 packages paillettes, 13/16 inch in diameter, in red, pink, olive, and turquoise, or all in 1 color

white glue

**Completed size:** 13 by 26 inches (excluding frame)

**Color code:** R—medium blue, S—light olive, T—darker olive, U—turquoise, V—aqua, W—orange, X—red, Y—hot pink, Z—hyacinth blue

## Instructions

1. Enlarge pattern according to instructions on page 19. Each square equals 2 inches. Pattern should measure 13 by 26 inches.

2. Press all fabric pieces with steam iron.

3. Tape pattern to background fabric so that there are 2 inches of fabric surrounding pattern. Follow directions on page 16 for use of tracing wheel and carbon. Make marks to indicate placement of design pieces.

4. Tape fabric scraps, one by one, to back of pattern, and trace flowers, stems, leaves, squares, and circles. You may draw shapes freehand if you prefer. Cut out as you trace, allowing ¼ inch around edges for turning under.

5. It is suggested that one rectangle be appliquéd at a time. Separate all pieces according to section, and keep in envelopes until you are ready to use them. Keep all border pieces together in another envelope. Starting with one rectangle, pin stem and a few leaves in position. Use whip stitch, as shown in Diagram 25, to whip edges under. Pin a few more, and whip them down. Continue in this manner until all are worked. Go on to next rectangle and continue until all are done.

6. To make the lines between rectangles,

couch red floss to fabric with sewing machine, as shown in Diagram 56. This time, however, make lines straight, instead of curved. Couch the vertical line first and then the two horizontal lines.

7. Make the border edge with floss, as shown in Diagram 83. Use red floss for chain stitch on the outer edges. (See page

**Diagram 83**

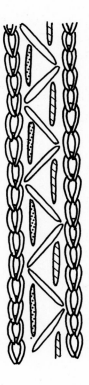

130 and Diagram 80.) Using olive floss, make zigzag stitch by hand, within the two red chain-stitched edges. Make points of zigzag stitch about ½ inch apart. Work running stitches with blue and aqua between zigzag points, as shown in Diagram 83.

8. Pin a few squares and circles of border, and whip them down. Continue in this manner until all are done.

9. Position of sequins is indicated by small circles on pattern. Vary colors randomly as you work, or use one color. Some circles are larger than others. For larger circles, trim sequins as shown in Diagram 82 and glue in position. Allow 1 hour for drying. Using floss in varying colors, make chain stitch around edges. (See Diagram 81.)

10. Work smaller circles, one at a time. Pierce and cut fabric shape, as shown in Diagram 84. (Make sure you cut only top layer of fabric.) Trim sequin as before. Place a drop of glue inside the hole, and insert sequin. There is no need to allow drying time since sequins are placed one at a time and will not shift while working. Using tip of needle, turn under edge of the hole. Work a chain stitch around with thread rather than floss for a more delicate edge.

11. Tape pattern to design and mark corners. Untape pattern. Design is now ready for stretching and framing, as described on page 22.

**Diagram 84**

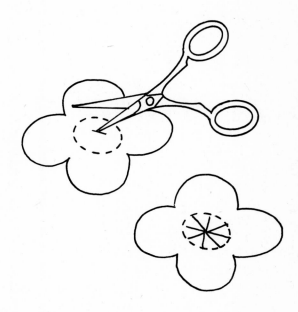

## Pattern 32: Wall Hanging

# Mod Gods

*(Technique 7)*

*This design uses exciting Mexican motifs. They were enlarged from a book called* De- sign Motifs of Ancient Mexico, *by Jorgé Enciso, published by Dover Publications. These designs originally appeared on clay-baked stamps, which were used to decorate pottery, cloth, paper, and hides.*

*In this wall hanging, the motifs are brought up to date with the use of color. I chose bright colors, just as contemporary Mexican folk artists do, to enhance these ancient motifs. These motifs adapt beautifully to the reverse appliqué technique.*

*From a distance, the design looks like a maze of tiny patchwork. Upon closer scru-*

*tiny, however, the illusion is revealed. The printed fabric is the trick. Choose an exotic print for each underlayer to contrast with the others, and don't be afraid of using too many bright colors. You will experience a small surprise every time one of the prints reveals itself under your needle. You are bound to have a lot of fun making this.*

### Materials

**1 cotton broadcloth rectangle, 18 by 22 inches, in gold**
**1 cotton broadcloth rectangle, 10 by 11 inches, in gold**
**1 cotton broadcloth rectangle, 11 by 18 inches, in cerise**
**1 cotton broadcloth rectangle, 10 by 12 inches, in orange**
**1 cotton broadcloth rectangle, 10 by 12 inches, in turquoise**
**5 cotton broadcloth print rectangles, each 1 inch smaller than 1 of above pieces and in contrasting color to it**
**1 cotton broadcloth rectangle, 4½ by 5 inches, in black**
**1 upholstery fabric rectangle, 30 by 38¾ inches, in dark green**
**scrap of fabric, in red**
**embroidery scissors**
**thread in gold, cerise, orange, and turquoise**
**1 fabric rectangle, 30 by 35½ inches, (optional) (for lining)**
**wood stain in any color**
**31 inches dowel rod, ⅝ inch in diameter**
**2 wooden finials (from hardware store)**
**28 inches lath, ¼ by 1 inch**

**Completed size:** 28 by 34 inches (excluding finials). Completed size of inner design: 24 by 28 inches.
**Color code:** A—gold, B—cerise, C—orange, D—turquoise, E—black, F—red

### Instructions

1. Enlarge pattern according to instructions on page 19. Each square equals 2

A

C

B

D

A

E

D

F

133

inches. Each panel should be drawn on separate sheet of paper. Overall pattern should measure 24 by 28 inches.

2. Press fabric pieces with steam iron.

3. One by one, tape patterns to appropriate fabrics. Follow directions on page 16 for use of tracing wheel and carbon, and trace design. Omit facial details on large design since black fabric will be inserted for face.

4. Start with large gold design. Pin the corresponding printed fabric piece, face up, to back of traced design on gold. Baste the two together if you wish. Refer to Pattern 7, steps 5 through 15, for technique details on cutting, slitting, whipping down edges, replacing cutaway details, and appliquéing them back. Cut only one detail at a time and work it through before going on to next detail. Cutting the entire design at one time would make it ungainly and difficult to keep in correct position. This design differs from the one in Pattern 7 in that it has— with the exception of the face area—only one layer of fabric underneath. In other words, you will need to cut through only one layer to reveal underneath layer.

5. Starting with the outside edge of the figure, slit, turn edges under, and whip down until starting point is reached. As you work, pin down the inner cutaway part of design to keep it in position. (See Diagram 85-A.) Progress to inner parts of design, as shown in Diagrams 85-B and 85-C.

6. Work all of design, saving face detail for last. Trim black fabric scrap to fit face panel. Cut away inner part of gold face panel and discard. (See Diagram 86.) Insert black piece and pin in place. (See Diagram 87.) Clip and turn gold edge under, whipping it down to black. Trace facial details on black, as shown in Diagram 88. Cut the inner mouth part away, and insert red scrap. This should be large enough to cover entire mouth area. Whip edge of black to red. Replace the cutaway part and appliqué it back into position. Work the nose area, whipping edges down to print fabric. Slit lower eye line and insert scrap of turquoise, large enough to cover entire eye area. Whip black edges to it. Repeat for other eye. Diagram 89 shows finished result.

7. Work other sections of design in the same manner. Occasionally, the exposed printed fabric may create an undesirable facial expression. If this occurs or if you would like more facial definition, try inserting a scrap of solid color fabric under facial area. In this design, I inserted a scrap of cerise beneath mouth and eyes in lower right corner. Solid colors inserted this way will usually improve any unwanted effects.

8. Replace patterns to panels and mark corners. Remove patterns, and connect corner marks with chalk line.

9. Trim edges of panels, allowing ½ inch all around for seaming and turning under.

10. Face to face, seam lower edge of orange panel to upper edge of turquoise panel on chalk line. In same way, seam upper edge of small gold panel to lower edge of turquoise and lower edge of large gold panel to upper edge of cerise. Press seams open. Seam these two large pieces together, making sure that corners of gold, cerise, and turquoise panels meet.

11. Turn border edges under on chalk line, and press flat.

12. Position design on green upholstery fabric so that there are 3 inches of green on each side and 4¾ inches of green on bottom. Pin in place.

13. Use gold thread and narrow-width zigzag stitch, set at 10 stitches to the inch, to attach panel to upholstery fabric. Stitch along folded edge of panel.

14. Turn side edges of hanging under 1 inch, and press flat. Turn lower and upper

Diagram 85-A

Diagram 85-B

**Diagram 85-C**

edges under 2 inches and press.

15. Topstitch lower edge 1⅝ inches from fold. Topstitch upper edge 1½ inches from fold to form a slot.

16. With top edge lining up with stitched line under top fold, fold under and press edges of lining fabric to match size of the hanging.

17. Hem down lower edge of lining by machine. Press. Pin or baste lining back to back with hanging. Stitch top and side edges together by hand or machine. Gently press.

18. Stain wooden dowel rod and finials, following directions that came with stain.

19. Insert dowel rod through upper slot of hanging. Glue finials to ends of dowel. Glue lath to back of lower edge, between hanging and lining.

**Diagram 86**

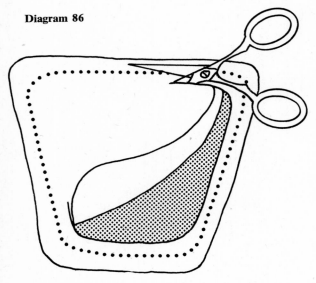

**Diagram 87**

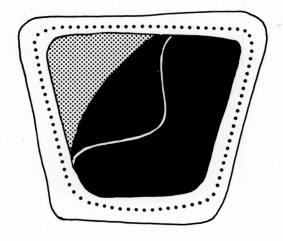

**Diagram 88**

**Diagram 89**

## Pattern 33: Wall Hanging

# Mexican Sunshine

*(Technique 8)*

*The design in this hanging is also an adaptation version of Mexican motifs. It offers an interesting variation to the reverse appliqué technique. Instead of making the stitches as tiny as possible—the way the Cuna Indians do—we will deliberately make them quite large! Thus, the stitches become an integral part of the texture. I used linen floss to achieve this effect, but any embroidery floss will do.*

### Materials

1 cotton broadcloth rectangle, 17 by 22 inches, in gold

1 cotton broadcloth rectangle, 19 by 24 inches, in black

scraps of fabric, in olive, turquoise, and orange

1 upholstery fabric rectangle, 27½ by 33 inches, in olive

2 upholstery fabric rectangles, 5½ by 9½ inches, in olive (for loops)

embroidery scissors

thread in olive

embroidery needle

embroidery floss in black, olive, turquoise, and orange

1 fabric rectangle, 25½ by 31 inches (optional) (for lining)

wood stain in any color

23 inches dowel rod, ⅝ inch in diameter

2 wooden finials (from hardware store)

25½ inches lath, ¼ by 1 inch

**Completed size:** 25½ by 30½ inches (excluding finials). Completed size of inner design: 20 by 25 inches.

**Color code:** G—gold, H—black, I—olive, J—turquoise, K—orange

### Instructions

1. Enlarge pattern according to instructions on page 19. Each square equals 2 inches. This pattern shows left and center motif. Broken line indicates the vertical center line. Right motif is repetition of left motif. Half of pattern, including center motif should measure 11 by 25 inches.

2. Press fabric pieces with steam iron.

3. Tape pattern to gold fabric so that there is 1 inch of fabric surrounding top, bottom, and left edges. Follow directions on page 16 for use of tracing wheel, pencil, and carbon. Trace design, omitting those small inner shapes that are within others. These will be cut away and removed later. Mark broken vertical line in three or four places and spots where top and bottom of design cross this line. Untape pattern and turn it upside down. Tape it to the other side of gold fabric, lining up the broken vertical lines and allowing 1 inch of fabric around top and bottom edges. Trace right side of

**Pattern 33**

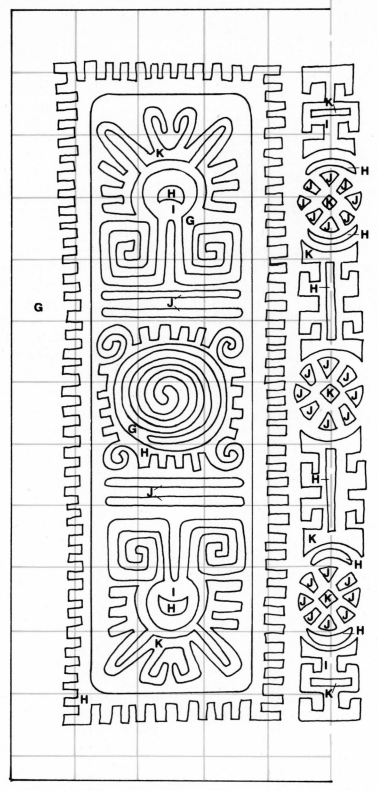

140

motif in same way you did left.

4. Refer to Pattern 7, steps 5 through 15, and Pattern 8, steps 4 through 10, for details on cutting, slitting, whipping down edges, replacing cutaway details, and appliquéing them back. You will be cutting only one detail at a time and working it through before going on to next detail. Cutting a complicated design such as this, all at once, would make it clumsy and difficult to work with.

5. Do turquoise shapes first, then olive, and then orange, piecing in the underlayers, as described in technique of Pattern 8. Use floss of contrasting colors to make stitches. Trace or draw freehand with chalk pencil, the small shapes within larger shapes, such as the two orange narrow horizontals within olive shapes at top and bottom of central motif. Piece in underlayers of orange, and work as before. Complete design in this manner until all but black areas are worked.

6. Pin black fabric underneath design so that entire design is covered from behind. Baste around edges.

7. Slit and whip down turned-under edges to expose the black where indicated. Don't forget the four black crescent shapes within the olive and the vertical slits within orange of central motif.

8. Tape pattern over design and mark corners. Untape pattern. Connect corner marks with chalk line.

9. Turn edges under all around on chalk line and press flat.

10. Position design on upholstery fabric so that there are 3¾ inches of the olive surrounding edge of design. Pin in place.

11. Using narrow-width zigzag stitch, set at 12 stitches to the inch, sew panel to the upholstery fabric around folded edge.

12. Turn edges of hanging under 1 inch and press flat.

13. Fold under and press edges of lining fabric to match size of hanging.

14. Hem lower edge of hanging by machine. Press. Do same for lining. Pin or baste lining to hanging, back to back. Stitch edges together by hand or machine, and gently press flat.

15. Press under the long edges of the two upholstery fabric rectangles, designated for loops. Topstitch these edges on machine. Position them to top of hanging so that the outside edges line up with outside edges of design panel. Pin undersides of loops to top, and seam in place. Fold over and sew ends to back of hanging. (See Diagram 71.)

16. Stain wooden dowel rod and finials, following directions that came with stain.

17. Glue finials to ends of dowel. Insert dowel through loops. Glue lath to back of lower edge of hanging, between hanging and lining.

# Appliqué
# in the Home

Every home should have its own personal identity. The families of those talented people who can use a needle and thread to create projects for the home are indeed lucky. These projects seem to add beauty and warmth to a home, in a way that store-bought items simply can't match. They make home truly special and different from any other place.

Whether it is in the form of an unusual quilt, a supergraphic room divider, or a few small pillows, fabric seems to evoke a cozy kind of security. It does so from the moment of a person's birth all the way through life. It is even more endearing when someone close has worked on it and created something special. Use pattern after pattern to enhance your home with fabric designs, for even if you prefer the modern look of plastic and chrome, a touch of needled fabric is still needed to keep it from looking cold.

This chapter will provide ideas to start you thinking. Perhaps the entire family will want to create one of these projects together.

*Pattern 34: Decorated Mirror*

# American Folk Flowers

*(Technique 1)*

*Here is an easy project that adds a decorative touch to the bedroom mirror or to that fast-peek mirror near the front door. With a little help from you, it makes a nice project for a child to work on.*

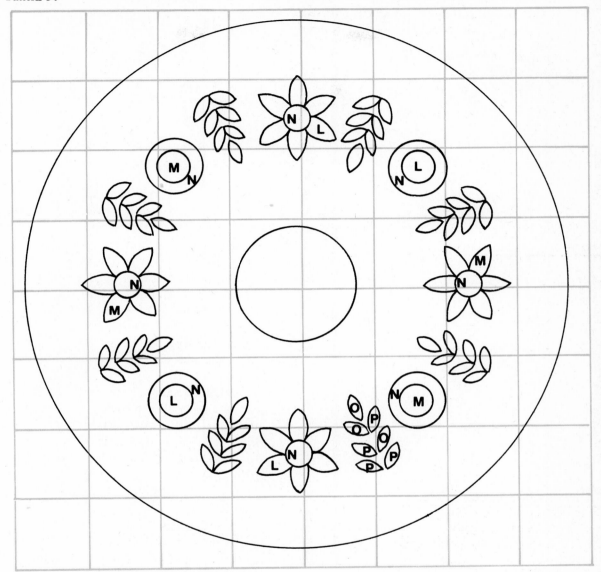

## Materials

1 fabric square, 16 by 16 inches, in any neutral color

1 felt square, 12 by 12 inches, in any desired color

9- by 12-inch rectangles or scraps of felt, in orange, magenta, violet, lime, and bright green (If rectangles are purchased, buy 1 of each color.)

1 styrofoam wreath form, 12 inches in diameter, with a 7-inch opening and a curved top surface (available at craft-supply shops or variety stores)

glue

fabric glue

1¼ yards edging, in orange, magenta, violet, lime, or bright green (for outer edge)

⅔ yard edging, in orange, magenta, violet, lime, or bright green (for inner edge)

any square or round mirror, larger than 7 but

smaller than 12 inches in diameter (This one was made with an 11½-inch frameless mirror.)
1 curtain ring (if mirror has no hanger of its own)

**Completed size:** 12 inches in diameter
**Color code:** L—orange, M—magenta, N—violet, O—lime, P—bright green

### Instructions

1. Enlarge pattern according to instructions on page 19. Each square equals 2 inches. Pattern should measure 16 by 16 inches.

2. Press fabric pieces.

3. Tape pattern to 16- by 16-inch fabric. Follow directions on page 16 for use of tracing wheel and carbon. Make marks to show placement of flowers and leaves. Trace circular edges. Cut out the outer circled edge.

**Diagram 90**

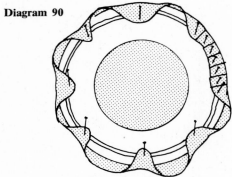

4. Lay wreath form face down on wrong side of fabric, centering it so that there is an equal amount of fabric surrounding the edge. Apply glue around the outer edge of back. Bring edge of fabric up and around form. To pin it down, place pin at top, bottom, and center of sides. Then pin in between these. Add more pins, making neat tucks with fabric. (See Diagram 90.) If you are using a heavy fabric that is too thick for tucking, clip away some of the excess. Allow 1 hour to dry and remove pins.

5. Following pattern, cut away inner circle of fabric. Make 1-inch clips all around inner edge. Apply glue around the inner

**Diagram 91**

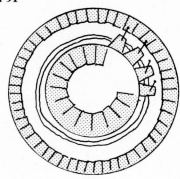

edge of back of form. Pin the clipped segments to back of form, as shown in Diagram 91. Be sure to stretch fabric tautly over curved surface of front so that edges are smooth. Allow 1 hour to dry. Remove pins.

6. One at a time, tape appropriate colors of felt to back of pattern and trace floral shapes. Repeated shapes need be traced only once and then used as models from which to cut the rest. Cut out all shapes. You may want to use pinking shears to cut the violet circles.

7. Place all shapes face down on newspaper and apply glue to backs.

8. Place all shapes in position on front of fabric circle. Press down well.

9. Glue edging to inner and outer edges of form. Pin it down so that it holds in place until dry. Allow 1 hour for drying, and remove pins.

10. Making sure that mirror is clean, glue frame to it with plenty of fabric glue. Clean away any glue that may have gone on mirror.

11. If you are using a mirror that is unfinished on the back and has no hanger of its own, cut a 12-inch-diameter circle from the 12-inch square of felt and glue it to back of frame and mirror. Sew a curtain ring to upper center felt back. Apply some glue over sewn stitches to reinforce felt and to make sure that curtain ring is securely attached to back of mirror.

146

# Stars of Morocco

*(Technique 2)*

*Here is an interesting pillow made of tiny pieces of felt, reminiscent of the richly-tiled mosaic architecture of Morocco. It may seem a bit mind-boggling at first, but if you do just a section at a time, you will see that it is not such a tremendous undertaking, after all. It is certainly well worth the effort, if your mind often takes you to such exotic places as Marrakech and Casablanca. Make one or two of these pillows for a touch of the casbah in your home.*

## Materials

⅔ yard felt, in bronze

9- by 12-inch rectangles or scraps of felt, in turquoise, tan, and pale avocado (If rectangles are purchased, buy 1 of each color.)

thread in clear nylon or bronze

1 pillow form, 20 by 20 inches (If you are making your own, use two 21- by 21-inch squares of muslin and 3 pounds polyester fiberfill.)

1 zipper, 18 inches in length, in bronze (optional)

**Completed size:** 20 by 20 inches

**Color code:** Q—bronze, R—turquoise, S—tan, T—pale avocado

## Instructions

1. Enlarge pattern according to instructions on page 19. Each square equals 2 inches. The pattern represents one quarter of the design. This enlarged quarter should measure 10 by 10 inches.

Point A

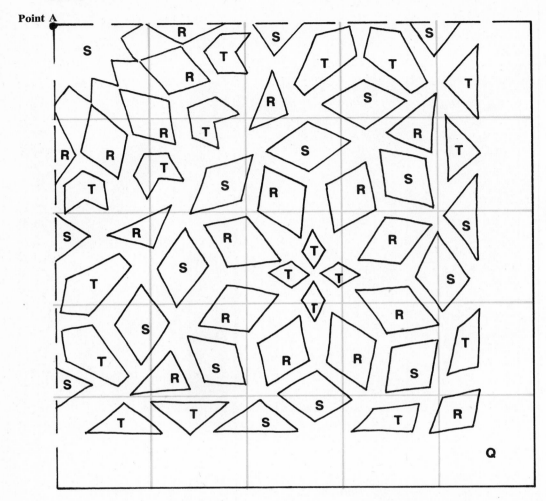

2. Cut a 22- by 22-inch square from bronze felt. Press felt pieces with steam iron.

3. Place point A at center of felt square and make a dot on felt at this point. Tape pattern down, making sure that the edges of pattern are parallel to edges of felt square. Follow directions on page 16 for use of tracing wheel and carbon. Make marks to indicate placement of all pieces. Extend broken lines slightly to margin of felt, as shown in pattern.

4. Untape pattern, and turn it one-quarter-way to its right side so that point A is now at upper right-hand corner. Tape pat-

tern to adjacent quarter of felt, lining up extended vertical lines and point A with center mark on felt. Trace shapes. Repeat procedure until entire design is traced, turning pattern one-quarter-way to right each time and lining up marks.

5. One at a time, tape appropriate colors of felt to back of pattern and trace shapes. Repeated shapes need be traced only once and then used as models from which to cut the rest. Cut out all pieces.

6. Lay out design, starting with central circular motif. Pin all pieces in place. You may use a tiny bit of fabric glue instead of

148

pins if you prefer. If so, allow ½ hour to set. You might also prefer to work on one quarter of design at a time.

7. Using narrow-width zigzag stitch, set at 20 stitches to the inch, sew pieces in place.

8. Steam press design flat.

9. Replace pattern in position over each quarter of design and trace corner marks. Remove pattern and, using yardstick for guide, connect marks with chalk line. Cut carefully on marked line. Place design on remaining bronze felt and cut another piece the same size.

10. Pin the two squares together, with design on outside. Sew three sides together, using a wide zigzag stitch, set at 10 stitches to the inch.

11. Insert pillow form. Pin the fourth side edges together. It may be too awkward to sew this side on sewing machine. Pillow form must be pushed away from edge as you sew so that edge will be flat. If it is too difficult to do this by machine, sew it by hand with whip stitch. When pillow needs to be cleaned, gently rip open this side and resew after cleaning. A zipper may be placed on this edge for easy removal of cover. Sew zipper in place, 1 inch from each end, and sew each of these ends together. Then proceed to sew the other three sides.

*Note:* To make your own pillow form, pin the two 21- by 21-inch squares of muslin together. Seam three sides and one half of fourth side together, making ½-inch seams. Turn inside out. Stuff with polyester fiberfill. Sew opening together by hand with whip stitch, stuffing pillow until full.

# Cut Flowers

*(Technique 2)*

The next four patterns are for more floor pillow designs. They can be used individually or together, as shown in the photograph. They are all reminiscent of the Art Nouveau style. Having extra floor pillows provides extended seating for casual parties.

## Materials
⅔ yard felt, in royal blue

9- by 12-inch rectangles or scraps of felt, in light turquoise, medium turquoise, lime, light olive, dark olive (If rectangles are purchased, buy 2 of dark olive and lime and 1 of all others.)

thread in clear nylon or royal blue

1 pillow form, 20 by 20 inches (If you are making your own, use two 21- by 21-inch squares of

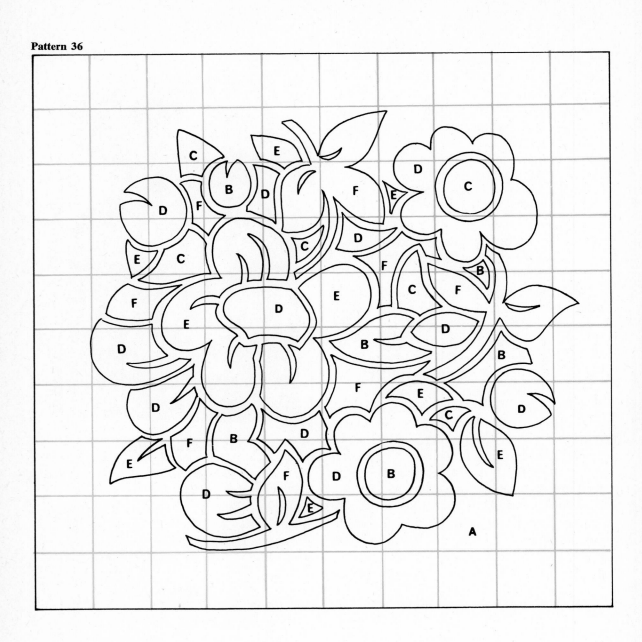

muslin and 3 pounds polyester fiberfill.)

1 zipper, 18 inches in length, in royal blue (optional)

yarn needle

yarn in turquoise

**Completed size:** 20 by 20 inches

**Color Code:** A—royal blue, B—light turquoise, C—medium turquoise, D—lime, E—light olive, F—dark olive

### Instructions

1. Enlarge pattern according to instructions on page 19. Each square equals 2 inches. Pattern should measure 20 by 20 inches.

2. Press felt pieces with steam iron.

3. Cut one 22- by 22-inch square of royal blue felt. Tape pattern to it so that there is 1 inch of felt surrounding edge. Follow directions on page 16 for use of tracing wheel and carbon. Make marks to show placement of all pieces. Untape pattern.

4. Tape appropriate colors of felt one at a time to back of pattern, and trace shapes. Cut out as you trace.

5. Lay out design on the royal blue background. Pin all shapes in position. Baste them down if you wish.

6. Using narrow-width zigzag stitch, set at 20 stitches to the inch, sew flowers and leaves in place.

7. Steam press design flat.

8. Place pattern over design in position, and trace corner marks. Remove pattern. Connect these marks with chalk line, using yardstick for guide. Cut carefully on marked line. Place design on remaining royal blue felt and cut another piece the same size.

9. Refer to Pattern 35, steps 10 and 11, for completion of pillow.

10. To make yarn tassels for corners, refer to Pattern 27, step 18. Instead of using eyelets, however, draw turquoise yarn through corners of pillow.

# Bouquet

*(Technique 2)*

*This bright bouquet design will help cheer up any room in your home.*

### Materials

⅔ yard felt, in lime

9- by 12-inch rectangles or scraps of felt, in royal blue, light blue, light turquoise, medium turquoise, bright green, light olive, and dark olive (If rectangles are purchased, buy 1 of each color.)

thread in clear nylon or lime

1 pillow form, 20 by 20 inches (If you are making your own, use two 21- by 21-inch squares of muslin and 3 pounds polyester fiberfill.)

1 zipper, 18 inches in length, in lime (optional)

**Pattern 37**

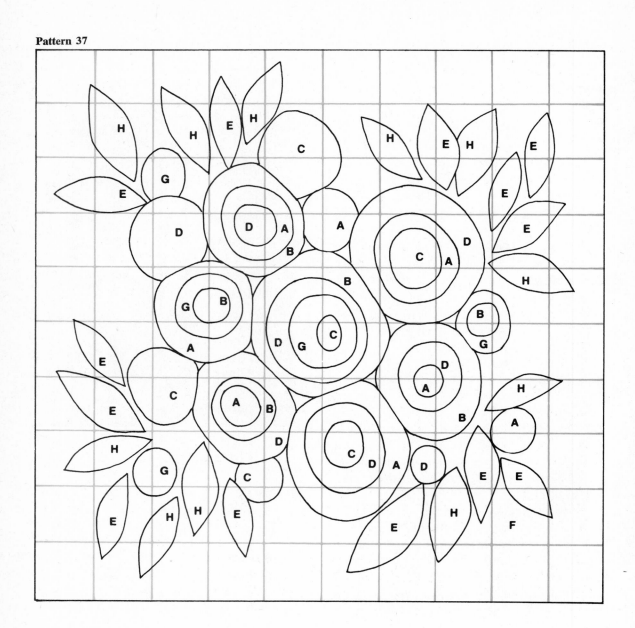

yarn needle
yarn in turquoise

**Completed size:** 20 by 20 inches
**Color code:** A—royal blue, B—light blue, C—light turquoise, D—medium turquoise, E—bright green, F—lime, G—light olive, H—dark olive

### Instructions

Follow steps of Pattern 36, substituting lime felt for royal blue. The circular shapes are placed one over the other. Sew one at a time, starting with center circle.

## *Pattern 38: Floor Pillow*

# Tiffany

*(Technique 2)*

*This design has a stained-glass look of old, treasured Tiffany lamps.*

### Materials

⅔ yard felt, in black

¼ yard felt, in gold

9- by 12-inch rectangles or scraps of felt, in yellow, orange, red, hot pink, magenta, deep magenta, light olive, and dark olive (If rectangles are purchased, buy 1 of each color.)

thread in clear nylon or black

1 pillow form, 20 by 20 inches (If you are making your own, use two 21- by 21-inch squares of muslin and 3 pounds of polyester fiberfill.)

1 zipper, 18 inches in length, in black (optional)

yarn needle

yarn in magenta

**Completed size:** 20 by 20 inches
**Color code:** G—light olive, H—dark olive, I—gold, J—yellow, K—orange, L—red, M—hot pink, N—magenta, O—deep magenta

### Instructions

1. Enlarge pattern according to instructions on page 19. Each square equals 2 inches. Pattern should measure 20 by 20 inches.

2. Press felt pieces with steam iron.

3. Cut one 22- by 22-inch square of black felt. Tape pattern to it so that there is 1 inch of felt surrounding edge. Follow directions on page 16 for use of tracing wheel and carbon. Make marks to indicate placement of all pieces other than flowers and leaves. Untape pattern.

4. One at a time, tape appropriate colors of felt to back of pattern and trace shapes. Cut out as you trace.

5. Lay out shapes on black square and pin in place. Baste them down if you wish.

6. Using narrow-width zigzag stitch, set at 20 stitches to the inch, sew shapes in position on black felt.

7. Retape pattern to design, and using tracing wheel and carbon, make marks to show placement of flowers and leaves. Untape pattern.

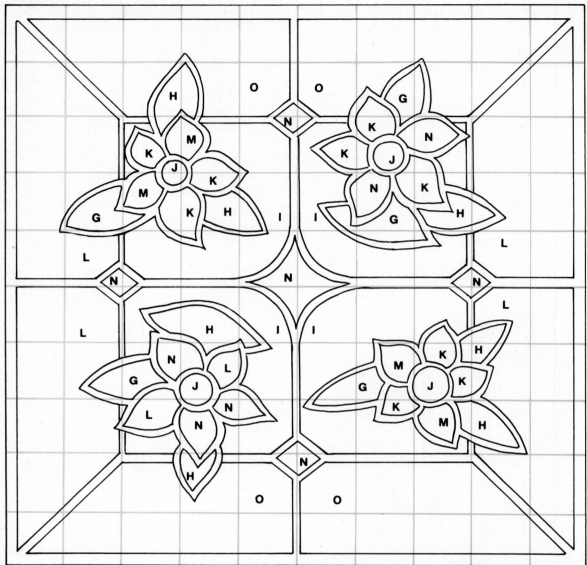

8. Tape scraps of appropriate colors to back of pattern and trace inner edge of flower and leaf shapes. Once they have been traced and cut, tape pattern to remaining black felt and trace outer edge of flower and leaf parts.

9. Place cutout flower and leaf parts in position on traced black felt and pin in place. Use same zigzag stitch as above, and sew them down.

10. Cut out the four flower designs so that they are outlined with ¼ inch of black felt.

11. Pin the four flower designs to proper places on design piece, and sew them down with same zigzag stitch.

12. Steam press the design flat.

13. Place pattern on design and trace corner marks. Remove pattern. Using yardstick for a guide, connect marks with a chalk line. Cut carefully along marked line. Place design piece on remaining black felt, and cut another piece the same size.

14. Refer to Pattern 35, steps 10 and 11, for completion of pillow.

15. To make yarn tassels, refer to Pattern 27, step 18. Instead of using eyelets, however, draw magenta yarn through corners of pillow.

## Pattern 39: Floor Pillow

# Art Nouveau

*(Technique 2)*

*Let these lovely colors add warmth at home.*

## Materials

⅔ yard felt, in black

1 felt rectangle, 10 by 18 inches, in hot pink

1 felt rectangle, 10 by 18 inches, in orange

1 felt rectangle, 10 by 18 inches, in red

1 felt rectangle, 10 by 18 inches, in deep magenta

9- by 12-inch rectangles or scraps of felt, in magenta, dark olive, light olive, and yellow (If rectangles are purchased, buy 1 of each color.)

thread in clear nylon or black

1 pillow form 20 by 20 inches (If you are making your own, use two 21- by 21-inch squares of muslin and 3 pounds polyester fiberfill.)

1 zipper, 18 inches in length, in black (optional)

yarn needle

yarn in magenta

**Completed size:** 20 by 20 inches

**Color code:** G—light olive, H—dark olive, I—yellow, J—orange, K—red, L—hot pink, M—magenta, N—deep magenta

### Instructions

1. Enlarge pattern according to instructions on page 19. Each square equals 2 inches. Pattern should measure 20 by 20 inches.

2. Press felt pieces with steam iron.

3. Cut one 22- by 22-inch square from black felt. Tape pattern to felt so that there is 1 inch of felt surrounding it. Follow directions on page 16 for use of tracing wheel and carbon. Make marks to indicate placement of four squares. Untape pattern.

4. Cut the four 9½-inch squares from appropriate colors of felt.

5. Place the four squares on black piece, and pin in place.

6. Using narrow-width zigzag stitch, set at 20 stitches to the inch, sew down squares.

7. Follow Pattern 38, beginning with step 7. On this design, however, cut the black strips that connect flowers and leaves to edges of squares separately, and sew them down in position.

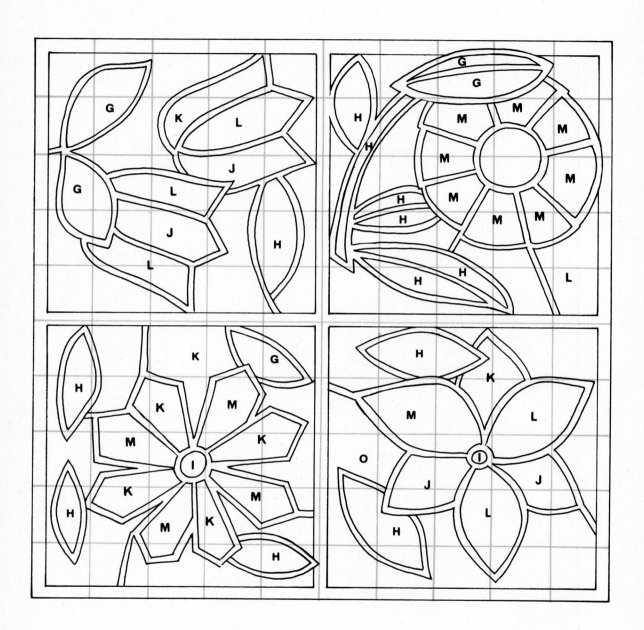

# Mediterranean Tiles

*(Technique 2)*

Perhaps you have always wanted to make a special area rug but just couldn't face the hours, months, or even years, involved to complete one. Here is one that can be made in two days. It is made of felt and can be easily sewn on the sewing machine. Each tile is made individually and then sewn together to form a row. The rows are then sewn together, just like a patchwork quilt. Thus, you have eliminated the cumbersome maneuvering of bulky fabric under the arm of the sewing machine. It can be made into any size needed.

The tiles are similar to those found in Mediterranean countries. Use your rug to create the atmosphere you wish. The layer of Dacron quilt batting, sandwiched between the two layers of felt, gives a dimensional look to each tile. When you purchase the felt, make certain that its content is at least 50 percent wool. Some felts have more rayon than wool content. You will need the heavier type for better wear.

### Materials
½ **yard felt, in orange**
½ **yard felt, in magenta**
½ **yard felt, in royal blue**
½ **yard felt, in turquoise**
**compass**
**1 bonded Dacron batting rectangle, 32 by 40 inches**

**Pattern 40**

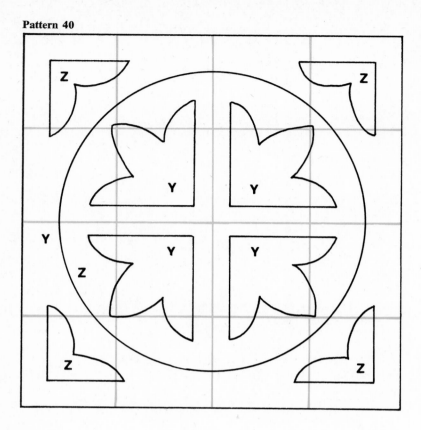

thread in clear nylon, white, or black

**4 yards fringe, in orange, magenta, royal blue, or turquoise**

**1 package rug tape (to prevent skidding of rug)**

**Completed size:** 31 by 38½ inches (excluding fringe). Each square is 8 by 8 inches. Some shrinking will occur as rug is worked.
**Color code:** *Tile A,* Y—magenta; Z—turquoise; *Tile B,* Y—turquoise; Z—orange; *Tile C,* Y—royal blue; Z—magenta; *Tile D,* Y—orange; Z—royal blue

### Instructions

1. Enlarge pattern for tile according to instructions on page 19. Each square equals 2 inches. Pattern should measure 8 by 8 inches. Use compass to draw circle.

2. Press felt pieces with steam iron.

3. For each tile, cut two felt pieces in appropriate colors. (See Diagram 92.) *Tile A* is magenta, *Tile B* is turquoise, *Tile C* is royal blue, and *Tile D* is orange. The tiles are all cut with a 1-inch underlap allowance, indicated by broken lines on diagram. Therefore, a tile with two broken lines should be cut 9 by 9 inches, a tile with one broken line should be cut 8 by 9 inches, and a tile with no broken line should be cut 8 by 8 inches. With chalk, mark the broken lines on each tile piece. Two squares are needed for each tile because one will be used for the top layer and one will be used for the bottom.

4. Tape pattern to a piece of remaining felt. One by one, trace the parts of the design. Cut these out, and use them as models from which to cut the rest. When you finish cutting, you should have five circles, twenty

158

3-prong shapes, and twenty 2-prong shapes in each color.

5. Cut 20 squares, each measuring 7¾ by 7¾ inches, from the Dacron batting.

6. Position circles and prong shapes on each top layer tile piece. Pin in position. This can be done either by eye or by tracing.

A little irregularity in positioning will be acceptable.

7. Place bottom layer of each tile underneath top layer, with a layer of Dacron batting between. Be sure batting is placed under part of tile that is seen and not beyond the broken lines. Pin all three layers together.

**Diagram 92**

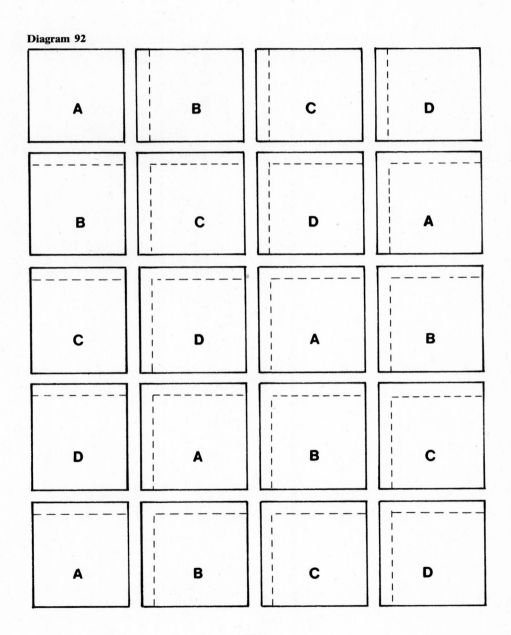

8. Using a medium-width zigzag stitch, set at 15 stitches to the inch, sew all non-underlapped edges. Using a narrow-width zigzag stitch, set at 20 stitches to the inch, stitch all shapes in position on tiles. Sew all underlapped edges of tiles along chalk mark with a straight stitch.

9. Press tiles with steam iron.

10. Lay out tiles as shown in Diagram 92. Sew tiles together, one row at a time. Starting with first horizontal row, pin and stitch *Tile A* to *Tile B* with B underlapping A. Repeat for *Tile B* to *Tile C* and *Tile C* to *Tile D*. Continue in this manner until all horizontal rows are sewn. Then stitch the rows together, adding one row at a time. Be sure each row is sewn together to form a straight line. Use a yardstick to guide the edge while pinning tiles together.

11. Sew fringe around edge of rug. Press to make sure the sewn edge lies down flat.

12. Attach rug tape to back of rug to prevent skidding. Follow directions that come with tape.

*Note:* If you want your rug in a different size or proportion, add more squares to each row as necessary.

# Folk Art

*(Technique 3)*

*Have you ever longed for one of those Swiss Alp or early Pennsylvanian, handcrafted and painted furniture pieces? Perhaps you have thought about painting a chest yourself but do not have enough confidence in your painting ability to attempt it. If so, why not try to appliqué a design and stretch it over the drawer fronts to achieve the same effect?*

*Buy an unpainted, ready-to-refinish chest, or use an old one that needs a fresh coat of paint or stain. You might be able to find an old treasure in a junk or antique shop, but any style, old or contemporary, will do.*

*You may have to make adjustments in the*

**Pattern 41**

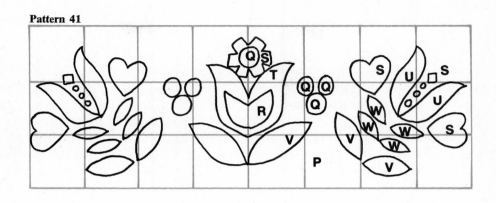

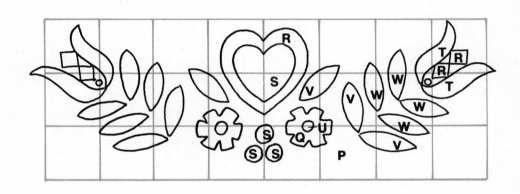

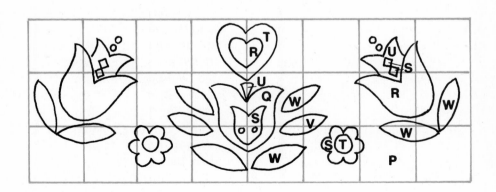

*elements of the design to fit the size you need, but this can be easily done. The chest used here does not have handles. The drawers are pulled out from the bottom edge.*

### Materials

1 chest of drawers, any size with any number of drawers (For a two-drawer chest, omit one of the designs; for a four-drawer chest, repeat two of designs; etc.)

fabric such as linen or sailcloth, required measurement, in turquoise or any other color you prefer (To determine how much fabric is required, measure the drawer front, add 1 inch all around, and multiply by the number of drawers.)

9- by 12-inch rectangles or scraps of felt, in white, orange, hot pink, magenta, violet, chartreuse, and lime (If rectangles are purchased, buy 1 of each color.)

thread in turquoise or one of other colors if preferred

staple tacker and staples

razor blade or art knife

white glue

**Completed size:** As needed. Drawer shown here is 7 by 20½ inches.
**Color code:** P—turquoise, Q—white, R—orange, S—hot pink, T—magenta, U—violet, V—chartreuse, W—lime

### Instructions

1. Enlarge pattern according to instructions on page 19. Measure height of each drawer, and divide by three. Draw squares to equal that measurement.

2. Cut drawer fabric into strips to fit over drawer front, allowing at least 1 inch all around for stretching and stapling. Press fabric.

3. Remove handles and hardware, if any, from drawers. Mark the position of the hardware and outside edges of drawers on fabric. Mark the center top and bottom of drawer along edge.

4. Tape pattern to drawer fabric, lining up center of central motif with center mark on fabric. Follow directions on page 16 for use of tracing wheel and carbon. Make marks to indicate placement of shapes.

5. If necessary, to accommodate for hardware or longer proportion of drawer, shift pattern to left, tape it, and trace position of remaining motifs. Repeat this for right side. Do same for all drawers.

6. One by one, tape appropriate colors of felt to back of pattern and trace all shapes. Cut out. Use a hole punch, if you have one, to cut out the tiny dots of magenta felt.

7. As you cut, position shapes onto fabric, and pin in place.

8. Use a running stitch, as shown in Diagram 13, to sew shapes in place. Make a very delicate stitch that can be seen only upon close observation. Continue in this manner until all drawers are completed.

9. Remove drawers from chest. Make marks at top and bottom center. Place design on one drawer, with the top center marks matching. Bring edge of fabric over top to inside edge of drawer, and staple once to hold in place. Continue to staple upper edge of fabric to inside top edge of drawer, evenly spacing staples as close together as possible.

10. Repeat this for bottom edge of drawer, stretching the fabric tightly so that it is flat but not tight enough to pucker. (With some fabrics, it is helpful to moisten the edge so that it bends smoothly over drawer edge.) Staple ends of drawers in same way.

11. Clip excess fabric from corners. Moisten if fabric is stubborn. Fold the corners neatly and staple down, making sure fabric is pulled taut on front side.

12. With razor blade or art knife, neatly trim away fabric beyond the staples. Place a line of white glue evenly along trimmed edge to prevent fraying. It is also a good

idea to spray drawer fronts with fabric protector to retard soilage. Replace hardware.

13. Repeat same procedure for all drawers. You may have encountered some difficulty in stapling the first drawer. However, once you have completed it, you will find the rest easier. Replace all drawers in chest.

*Pattern 42: Chairs*

# Dutch Designs

*(Technique 4)*

*This is a great idea for a young person who is decorating his or her first apartment on a very limited budget. Director's chairs come in a large assortment of colors and are inexpensive to buy. It is fun to add a personal touch to their exciting colors. A teenager might also enjoy having them in his or her room. They are well suited for family rooms and vacation cabins and, if needed, can always go outside on the patio. Do not leave them outdoors too long, however, since sunlight tends to fade felt colors and rain would certainly ruin them.*

## Materials
**1 canvas director's chair, in plum or turquoise**
**9- by 12-inch rectangles or scraps of felt, in hot pink, magenta, orange, green, white, and either turquoise or violet (If rectangles are purchased, buy 1 of each color.)**

**Pattern 42-A**

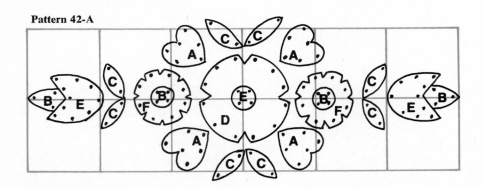

**Pattern 42-B**

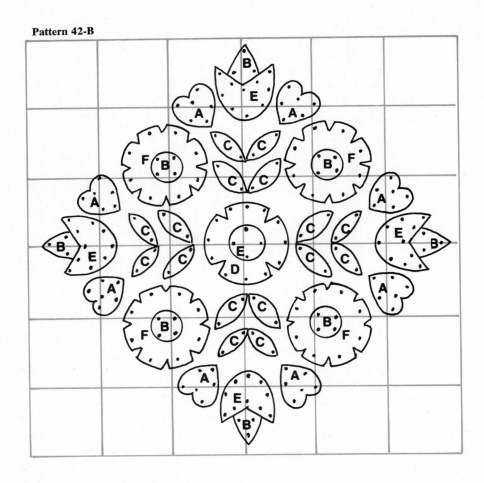

164

white glue

yarn needle

lightweight yarn in color to match canvas

½ yard fabric, in color to match canvas (for lining)

**Color code:** A—hot pink, B—magenta, C—green, D—white, E—orange, F—turquoise (for plum chair), or violet (for turquoise chair)

### Instructions

1. Enlarge patterns according to instructions on page 19. Each square equals 2 inches. Pattern A should measure 4 by 12 inches, and Pattern B should measure 12 by 12 inches.

2. Press felt pieces.

3. Remove canvas seat and back from chair. Tape Pattern A to back and Pattern B to seat, centering design. Follow directions on page 16 for use of tracing wheel and carbon. Make marks to indicate placement of pieces. Untape patterns.

4. One by one, tape appropriate colors of felt to back of pattern and trace shapes. Repeated shapes need be traced only once and then used as models from which to cut the rest. Cut out all pieces.

5. Lay out pieces in position on chair seat and back.

6. Use a minimum amount of glue to hold each piece in place. Allow ½ hour for glue to set.

7. Using yarn to match canvas and following small dots on patterns, make French knots throughout design. See page 41 and Diagram 19 for review on French knots.

8. For a nice finishing touch and to cover yarn ends and knots, line both seat and back on reverse sides. Cut a piece of fabric 17 by 19 inches for chair seat and a piece 8 by 17 inches for chair back. Turn under edges, ½ inch all around, and press. Glue this edge to back of canvas, applying glue evenly. Allow plenty of time for thorough drying.

9. When seat and back are finished, slip back onto chair. If you have made both a plum and a turquoise chair, mix or match backs to seats. Make sure linings are completely dry before you sit on chair.

*Pattern 43: Screen*

# Summer Suns

*(Technique 5)*

*Use this screen as a room divider, to hide a small, untidy work area from view, or in any other way you choose. The sun faces will certainly brighten up any room. Use assorted colors of felt for the panels with sunny-colored fabric or felt scraps for the appliqués.*

*It will not be difficult to build the screen*

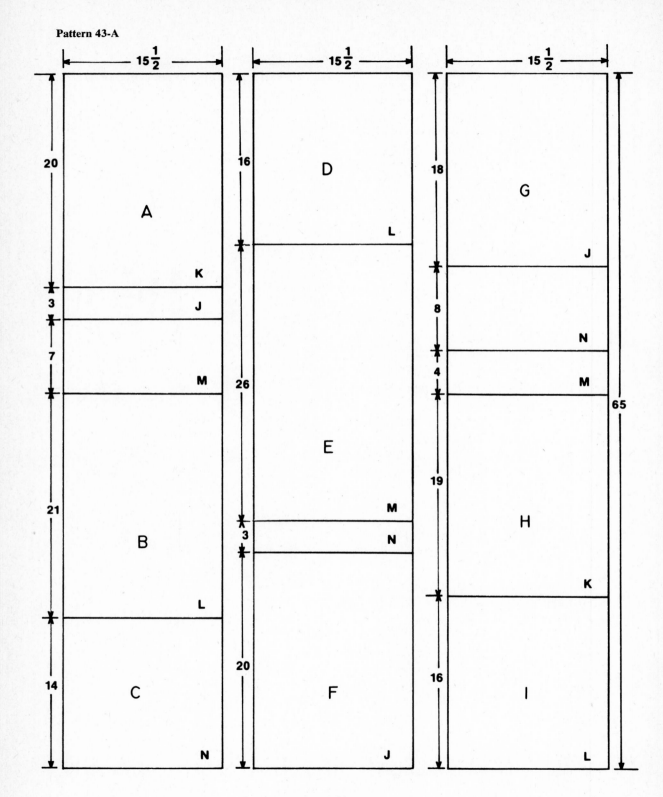

Pattern 43-A

166

*yourself. However, if you prefer, buy an inexpensive one or use an old one in need of restoration. If you do decide to use an old one, the proportions of this design may have to be changed to fit. This is done simply by enlarging the design areas of the pattern to fit the width of the screen panels. Then adjust the plain panels to fit the necessary height. The following directions are for a screen you have built yourself. Following these directions are further directions on how to build this screen.*

## Materials

½ yard felt, in lemon
½ yard felt, in golden yellow
½ yard felt, in yellow-orange
½ yard felt, in orange
½ yard felt, in gold
fabric scraps in stripes, dots, checks, and prints, in above colors (Felt pieces may be used where desired.)
thread in yellow, orange, and brown
yarn in yellow and orange

**Completed size:** 55½ by 69 inches
**Color code:** J—lemon yellow, K—golden yellow, L—yellow-orange, M—orange, N—gold

## Instructions

1. Cut felt panels according to color and size designated in Pattern 43-A. The lower right-hand letter stands for color of panel. Add 2 inches around outer edges of each panel piece to allow for stretching and ½ inch around seamed edges.

2. Enlarge sun panel patterns in Pattern 43-B according to directions on page 19. Each square equals 2 inches. Draw each panel on a separate sheet of paper.

3. One by one, tape patterns to appropriate colors of felt. Follow directions on page 16 for use of tracing wheel and carbon. Make marks to indicate placement of sun shapes. Trace all thin line details on panels

B, F, H, and I. Untape patterns.

4. The decision as to which fabrics to use for sun designs is up to you. One by one, tape chosen fabrics to back of patterns and trace shapes. Untape fabrics.

5. Lay panel pieces out on floor and arrange fabric pieces in position. Pin in place. Any changes in fabric choice will have to be made now.

6. With one panel at a time, hand- or machine-baste shapes down. Satin-stitch, using matching or contrasting thread, with wide zigzag stitch. (See Diagrams 23-A and 23-B.)

7. Satin-stitch thin lines of facial details on panels A, B (smile), E, G, H (smile and ray lines), and I.

8. Couch on yarn for entire F panel and for ray lines on panels B and I. This can be done either by machine, as shown in Diagram 56, or by hand, as shown in Diagram 75. Or, if you prefer, you may satin-stitch these lines instead of couching them.

9. Press all completed panels.

10. Replace patterns on appropriate sun design panels and mark corner marks. Connect marks with chalk line on edges that will be seamed together. Outside edges need not be marked.

11. Lay out all panels in position on floor, as shown on Pattern 43-A. On wrong side of fabric seam panels together across chalk lines. You will now have three separate panels.

12. Press seams open. Panel pieces are now ready to be stretched on screen panels. If you are not constructing your own screen, carefully cut panel pieces to fit screen panels exactly. Glue them to front of panels, around the edges only.

## Materials (Construction of Screen)

1 Masonite panel, ⅛ inch by 4 feet by 8 feet
8 lengths pine molding, each 6 feet by ¾ inch by 1½ inches, with two rounded edges if

**Pattern 43-B**

A

B

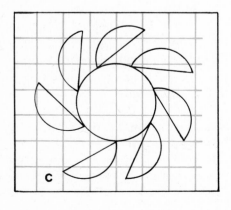

C

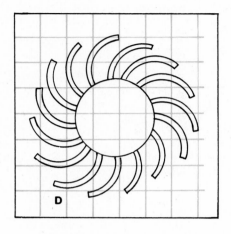

D

E

168

F

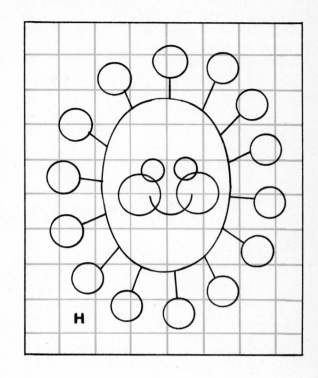

H

G

I

available
electric saw
fine sandpaper
clear sealer
adhesive tape
staple tacker
U-shaped staples, with ⅛-inch legs
24 corrugated fasteners
wood glue
plastic wood pencil
spray paint, in brown
6 brass hinges with screws, ¾-inch size
6 plastic guides, ½-inch size

### Instructions

1. (See Diagram 93.) Cut six A-moldings to measure 5 feet 9 inches. Make 45-degree miter cuts at top end of each. Cut a rabbet 2½ inches from bottom end to accommodate B-molding. Cut a groove ⁵⁄₁₆ inch deep and ¼ inch wide, beginning at miter and ending at rabbet. (See cross section in Diagram 94.)

2. Cut three 16-inch-long B-moldings. Cut the same groove as above across full length.

3. Cut three 18½-inch-long C-moldings, one for each panel. Cut 45-degree miter on each end, and cut groove full length.

4. Cut Masonite panel into three equal panels, measuring 1¼ feet by 5 feet, 5½ inches high. (See Diagram 95 for cutting layout.) Sand sharp edges and all corners of each panel. Remove any dirt or dust that may be on panels.

5. Seal moldings and edges of Masonite with clear sealer. Allow drying time as directed on can.

6. Stretch the finished felt sun panels by wrapping them, one at a time, around the rough side and edges of Masonite panels. Leave smooth side of Masonite exposed for now—it will be painted later. To make sure design is straight and even, tape down pieces to back of panel with adhesive tape before

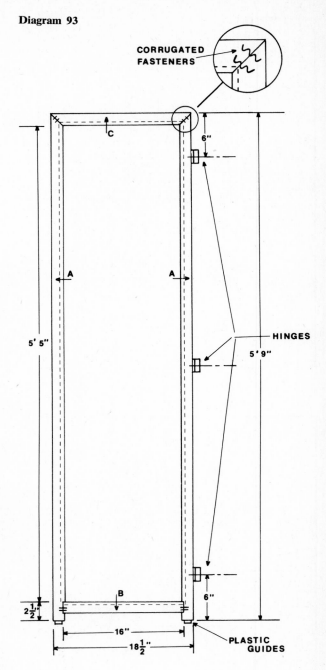

Diagram 93

CORRUGATED
FASTENERS

C

6"

A          A

HINGES

5' 5"          5' 9"

B          6"

2½"

16"

18½"          PLASTIC
GUIDES

Diagram 94

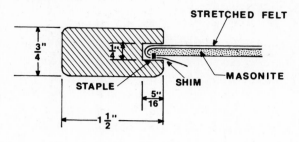

stapling. When stapling, staple close to the edge on back, spacing staples fairly close together. Do not cut off excess materials until panels are framed.

7. For each panel, apply glue to groove of B-molding and slip panel into it. Apply glue to A-molding and insert panel and then to C-molding and insert panel. Use corrugated fasteners, as indicated on Diagram 93, to secure moldings at all four corners. If there are any openings in jointed connections, fill them with plastic wood pencil and lightly sand over.

8. Shim with wood shavings, where indicated on Diagram 94, to secure position of panel in groove.

9. Allow for drying as directed on glue container. Cut away excess material from back of panels.

10. Carefully mask all front panels. Spray paint the moldings and backs of panels. Allow drying time as indicated on paint can.

11. Hinge panels together, placing hinges as indicated on Diagrams 93 and 96.

12. Apply plastic guides to bottom of each A-molding as indicated in Diagram 93.

Diagram 95

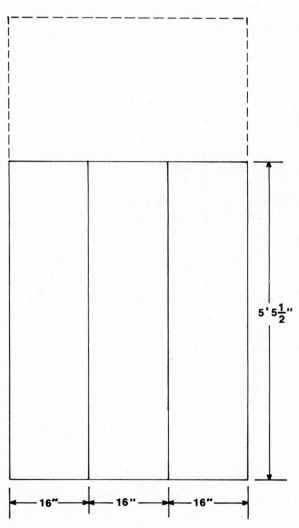

Diagram 96

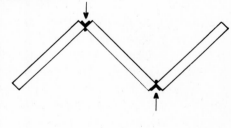

171

# Thunderbird

*(Technique 5)*

These thunderbird designs are adapted from those of the Pueblo Indians of New Mexico. Long appreciated by the people who live near their lands, American Indian crafts have gained more respect in recent years than ever before and are beginning to find their way into more and more homes. These designs were taken from North American Indian Design Coloring Book, *by Paul E. Kennedy, published by Dover. They are very simple to make and can be used to replace a worn or faded seat cover for almost any chair. Since the seat cover construction will depend on the kind of chair seat you have, no instructions are given here for fin-*

ishing. You may need only to remove the old slip cover and use it as a pattern for the new one. However, if the chair is constructed in such a way as to make reapplying the seat cover too complicated for you to do, take the design piece to an upholsterer. Be sure to leave ample allowance around the edge of the seat so that the upholsterer has enough material to work with and can then trim it down to the proper size.

## Materials

1 upholstery fabric square, 24 by 24 inches, in black
1 upholstery fabric scrap, 11 by 12 inches, in sand tone
small scraps of upholstery fabric, in turquoise and dark coral
thread in black

**Color code:** O—sand tone, P—turquoise, Q—dark coral

### Instructions

1. Enlarge whichever pattern you choose according to instructions on page 19. Each square equals 1½ inches. Curved bird pattern should measure 10½ by 12 inches and angular bird pattern should measure 9 by 12 inches.

2. Press all fabric pieces.

3. Center pattern onto black fabric, and tape it down. Follow directions on page 16 for use of tracing wheel and carbon. Trace outline of thunderbird. Untape pattern.

4. Tape sand tone scrap to back of pattern. Trace thunderbird and enough markings to show position of inner details. Untape, and do same for turquoise and coral scraps.

5. Cut out all turquoise and coral shapes except those coral pieces that touch turquoise on angular thunderbird.

6. On the angular thunderbird, sew the turquoise pieces to coral fabric where called for. Baste by hand or machine, as shown in

Diagrams 23-A and B, and then sew a zig-zag satin stitch. Trim away excess coral fabric overlapped by turquoise, and cut out rest of coral shape.

7. Position the pieces on the thunderbird, and pin in place.

8. Using zigzag satin stitch, sew down all pieces. Press and cut out thunderbird.

9. In proper position, pin the thunderbird on black fabric, and with same zigzag stitch sew around edge. Seat cover is now ready to be fitted to your chair.

**Pattern 44**

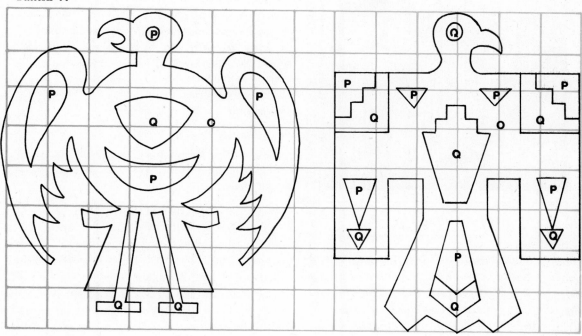

## Pattern 45: Room Divider

# Hearts and Flowers

*(Technique 6)*

*This dramatic room divider, though large in size, is really very simple to make. The design is basic, easy, and quickly appliquéd by hand. It consists of twenty-four sections, joined together to form eight streamers with three sections each. There are two streamers in one design unit. Make as many design units as you need to achieve the effect you want.*

*Use the room divider to conceal your laundry room or utility area. You can also add more units and use it to split a very large room into more intimate areas. Its bold design will lighten any contemporary room in need of some vitality. It would also look*

*fine hanging right on your wall as a super-graphic wall hanging.*

### Materials

assorted fabric pieces (This one was made of a mixture of basket-weave and diagonal-weave fabrics in varied weights.)

2 yards fabric, in scarlet

1 yard fabric, in brick red

1 yard fabric, in magenta

1 yard fabric, in violet

½ yard fabric, in dark brown

½ yard fabric, in light brown

¼ yard fabric, in ocher

scraps of broadcloth or similar weight fabrics in ocher, orange, scarlet, lavender, violet, turquoise, shades of green, in solids and prints

1 fabric rectangle, 1¼ by 5⅓ yards, or 24 9¼- by 33¼-inch strips of varied fabrics (for lining)

thread in matching colors

16 drapery weights

curtain rod, extending to 64 inches

**Completed size:** 64 by 94 inches

**Color code:** R—scarlet, S—brick red, T—magenta, U—violet, V—dark brown, W—light brown, X—ocher

### Instructions

1. Enlarge Patterns 45-B 1, 2, and 3 according to instructions on page 19. Each square equals 2 inches. Each pattern should measure 8 by 32 inches.

2. Press fabric pieces with steam iron.

3. Following color and dimension specifications in Pattern 45-A, cut fabrics into strips, adding ⅝ inch for seam allowance. The lower right-hand letter indicates color for each panel.

4. Using photograph of project as a guide, tape appropriate pattern (45-B 1, 2, or 3) to appropriate color strip so that there is a ⅝-inch margin of fabric surrounding top and sides of pattern. Follow directions on page 16 for use of tracing wheel and carbon. Make marks to show placement of

**Pattern 45-A**

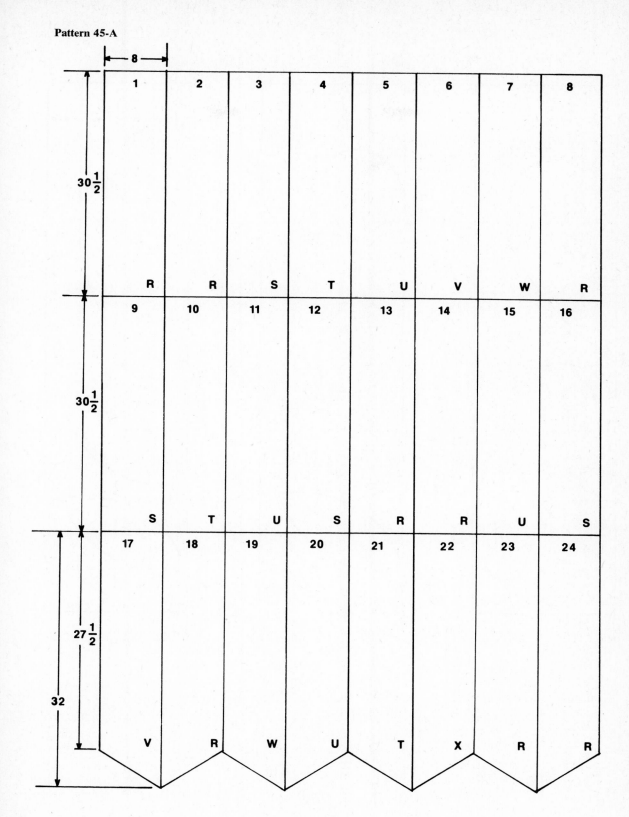

**Pattern 45-B**

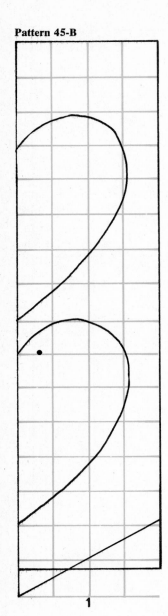

1

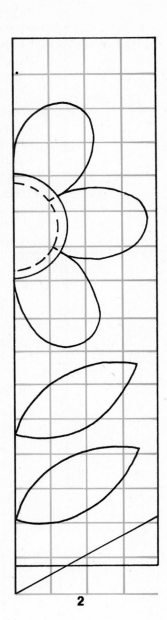

2

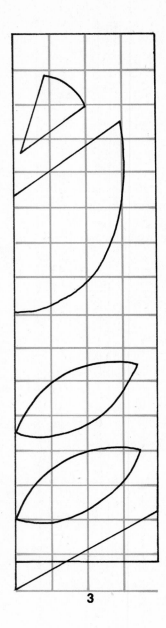

3

176

hearts and flowers. Untape patterns.

5. Tape fabric scraps to backs of patterns, and trace the flower and heart shapes. Allow ¼ inch around edges for turning under and an extra ½ inch along those that touch border of designs. Cut out all pieces.

6. In proper position, lay out the cut strips on floor, following Pattern 45-A. Number each piece on back with pencil, chalk, or marked tape so that later they can be easily arranged back in order.

7. Place the heart and flower shapes in position. You may decide to make some changes at this point. Exchange or recut until you have found the arrangement you like best. Use prints and solids randomly so that a good mixture of each is sprinkled throughout. When your decision is final, pin each piece in place.

8. Using whip stitch, as shown in Diagram 25, whip down edges of appliqué pieces. On the daisy design, whip down petals first and then center circle.

9. When all pieces are appliquéd, tape patterns to each in position. With carbon side up, place carbon paper against wrong side of fabric. Trace outline of each panel so that it will appear on back.

10. When tracing panels 17 through 24, place carbon paper between pattern and fabric with carbon side down against fabric. Trace the angled line at bottom to produce wedge shape, so that the line is on front of fabric, instead of back.

11. On wrong side, seam panels together along traced outline. Begin by seaming panel 1 to panel 9, and 9 to 17. Continue in this manner until you have eight three-paneled streamers. Press seams open.

12. If one color is chosen for lining, cut eight 9¼- by 95¼-inch strips. You may prefer using several colors for the lining. If so, cut separate strips, following dimensions in Pattern 45-A, and position them according to color arrangement you prefer. Number strips to correspond with the design strip it will be sewn to. Place marks for seams at top and bottom edges of each middle lining strip, 31 inches apart. Seam top, middle, and bottom sections together. You should now have eight lining strips. Press seams downward.

13. Face to face, pin each design strip to each lining strip.

14. Seam along traced line on wrong side of design strips, leaving bottom edges open. Stop stitches 1¾ inches from top, and seam across top edge on marked line. Resume stitching on the other side, 1¾ inches from top seam. (See Diagram 97. The 1¾-inch space is allowance for rod to pass through.)

Diagram 97

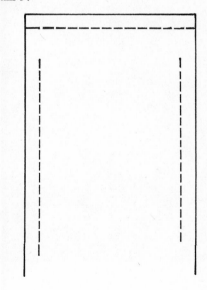

15. Turn streamers inside out and press edges flat. Turn under unseamed portion at top of streamers, and press down so that edges are straight.

16. Turn bottom edges of streamers un-

der, following traced line. Turn lining edge under to correspond. Place two weights on inside bottom of each streamer, as shown in Diagram 98, and sew to seams. Sew lower edges of design and lining streamers together, by hand or with zigzag stitch on machine.

17. Keeping sequence of design, slip rod through the top of each streamer.

Diagram 98

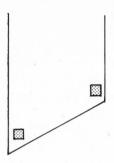

*Pattern 46: Pillows*

# Hawaiian Echoes

*(Technique 6)*

*The beautiful quilts of Hawaii were the inspiration for the motifs on these pillows. Hawaiian quilt-making is done first by cutting an intricate design of rich tropical foliage or other shapes, from a piece of paper* *the size of the quilt and folded into eighths. The paper is then unfolded and the design transferred to fabric, where it is appliquéd to the background and then quilted. Although much more complicated, this method of cutting the design is not unlike the way children are taught to create designs from folded paper.*

*In this pattern, the designs are cut to pillow size. You may cut your own design or copy these. Quilting is the process of sewing a completed design to a backing fabric with a layer of quilt batting in between. You may omit the quilting if you prefer.*

## Materials
### Large pillow:
2 cotton broadcloth squares, 20 by 20 inches, in violet

1 cotton broadcloth square, 17 by 17 inches, in turquoise

thread in matching colors

1 pillow form square, 18 by 18 inches (If you are making your own, use two 19- by 19-inch squares of muslin and 1½ pounds polyester fiberfill.)

1 zipper, 16 inches in length, in violet (optional)

If design is to be quilted:

1 muslin square, 20 by 20 inches

1 bonded Dacron quilt batting square, 18 by 18 inches

### Medium pillow:
2 gingham squares, 18 by 18 inches, in turquoise

1 gingham square, 13 by 13 inches, in orange

thread in matching colors

1 pillow form square, 16 by 16 inches (If you are making your own, use two 17- by 17-inch squares of muslin and 1 pound polyester fiberfill.)

1 zipper, 14 inches in length, in turquoise (optional)

If design is to be quilted:

1 muslin square, 18 by 18 inches

1 bonded Dacron quilt batting square, 16 by 16 inches

### Small pillow:
2 cotton print squares, 16 by 16 inches, in orange

scraps of cotton, in violet

thread in matching colors

1 pillow form square, 14 by 14 inches (If you are making your own, use two 15- by 15-inch squares of muslin and ¾ pound polyester fiberfill.)

1 zipper, 12 inches in length, in orange (optional)

If design is to be quilted:

1 muslin square, 16 by 16 inches

1 bonded Dacron quilt batting square, 14 by 14 inches

**Completed sizes:** *large,* 18 by 18 inches; *medium,* 16 by 16 inches; *small,* 14 by 14 inches

## Instructions
1. Cut paper into a 16-inch square for large design or a 12-inch square for medium design. The small design is made from cutaway portions of medium design. Another complete design could be made from the cutaway portion of the larger design, although not included here. Fold paper in half twice to form a square, and fold square diagonally in half. (See Diagram 99.)

**Diagram 99**

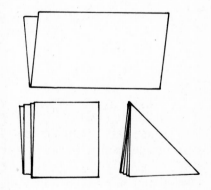

2. Enlarge pattern onto folded paper according to directions on page 19. (Broken lines indicate folded edges.) Each square equals 1 inch. Cut out designs on drawn lines. Unfold paper. If you wish, experiment with and cut your own designs.

179

**Pattern 46**

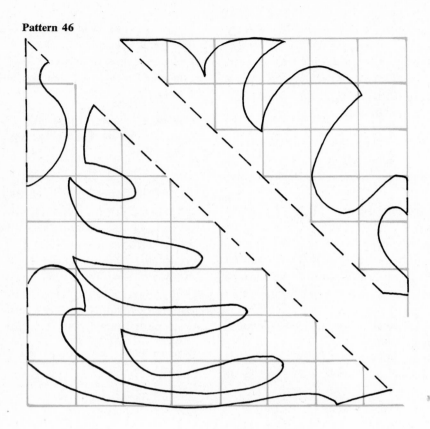

3  Press all fabric pieces.

4. Pin paper pattern on smaller fabric square, and trace around the edge with pencil.

5. Center and pin traced fabric piece to pillow square.

6. Start cutting the edge of design, leaving an allowance of ⅛ inch for turning under. Cut only a little at a time, and then sew down the portion you have cut. To sew, use whip stitch, as shown in Diagram 25, and whip down edges. Clip corners and inward curves where necessary to follow shape of traced edge.

7. To quilt pillow, pin appliquéd design, face up, to square of muslin with Dacron batting in between. Begin at center of design, and baste diagonally across the three layers, as shown in Diagram 100. This will hold the layers together while quilting is done. *Note:* Quilting is optional. In this pattern the large and small pillows were quilted and the medium pillow was not.

8. Start at center of design and work outward. Place a running stitch, as shown in Diagram 13, inside each appliqué shape, ¼ inch from edge, and another running stitch outside appliqué shape, ¼ inch from

**Diagram 100**

**Diagram 101**

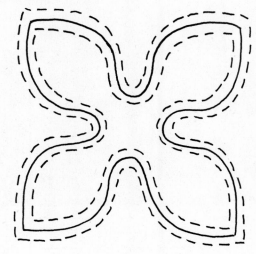

181

edge. (See Diagram 101.) In Hawaiian quilting, the shapes are continuously outlined by these lines of running stitches, over the whole surface. You may do this on the pillows if you wish, making the quilting lines ¼ inch apart. It is not essential, however, and was not done on these pillows. Remove basting.

9. Place worked design face to face with square of matching fabric. If you will not be inserting a zipper, seam the two together around three edges. Make seams 1 inch from edge, unless quilted. Bear in mind that quilting draws up the fabric so that it shrinks in size. Therefore, if pillow top was quilted, make seams ¾ inch from edge. Clip corners and turn inside out. Insert pillow form. With edges turned to inside, pin fourth side together. Whip together by hand to close up. If you do wish to insert zipper, sew it in place before seaming the other three sides. See Pattern 35, step 11. This will also explain how to make your own pillow form.

*Pattern 47: Place Mats*

# Fiesta

*(Technique 6)*

*Although the quilts of Pakistan were the inspiration for these place mats, the colors used add a Mexican flavor to them. The design is made in much the same way as the Hawaiian pillows. Rectangles of paper are folded, cut, snipped, and then unfolded to*

182

*make patterns for the designs. Children will probably love doing the folding and snipping. Make as many place mats as you need.*

## Materials (for 2 place mats)
½ yard sailcloth or poplin, in orange, magenta, turquoise, or green
2 cotton broadcloth rectangles, 5 by 12 inches, in contrasting colors

**Completed size:** 13½ by 19 inches
**Color code:** 2 colors for each mat

### Instructions
1. Cut paper into rectangles to measure 4 by 11 inches. Fold each in half twice. Enlarge each pattern on a folded rectangle according to directions on page 19. (Broken lines indicate folded edges.) Each square equals 1 inch. Cut out designs on drawn

**Pattern 47**

183

lines. Unfold. If you wish, experiment with your own designs.

2. Press all fabric pieces.

3. Pin cutout design on each broadcloth rectangle to be used. With pencil, trace outline and inner shapes. Cut design around outer edge, leaving a ⅛-inch allowance for turning under.

4. Cut the place mat fabric into rectangles, each measuring 14½ by 20 inches. Pin design to place mat so that it is 1½ inches from side edges and 1¾ inches from the top and bottom edges.

5. Turn under edges and whip down, as shown in Diagram 25. Cut and slit all inner cutouts, and clip and whip down edges. Refer to Pattern 7, steps 5 to 15, for slitting and whipping details.

6. Press edges of place mat under, folding twice to hide all raw edges. Clip corners of excess fabric. Stitch down, using zigzag or straight stitch.

*Pattern 48: Pillow*

# Landmarks

*(Technique 7)*

*Nicholas Sidjakov's illustrations in the children's book* Steffan, *published by Parnassus Press, gave me the idea for this pillow. The illustrations in this delightful book lend themselves well to the technique of the San Blas Indians. If you have been practicing*

**Pattern 48**

*this technique and are becoming proficient at it, you might want to try this design. Keep in mind that the slits made here are very tiny.*

### Materials

½ yard cotton, in rust

1 cotton square, 16 by 16 inches, in turquoise

1 cotton square, 16 by 16 inches, in magenta

thread in rust and turquoise

1 pillow form square, 16 by 16 inches (If you are making your own, use two 17- by 17-inch squares of muslin and 1 pound polyester fiberfill.)

1 zipper, 14 inches in length, in rust (optional)

**Completed size:** 16 by 16 inches

**Color code:** Y—rust, Z—turquoise. All cutouts are magenta.

### Instructions

1. Enlarge pattern according to instructions on page 19. Each square equals 2 inches. Pattern should measure 16 by 16 inches.

2. Press fabric pieces. Cut rust fabric into two 18- by 18-inch squares.

3. Tape pattern to one rust square so that there is 1 inch of fabric surrounding edge of pattern. Follow directions on page 16 for use of tracing wheel and carbon. Trace outline of building, omitting all inner details. Untape pattern.

4. Place rust fabric on top of turquoise square and magenta underneath turquoise. Pin the three together and baste around edges.

5. Pierce the rust fabric ⅛ inch inside traced line, and cut a little at a time. Then turn this edge under and whip down to turquoise. Review Pattern 7, steps 5 through 15 and Pattern 8, steps 4 through 10, for details on cutting, slitting, clipping, and whipping down the edges.

6. When outline is complete, retape pattern to fabric. Using tracing wheel, carbon, and a hard pencil, trace inner details.

7. Do all details, slitting, cutting, and whipping down edges to magenta layer. The six windows in the lower right-hand corner are made by replacing the cutaway inner part of building, cutting them into window shapes, and appliquéing them onto magenta. Complete design.

8. Place the design piece face to face with second rust square. If you are not going to insert a zipper, seam the two together, 1 inch from edge, around three sides. Clip corners and turn to inside out. Insert pillow form. Pin fourth side together with edges turned to inside. Whip together by hand to close up. If you do wish to insert zipper, sew

in place before seaming the other three sides. See Pattern 35, step 11. This also will explain how to make your own pillow form.

*Pattern 49: Quilt*

# Mexican Images

*(Techniques 7 and 8)*

*Here is an unusual quilt of Mexican inspiration, made with the San Blas reverse appliqué technique. If you feel that making an entire quilt is too laborious a job for you to cope with, bear in mind that these quilt blocks can have many other uses. For example, you can pick out one of them and make it into a small wall hanging or pillow. Better yet, the four main design pieces can be put together to make a fine wall hanging.*

186

**Pattern 49**

A

B

C

D

187

**Pattern 49**

E

F

I

G

J

H

188

*If you do want to make the entire quilt, be prepared to allow a good length of time for it. The process is a long one unless, of course, you have help. This particular quilt was made in a year and a half. The blocks can be made whenever you have spare time and can be conveniently carried around with you. Since few people have enough space in their homes for a large quilting frame, this quilt was made with a quilt-as-you-go technique rather than stretched on a frame.*

Quilting *refers to the stitching that holds the filler in place within the blocks. This quilt actually has very little quilting. The appliqué blocks themselves are lined but not quilted. Since this is a light coverlet, no added filler is needed inside the blocks. The only areas to be quilted are the border and the spacing strips between the blocks. A light filler of outing flannel is placed inside, between the top and the lining, and a minimum amount of quilting is done to keep the filler in place. Each border block and strip is quilted separately.*

*The blocks and strips are then sewn together from the back. It is important that the sizes be accurate so that the parts fit.*

*A quilt is always a good way to use leftover fabric scraps. Choose vivid colors to keep in touch with the spirit of Mexico.*

## Materials

15 (minimum) cotton or blend rectangles, 12 by 16 inches, in vivid colors

16 (minimum) cotton or blend rectangles, 10 by 14 inches, in vivid colors

2⅝ yards cotton or blend fabric, in off-white

4¼ yards cotton or blend fabric, in any desired color (for lining)

polyester thread in matching colors

2¾ yards outing flannel (for filler)

scraps in vivid colors

**Completed size:** 68 by 74½ inches (coverlet for double bed)

Sizes of individual blocks and strips:

A, B, C, and D blocks: 9½ by 14 inches
E and F blocks: 9½ by 11 inches
G strips: 2 by 9½ inches
H strips: 2 by 46 inches
I blocks: 9½ by 17½ inches
J blocks: 11 by 23 inches

## Instructions

1. If you want to be able to launder the quilt, all fabric pieces should be washed before doing anything. It is better to allow fabrics to shrink now than to have them shrink later. Press all fabric pieces before cutting.

2. Enlarge quilt blocks according to instructions on page 19. Each square equals 2 inches. Use separate sheets of paper for each design.

3. Tape patterns for blocks A, B, C, and D to selected colored fabrics, and trace outer shapes of designs. Do not trace any of the shapes that are within other shapes, such as those in blocks A and B. Since block B is composed of eight smaller blocks, plan colors for entire block before tracing. All of blocks C and D can be traced now. In block C some of the facial details are cut away and replaced later in the faces.

It is a good idea to trace several designs at once and to plan the colors for them in advance so that they may be picked up at a moment's notice and taken along with you. However, it is not necessary to plan the colors for all the blocks before starting the quilt. In fact, it is more exciting to use whatever leftover scraps happen to come your way as you are working on your quilt.

4. Refer to Pattern 7, steps 5 through 15, and Pattern 8, steps 4 through 10, for cutting, slitting, clipping, and whipping details. Also refer to Pattern 32, steps 4 through 6, for other helpful hints.

Block B is made of eight tiny blocks. Since much detail is involved, omit some of

189

the smaller details if you wish. When the small blocks are completed, seam backs together to form one block and press seams open.

The underlayer of block C is made of two fabrics. One is folded over the other, as shown in Diagram 102. Baste these two fab-

**Diagram 102**

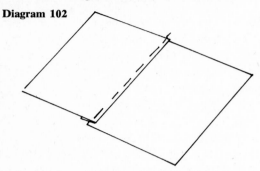

rics together, and press. Place the seam at middle of design so that the double image of the man is split into two colors, one above and one below.

Use reverse appliqué method 1 for border and two horizontal slits in block B. When these are complete, turn the design over and cut away any excess fabric. Pin in fabric for remaining part of design.

5. See Diagram 103 for cutting layout of the 2⅝-yard piece of off-white fabric. Follow piece measurements listed on page 189, add ½ inch all around for seams, and cut blocks E, F, I, J, and strips G and H. Measure carefully with yardstick and mark before cutting.

6. Tape block E and F patterns to appropriate blocks of cotton fabric. Trace design and untape patterns. Using any color underlayer you wish, work design.

7. See Diagram 103 for cutting layout of the 4¼-yard lining piece. Follow piece measurements listed on page 189, add ½ inch all around for seams, and cut out lining pieces.

8. Retape patterns A, B, C, and D, one at a time, on appropriate design pieces.

Mark corners and untape patterns. Transfer these marks to reverse sides of design pieces by placing carbon paper face up against wrong side of design. Connect these marks on reverse side with a pencil, using ruler for guide.

9. Working with one block at a time, pin each block face down to matching lining block. Seam around three sides on traced lines. Clip corners, turn inside out, and press edges. Sew remaining sides together,

**Diagram 103**

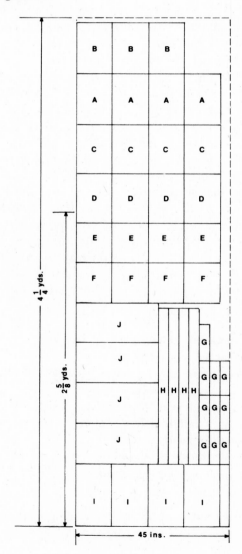

190

**Diagram 104**

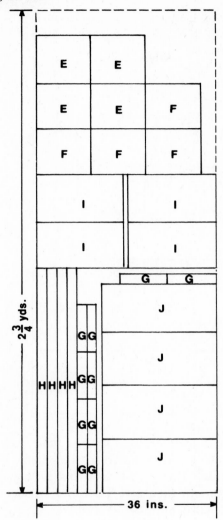

11. Start with G strips, and work one at a time. Baste strip of flannel to off-white strip. Place matching strip of lining to front side of off-white strip, and pin the three pieces together. With a ruler to help, draw the seam line on off-white strip around flannel.

12. Seam three sides on sewing machine. Clip corners, and turn inside out. Press edges, and sew fourth side by hand. Continue doing all ten G strips in this way. Check measurements constantly as you work.

13. Repeat this procedure for the four H strips and the E, F, I, and J blocks until all are lined and filled with a layer of flannel. Check measurements carefully.

14. Tape appropriate patterns to G and H strips and I and J blocks. Trace the zigzag quilting lines. Do not use dressmaker's carbon for this unless the package specifies that it is washable. Before taping, rub over the quilting lines on reverse side of the patterns with a soft pencil. After taping, trace lines with pencil. This will produce a faint line on front of fabric. If necessary, go over the lines with a hard lead pencil to make them visible. No lines need be traced on the E and F blocks.

15. Quilt the strips. This is done by carefully going over the traced zigzag lines with small running stitches, as shown in Diagram 13. Remove basting thread when each strip has been completed.

16. Quilt blocks E and F. This is done by putting a line of quilting stitches, ¼ inch around the edge of each block, just in far enough to catch the inner lining of outing flannel. Then quilt around the edge of the circles ¼ inch away from the circular motif. Remove the basting thread.

17. Quilt blocks I and J carefully, sewing along outline of design and placing another line of quilting ¼ inch from the edge. Remove any basting thread.

by hand, with small stitches. Measure each block upon completion to check measurements. If not accurate, rip out and sew it over. Continue until all fifteen blocks are complete.

10. Follow Diagram 104 for cutting layout of outing flannel piece. Cut out blocks according to measurements on page 189. Do not allow for seaming. Cut proper amount of block E pieces, block F pieces, block I pieces, block J pieces, H strip pieces, and G strip pieces.

Diagram 105

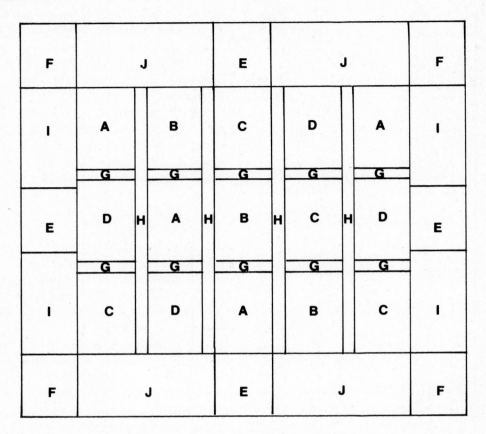

18. The blocks are now complete, and the quilt is ready to assemble. Lay out quilt blocks, following Diagram 105. Make changes in arrangement if you wish.

19. The quilt pieces are sewn together from the back. Place the two pieces to be

**Diagram 106**

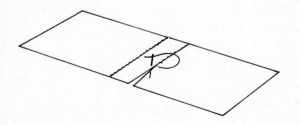

sewn together face down on a table, side by side. Use a whip stitch to join them. (See Diagram 106.) Sew G strips to adjacent blocks and then sew blocks to adjacent H strips until the central part of the quilt is complete.

20. Sew J blocks and appropriate E blocks together, and sew these strips to upper and lower edges of central portion. Sew the appropriate F, I, and E blocks together, and then join these to sides of center.

21. When quilt is complete, embroider your name and the date on it. Someday, perhaps the quilt will be handed down to your ancestors or discovered in an attic (if houses still have attics). If so, the new owners will certainly appreciate knowing who made it, and when!

192

# 6

# Appliqué
# Clothing

The person who can sew well is indeed fortunate when it comes to dressing. Many people are no longer content with mass-produced wardrobes. Most people want to express their individuality in the way they look. Appliqué work is a delightful way to make something unique out of a store-bought or pattern-made dress.

A visit to a boutique shop these days will uncover many interesting imported garments, trimmed with unusual ethnic handwork. Prices on such items, however, are usually out of an average budget's range. Once you have learned how to handle a needle and thread, you will be able to create a stunning gown or perhaps a small detail for a dress. Very often, these self-made creations are more suitable for you than the one you saw at the boutique shop. Furthermore, they are fun to do and certainly cost a lot less.

We should all follow the example of young people. They love to experiment. Once they have decorated their jeans with manufactured appliqués, they want to go on to something else.

Now that fashion has finally been liberated from strict discipline, we have the freedom to wear what we like. Those of us who have lived long enough to see styles come and go are quite bored by fashion headlines that remind us of the dictatorship of the fashion industry. Some of us prefer to go our own way with styles, wearing clothes that are right for us and adding a special touch to make them truly personal.

Entertaining at home with close friends is a wonderful opportunity to let your imagination operate freely. A hostess can create the atmosphere for her party with her gown. It also helps extend her personality.

While attending a folk dance session at a ski lodge, I couldn't help but notice how the instructor's lavishly embroidered peasant dress helped to emphasize the enthusiasm and love she felt for the dances.

Perhaps this chapter will give you some ideas on how to better express yourself through your clothing.

*Pattern 50: Bolero*

# India Inspiration

*(Technique 2)*

*Here is an easy-to-make felt bolero with overtones of the delicate mirror embroidery of India. It will add an exotic look to a very plain gown or to a pants and shirt outfit. It may be just what you need for your party.*

### Materials
½ yard felt, in bronze
½ yard felt, in orange
⅛ yard felt, in turquoise

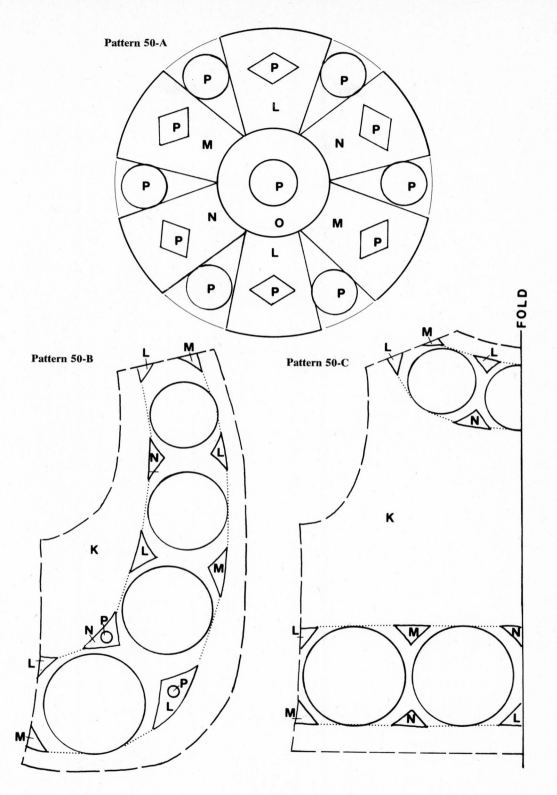

**Pattern 50-A**

**Pattern 50-B**

**Pattern 50-C**

FOLD

9- by 12-inch rectangles or scraps of felt, in magenta and gold (If rectangles are purchased, buy 1 of each color.)

bolero pattern in proper size

compass

thread in bronze

metallic mylar, paillettes, or aluminum cooking tins (See Patterns 25 and 31.)

white glue

lightweight yarn in turquoise, orange, and magenta

**Color code:** K—bronze, L—orange, M—turquoise, N—magenta, O—gold, P—metallic mylar

### Instructions

1. Using a compass, draw a circle in each of the following diameters: 2½ inches, 3 inches, 3½ inches, and 4 inches. Draw a 1-inch-diameter circle within the 2½-inch circle and a 1¼-inch circle within the others. Also draw another ½-inch circle in center of each. The petals in the circles, as shown in Pattern 50-A, can be drawn by eye. Now add the circle and diamond shapes. These rosette shapes do not have to be geometrically perfect. Cut out rosette circles.

2. Tape the circles to bolero front pattern, as shown in Pattern 50-B. (Broken lines indicate variable seam line of pattern. Your pattern may be shaped a little differently.) Petals may be tilted at random angles. Draw a line to connect circles, as shown by dotted line in Pattern 50-B. Draw remaining triangles, as shown, using drawn line to guide their position.

3. Cut two 4-inch circles, and tape them to pattern back along the lower edge, as shown in Pattern 50-C. Cut two 3-inch circles. Cut one in half, and tape both halves and the whole to pattern back along upper neck edge, as shown in Pattern 50-C. Draw triangles as in step 2.

4. Press felt pieces with steam iron.

5. Pin the pattern back and front to bronze felt, following directions of pattern, and cut it out. Omit facings. Cut on the cutting line of the pattern, although the edges will be trimmed away at the seam line later.

6. Follow directions on page 16 for use of tracing wheel and carbon. Make marks to show placement of rosettes and triangles. Unpin pattern.

7. Sew darts following pattern instructions, and press. Leave front and back unseamed.

8. Remove rosette patterns from pattern front and back, and tape them to the appropriate felt pieces. Trace petal and circle shapes. Repeated shapes need be traced only once and then used as models from which to cut the rest. Cut out holes that appear within petals, as indicated by the letter P for metal bits.

9. Position the cut shapes on bolero front and back as you cut. Pin in place.

10. Tape appropriate felt pieces to pattern front and back, and trace triangular shapes. Cut out and position them on front and back of bolero.

11. Cut out metallic bits from material you have chosen, and pin in position, underneath holes. Refer to Pattern 25, steps 12 and 13.

12. When all pieces are placed in position, glue them in place, using minimum amount of glue. Allow 1 hour for glue to dry. When dry, pick up design to make sure nothing falls off. Reglue any loose pieces.

13. Using straight stitch on sewing machine, sew around edge of all shapes, including metallic bit holes. The sewing machine will sew over the metallic material.

14. Cut small circles of metallic material, and position them between petals of circles, as indicated. Glue down.

15. Using yarns of all three colors, work a chain stitch around edges of metallic cir-

cles between the petals. (See Diagrams 80 and 81.)

16. Seam bolero and press seams. Trim away edges on seam line. Sew triangles in place on seams.

17. Use pattern to make another bolero from orange felt. Press seams open.

18. Pin bronze bolero back to back with orange, with open seams against each other. Pin all around armhole so that the orange forms an even border around the bronze bolero.

19. Use medium-width zigzag stitch, set at 20 stitches to the inch, and sew bronze to orange around edge.

20. Trim all around edge of orange, ¼ inch beyond bronze edge. Make sure edge is even all around.

21. Using turquoise felt, cut a long, narrow strip that is straight on one side and pinked on the other. (See Diagram 107.)

**Diagram 107**

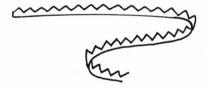

Pin strip close to bronze edge of bolero, starting at back of neck. Pin so that straight side is on the outer edge of bolero and pinked side is on the inner edge. Sew along the straight edge with same zigzag stitch as above. Cut another strip to continue if first strip is not long enough. Repeat pinning and sewing this strip to the armhole edge.

# Hungarian Szur

*(Technique 2)*

*The szur, worn exclusively by Hungarian men for festive occasions, is one of their most ancient forms of dress. It was elaborately embellished with intricate cutout felt work. This vest was inspired by the szurs. Intricate as it may appear, it is a much simplified version of the original szur designs. You use pinking shears to create the right effect.*

### Materials
⅝ **yard felt, in red, or in any desired color**
⅝ **yard felt, in olive, or in any desired color**
**vest pattern in proper size**
**thread in matching colors**
**compass**

197

**Pattern 51-A**

**Pattern 51-B**

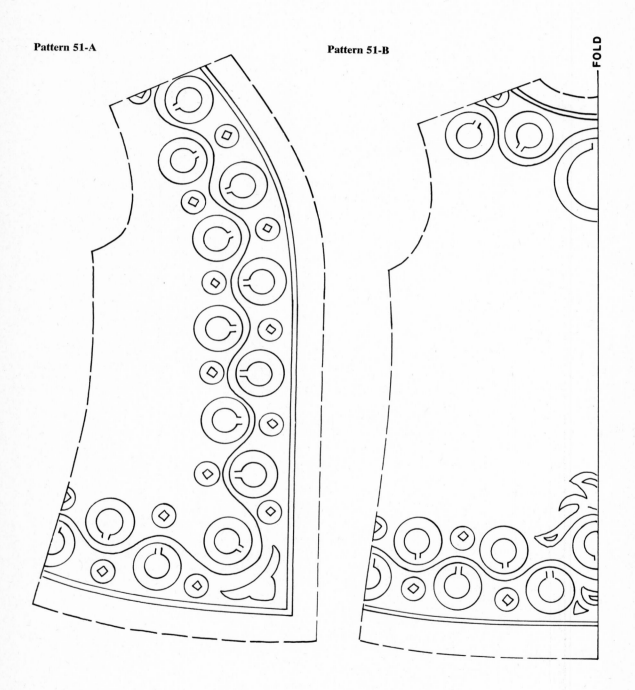

**4 yards or necessary amount folded woven bias edging, in gray or in any desired color**

**5 buttons (optional)**

### Instructions

1. Press felt pieces.

2. Follow pattern directions to make one red and one olive vest from felt. Omit pattern facings. Cut on the cutting line of the pattern, although the excess fabric will be trimmed away later. Olive vest is used for lining. Put aside for now.

3. Cut long strips of olive felt, about ½ inch wide. Use pinking shears for one edge, as shown in Diagram 107. Pin and sew all around edge of red vest about 1⅛ inches from seam line so that pinked edge faces outer edge of vest. If possible, place ends at lower corners of front.

4. Cut thirty-nine 2-inch-diameter circles of olive felt. Cut an incomplete circle within each circle, measuring about 1¼ inches in diameter, as shown in Diagram 108. With

**Diagram 108**

pinking shears, cut around this inner circle. (See Diagram 109.) Now fold the inner circle in half, varying the angle, as shown in Diagram 110. Cut out various shapes to get designs, such as those in Diagram 111.

**Diagram 109**

**Diagram 110**

5. Position these circles on vest front and back, according to Patterns 51-A and B. (Broken lines indicate variable seam line of pattern. Your spacing may vary, depending on size and length of your pattern.) Pin and using straight stitch, sew around edges of outer, and then inner, circles. Leave inner cutouts unsewn.

6. Cut one circle from olive felt, 3¾ inches in diameter. Cut an inner circle about 2½ inches in diameter. Create design shown in Diagram 112. Pin circle to center back, as shown in Pattern 51-B. Sew in place on circumferences.

**Diagram 111**

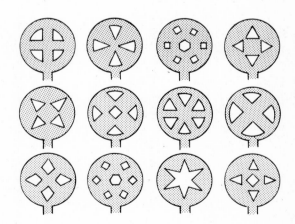

**Diagram 112**

**Diagram 115**

7. Cut long narrow strips from olive felt, again pinking one edge, as shown in Diagram 107. Pin this strip between the circles, following twisting line in Patterns 51-A and B. Sew in place.

8. Using pinking shears, cut thirty-four small circles, 1 inch in diameter. Cut a small diamond shape from the center of each. (See Diagram 113.) Position these as shown

**Diagram 113**

in Patterns 51-A and B, and sew in place.

9. Cut two corner shapes, as shown in Diagram 114. Following Pattern 51-A for positioning, pin and sew these to lower front corners.

**Diagram 114**

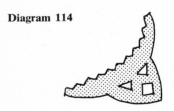

10. Cut shapes shown in Diagram 115. Pin and sew them to lower center back, as shown in Pattern 51-B.

11. Trim away edges on vest and vest lining, cutting on seam line. Repeat for armholes.

12. Pin olive lining to red vest, back to back, with open seams together. Baste edges together by hand or machine. Do same for armholes. Sew folded bias edging all around edge of vest and armholes.

13. Sew on buttons if you wish, and make vertical buttonholes.

*Pattern 52: Vest*

# Festive Folk

## (Technique 3)

*This vest echoes the colorful folk art of central Europe. It should be worn for the most festive events. Perhaps a young bride would like to make it for her bridegroom. Worn by either men or women, it helps set off and add to a celebration, of any kind. You might want to wear it to local art festivals, for holiday entertaining, or for any special occasion.*

### Materials

1 yard felt, in white

9- by 12-inch rectangles or scraps of felt, in gold, yellow, orange, magenta, royal blue, turquoise, bright green, and lime (If rectangles are purchased, buy 2 of each color.)

long vest pattern in proper size

thread in white

white glue

lightweight yarn in at least 3 matching colors

4½ yards or necessary amount folded woven bias edging, in any matching color

**Color code:** R—white, S—gold, T—yellow, U—orange, V—magenta, W—royal blue, X—turquoise, Y—bright green, Z—lime

### Instructions

1. Press felt pieces.

2. Follow pattern directions, and cut two vests from white felt. Cut around edges on cutting line of pattern, although this will be trimmed off at seam line later. Omit pattern facings.

3. Complete one vest as directed by pattern. It will be used for lining, so set it aside until later. Sew darts in vest to be used for design. Leave unseamed.

4. Enlarge pattern according to instructions on page 19. Each square equals 1 inch. The pattern serves only as a guide for cutting shapes. Positioning will have to be done by eye and adjustments will have to be made according to size of pattern. Broken lines indicate variable seam line of pattern.

5. Tape appropriate colors of felts to backs of pattern parts. Follow directions on page 16 for use of tracing wheel and carbon. Trace shapes. Repeated shapes need be traced only once and then used as models from which to cut the rest. Cut out all shapes. For shapes that are positioned on center fold of Pattern 52-B, tape pattern to felt and trace half of shape. Fold on fold line and cut out shapes as you trace. Cut shapes for reverse side. To do this use the shapes you have cut already as models to cut the rest and reverse their positions.

6. Lay out all shapes on vest front pieces and back by eye, following pattern as guide. Allow 2 inches around edge for border de-

**Pattern 52-A**

**Pattern 52-B**

FOLD

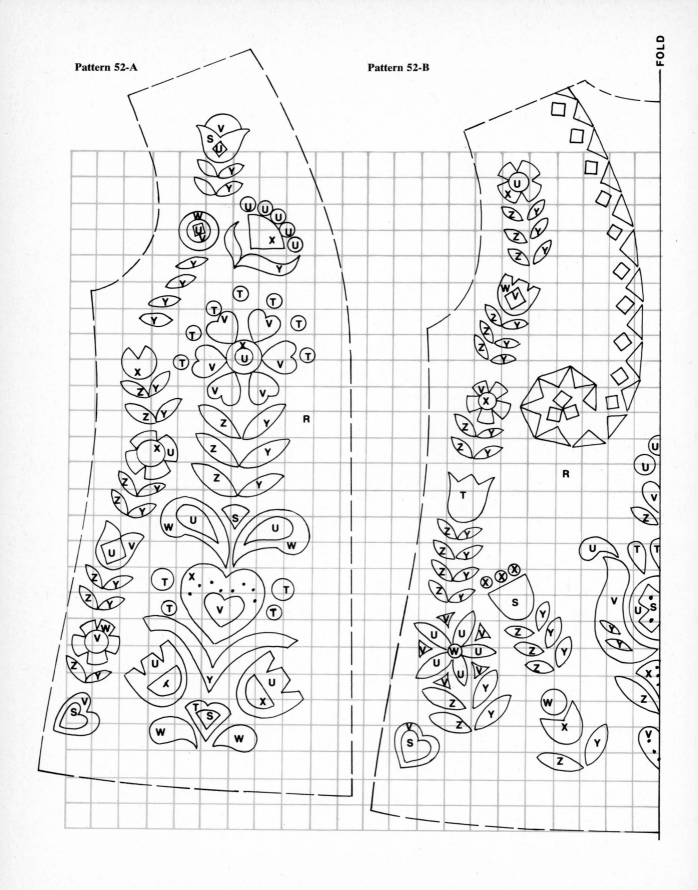

sign to be added later. If the vest has vertical darts on front, center large heart, flower, and related shapes along dart.

7. Using a minimum amount of glue, place each piece in position. Allow ½ hour for glue to set.

8. With yarns of contrasting colors, whip stitch down edges of all shapes, as shown in Diagram 14. Small dots in pattern indicate position of French knots. Make French knots according to Diagram 19 and instructions on page 41.

9. Seam front to back according to pattern instructions. Trim edges around vest on seam line, including armholes.

10. Cut gold triangles and yellow squares, following measurements in Diagram 116.

**Diagram 116**

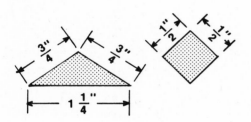

Cut as many as you will need. Start pinning triangles at center of lower back. Position them as shown in Diagram 117, and pin triangles ½ inch from edge of vest. Pin all around except for back neckline edge. Respace if necessary so that shapes at lower corner of vest front are positioned as shown in Diagram 118. Glue triangles in place, and then glue squares between them as shown in diagrams.

11. Beginning at back neckline, position triangles and squares by eye, as shown on pattern. Glue in place.

**Diagram 117**

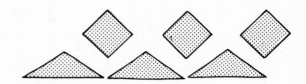

12. Whip shapes into place. Place one stitch in each corner of squares.

13. Pin lining to vest, back to back, with open seams together. Trim lining edge to match vest. Baste edges together by hand or machine. Repeat same for armholes. Sew folded bias edging all around edge of vest and armholes.

**Diagram 118**

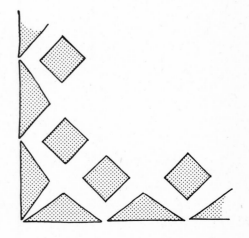

203

## Pattern 53: Dress Pocket

# Peasant Patterns

*(Technique 4)*

*Perhaps you have an old dress or skirt hanging in your closet, unworn. You don't want to get rid of it, yet you don't want to wear it either. It seems to be lacking something. Maybe all it needs is a colorful pocket to add new life to it. This pocket would be appropriate for a floral print as well as a solid color. You might even want to use it to add a bit of color to a simple hostess apron.*

### Materials

**1 fabric rectangle, 7½ by 10 inches, in any color to contrast with garment**
**scraps of felt, in white, turquoise, violet, hot pink, and orange**

**yarn needle**
**lightweight yarn in white and orange**
**thread in color to match pocket**
**dress, skirt, or apron**

**Completed size:** 6½ by 9 inches
**Color code:** A—white, B—turquoise, C—violet, D—hot pink, E—orange

### Instructions

1. Enlarge pattern according to instructions on page 19. Each square equals 1 inch. Pattern should measure 6½ by 9 inches.

2. Press fabric pieces.

3. Tape pattern to fabric rectangle so that there is ½ inch of fabric surrounding pattern. Follow directions on page 16 for use of tracing wheel and carbon. Make marks to show placement of shapes.

4. Tape appropriate scraps of felt to back of pattern, and trace. Repeated shapes need

204

be traced only once and then used as models from which to cut the rest. If you care to, use pinking shears to cut orange heart shape.

5. Lay out pieces on pocket fabric. Pin in place.

6. Following small dots on pattern, make French knots in contrasting colors of yarn. Refer to Diagram 19 and page 41 for review on French knots.

7. Turn side and bottom edges under ½ inch, and press. Turn top edge under twice to hide raw edges, making each fold ¼ inch.

8. Pin pocket to garment. Use a whip stitch to whip down side and bottom edges of pocket to garment. You may line the pocket if you wish.

*Pattern 54: Dress Ornament*

# Hexagon Motif

*(Technique 5)*

*The hexagon shape is often used in patchwork quilts. It is simply a matter of cutting out hexagons from your favorite scraps of fabric and appliquéing them in such a way so as to give a patchwork effect. The skirt border shown here was made from country prints of purples and violets, resulting in a provincial look. Diagram 119 shows other ways of using this motif. Choosing interesting fabrics will result in different effects. For a caftan, you might prefer the luxurious look of jewel-toned silks and satins. Cut up a red*

Diagram 119

206

*bandana or bits of gingham for your jeans. Decorate a shirt with many colors.*

## Materials
scraps of fabric, in any color
any garment, ready-to-wear or make-it-yourself
compass
thread in matching or contrasting colors

## Instructions

1. Using a compass, draw circle to desired size. Those used for the skirt border were made from 6-inch circles. (See Diagram 120.) Keeping compass at same radius, place the compass point on circumference of circle at point A and swing an arc from point B to point C. Lift compass and place it at point B. Swing another arc from point D to point A. Continue this around the circle until you have made six arcs forming the petal design. To form hexagon, connect the points with straight lines, using a ruler. This is your pattern.

2. Press fabric pieces.

3. Cut out pattern along straight edges of hexagon. Pin it to fabrics chosen, and with

**Pattern 54**

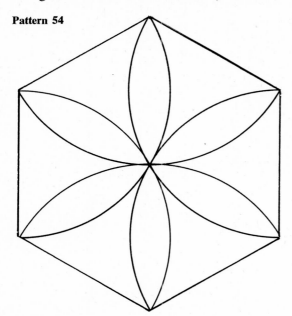

pencil, trace around edges. Cut out fabrics, leaving at least ½-inch allowance all around. This will be trimmed away later.

**Diagram 120**

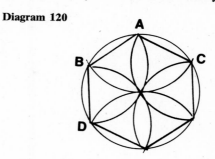

4. Pin pattern to fabric to be used for petals. Follow directions on page 16 for use of tracing wheel and carbon. Trace petal shape. It need be traced only once and then used as a model from which to cut the rest.

5. In proper position, pin these petals to the hexagon shapes. Baste in place by hand or machine. Use zigzag stitch to sew in place, as shown in Diagrams 23-A and B. Gently press.

6. Cut hexagons along traced edges. When all hexagons are complete and cut, position them on the garment and pin in place. See Diagram 121 for skirt border positioning. Twenty hexagons are needed for this formation. Basting first and using same zigzag stitch as before, sew them down. If you are making your own garment from a pattern, it is better to appliqué motifs before seaming. Last, place one hexagon over the side seams.

**Diagram 121**

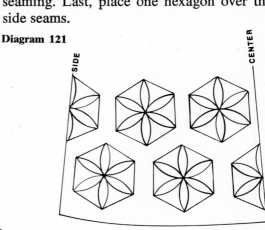

Pattern 55: Dress

# Paper Doll Parade

(Technique 6)

Little girls, gingham, and paper dolls all seem to go together. This little dress combines both gingham and paper doll shapes. You might prefer using prints, stripes, polka dots, or any combination for your little girl's dress. Why not let her cut her own paper doll pattern or help cut the one shown here?

Use any dress pattern or add the dolls to a ready-made dress. If you want to put them on a dress with a full gathered waistline, put a border of small dolls around the hem. (See Diagram 122.) For less work, just make two larger dolls. On a dress with no waistline, arrange the dolls from the neckline to the hem. The circles may be placed at random or omitted altogether.

## Materials
scraps of fabric, any type, in any colors
dress, ready-to-wear or make-it-yourself
thread to match

**Completed size:** Dress shown is a size 6. Dolls shown are 8 inches tall.

### Instructions
1. Enlarge doll pattern to size desired, following instructions on page 19. Decide on height of doll and divide that into four parts. Use this dimension for the squares. If you prefer, cut your own doll pattern.
2. Press fabric pieces.
3. Pin doll pattern to scraps of fabrics. Trace around edge with pencil.
4. Cut out doll shapes, leaving ⅛ inch allowance all around for turning under.
5. Pin doll shapes to dress front, as shown in pattern or in any desired arrangement. If you are making the dress yourself, it is better to appliqué the design before seaming. If this is done, be sure to make allowance for hem of dress. Cut circles of fabric. Place them at random or follow placement in pattern. (Broken line on pattern indicates variable seam line of dress.)
6. Using whip stitch, as shown in Diagram 25, sew dolls and circles in place.

Diagram 122

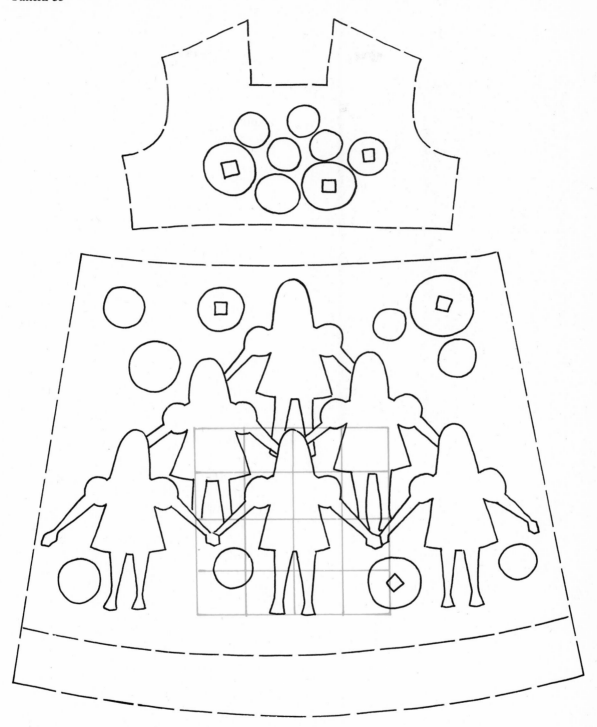

Pattern 56: Caftan

# Pakistan Quilt

(Technique 6)

Diagram 123

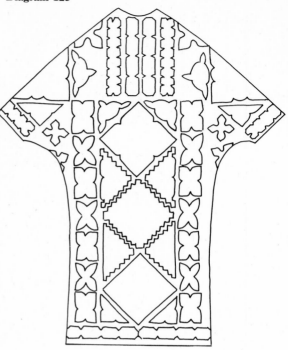

If you are now an expert appliqué crafts-man, this caftan will be easy for you. It is a time-consuming project, but is well worth the time it takes. Once you have completed it, you will have not only a dress but a work of art as well. Whether you use it for a host-ess gown, for a poolside cover-up, or for luxurious lounging at home, it will make an outstanding appearance for many years.

The quilts of Pakistan were the inspiration for the design. Folded paper is snipped, and opened. The lacy designs are outlined on fabrics and then appliquéd in place.

Your pattern may be a basic A-line dress or a lounge robe with full sleeves as shown here. The design can also be adapted to those loose styles that combine the sleeve into one piece with the front and back. Use a light, soft, flowing fabric for this style. (See Diagram 123.) You may arrange the designs in any way to fit your pattern style.

## Materials

pattern in proper size
fabric, amount designated on pattern, in eggplant
fabric scraps or ¼ yard of any lightweight fabric, in lavender, magenta, brick red, rust, burnt orange, green, and turquoise

**Color code:** F—eggplant, G—lavender, H—magenta, I—brick red, J—rust, K—burnt orange, L—green, M—turquoise

## Instructions

1. There are fourteen designs to be cut from paper. Cut two 2- by 12-inch strips for designs 1 and 2; four 8½- by 8½-inch squares for designs 3, 4, 5, and 6; two tri-

210

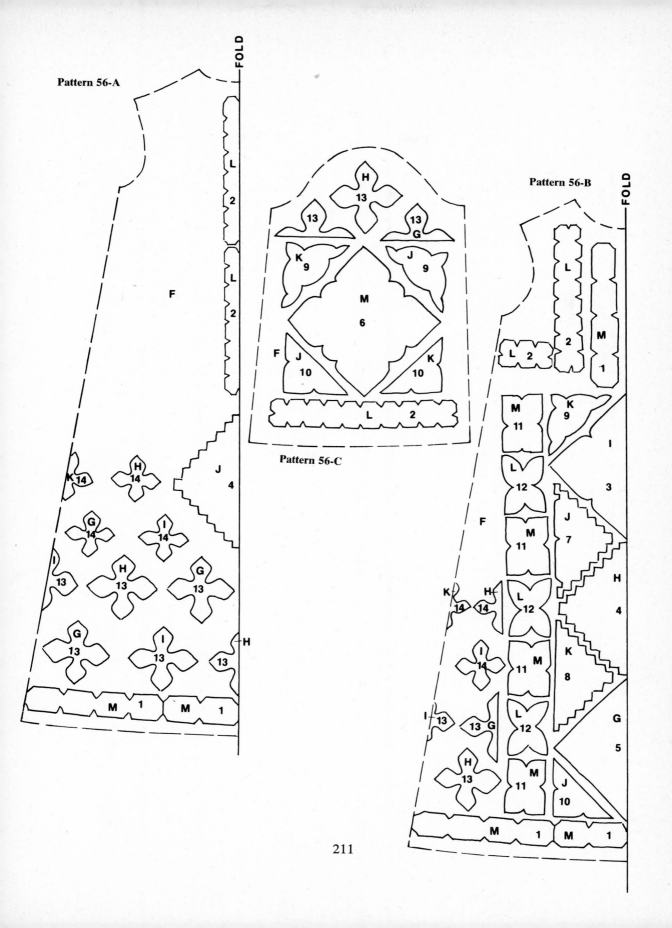

Pattern 56-A

FOLD

Pattern 56-B

FOLD

Pattern 56-C

211

angles, from one 7¼- by 7¼-inch square, cut diagonally, for designs 7 and 8; two triangles, from one 5- by 5-inch square cut diagonally, for designs 9 and 10; two 3½- by 4¾-inch rectangles for designs 11 and 12; one 4¼- by 4¼-inch square for design 13; and one 3¼- by 3¼-inch square for design 14.

2. Fold design strip 1 in half twice so that you have a 2- by 3-inch rectangle. Snip corners off, as shown in Diagram 124. Fold

**Diagram 124**

this diagonally and snip out pieces, as shown in Diagram 125-A. Unfold and refold diagonally across the other corners. Snip again, as shown in Diagram 125-B. Unfold. This is design 1.

3. Fold design strip 2 in half three times so that you have a rectangle measuring 1½ by 2 inches. Snip as shown in Diagram 126. Unfold. This is design 2.

**Diagram 125-A**                    **Diagram 125-B**

4. Fold design squares 3, 4, 5, and 6 into eighths, as shown in Diagram 99. Enlarge designs in Pattern 56-D. Each square equals 1 inch. Broken lines indicate folded sides. Draw squares directly on folded paper. Follow instructions on page 19 for enlarging. Draw design and snip out cutouts. Unfold. These are designs 3, 4, 5, and 6.

**Diagram 126**

5. Fold design triangles 7, 8, 9, and 10 in half twice to form smaller triangles. Repeat the enlarging and snipping process in step 4 for those shapes. For design 10, cut two strips of paper ¼ by 2 inches. Tape them to two edges, as indicated by dotted lines on design 10. These are designs 7, 8, 9, and 10.

6. Fold design rectangles 11 and 12 in half twice, and design squares 13 and 14 into eighths. Snip as in step 4. These are designs 11, 12, 13, and 14.

7. Cut out dress from fabric, following pattern directions. It is very important to allow at least 1 extra inch all around on parts of pattern that will be appliquéd, since appliquéing tends to draw the fabric up. Sometimes as much as 1 inch of shrinkage will occur in length and ¾ inch in width. Omitting this allowance might make the dress too tight. Mark the seam lines on fabric, but do not do the final cutting until appliquéing is complete. If you are using a loose, nonfit pattern, this need not apply.

8. Lay the cutout front out on floor, and position the paper designs on it. Try various arrangements of your own choice or follow those suggested in Pattern 56-A. Adjustments in spacing may have to be made in accordance with size of pattern. Broken lines on pattern indicate variable seam lines. Strips 1 and 2 may be lengthened or shortened if necessary. Begin by placing the central designs first. Use chalk to mark the placement you have decided upon.

9. Pin designs to appropriate fabrics, and trace around outside edges. Cut out shapes. Cut out, allowing at least ⅛ inch all around

for turning under. Make as many shapes of each design as needed.

10. Position pieces on front piece. Pin the pieces in position and baste. If design 1 has to curve around lower edge, make a tiny tuck in the center of pattern. (See Diagram 127.) This will give it a slight bend. Baste

**Diagram 127**

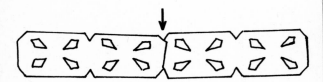

pieces before appliquéing, or if preferred, pin and appliqué a few at a time.

11. Turn under edges and whip down, as shown in Diagram 25. Cut and slit all inner cutouts. Clip and whip down all edges. Refer to Pattern 7, steps 5 to 15, for slitting and whipping details. .

12. Position pieces on back piece, as suggested in Pattern 56-B, and on sleeves, as suggested in Pattern 56-C. An alternate way is shown here for the back in order to simplify the work, but if you wish, you may repeat the front design on the back. If you are using one of the loose-fitting patterns mentioned before, seam back to front before pinning, basting, or appliquéing the sleeve area.

13. When appliqué is complete, repin patterns to front, back, and sleeves. Trim on cutting lines. Finish dress as directed by pattern. Appliqués that are on seam line are sewn on after seaming.

# African Shapes

*(Techniques 7 or 8)*

*This necklace was designed with an African look in mind. Its jewel-toned silks give it an exotic look, making it just the right accessory to wear with a basic evening dress. Cottons or satins would also do it justice.*

## Materials
**scraps of silk, satin, peau de soie, or cotton, in royal blue, magenta, hot pink, orange, and poison green**

**1 bristol board, 9 by 12 inches (Purchase from an art-supply store, or use a shirt board or artist's tablet back.)**

**thread in matching colors**

**white glue**

214

**Pattern 57**

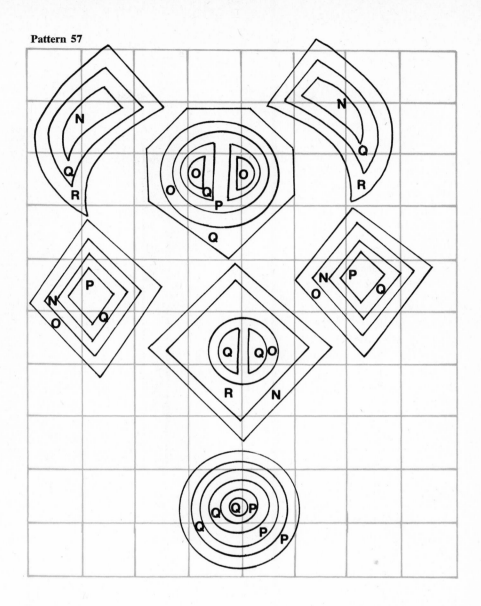

**gold wire choker (from craft-supply shop)**
**4 gold beads**

**Completed size:** 9¼ inches from center neckline to lowest point
**Color code:** N—royal blue, O—magenta, P—hot pink, Q—orange, R—poison green

### Instructions

1. Enlarge pattern according to direc-

tions on page 19. Each square equals 1 inch. Pattern should measure 8 by 10 inches.

2. Press fabric pieces.

3. Tape appropriate scraps of fabric to back of pattern. Follow directions on page 16 for use of tracing wheel and carbon. Trace outline of each of the seven shapes and the first inner shape within each. Omit those that are within the first ones. Cut along

outline of all seven, leaving at least 1 inch allowance all around.

4. Cut fabric to match sizes of all inner shapes. Pin or baste underneath larger shape.

5. Refer to Pattern 7, steps 5 through 14, for details of technique.

6. When all seven shapes are complete, turn them over and cut away excess fabric from underlayers. Trim top layer of each, leaving ½ inch all around for turning under.

7. Tape pattern to cardboard, and trace outline of each shape with a pencil and carbon. Untape pattern and cut out cardboard shapes.

8. Turn each fabric design over, face down. Place each cardboard shape over appropriate fabric shape. You will have to clip corners and curved edges in order to turn under. Working one piece at a time, place glue around edge of cardboard, bring edge of fabric over to back of cardboard, and press down. (See Diagram 128.)

**Diagram 128**

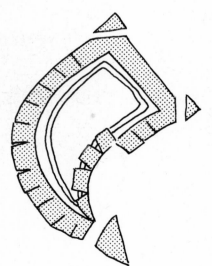

**Diagram 129**

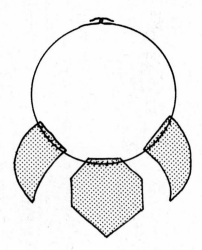

9. Cut matching piece of fabric for each shape, allowing ¼ inch all around. Place each on cardboard and fold around edge.

10. Whip around edges to finish off the back neatly.

11. Sew backs of the three upper shapes to the wire choker, as shown in Diagram 129.

12. Following pattern for position, connect the other four pieces to the top three by placing a bead at connecting corners with needle and thread, as shown in Diagram 130.

**Diagram 130**

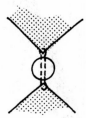

# Aztecan Motif

(Technique 8)

This yoke design may be placed on a dress, shirt, or top to be worn with pants. Diagram 131 shows several possibilities for its use. The design also has a border motif included in the pattern, but you may omit this if you wish. The circles in the middle of the yoke can be replaced with buttons. I used floss in this design to emphasize the stitches and to add texture to the yoke.

## Materials

pattern for dress, shirt, or top with jewel neckline
fabric and notions specified by pattern
fabric scraps, any type, in any color
embroidery needle
embroidery floss, in matching colors

**Completed size:** 8 inches from center of neckline to bottom of border; 6 inches without border

**Color code:** S—cerise, T—red, U—vermilion, V—gold, W—turquoise

### Instructions

1. Enlarge pattern according to instructions on page 19. Measure width of yoke from center front of pattern to edge of armhole. (See Diagram 132.) Divide this into four equal parts. Use this for the dimensions of squares.

2. Press fabric pieces.

3. Cut out garment as directed by pattern. Since appliqué work tends to draw up

Diagram 131

Diagram 132

and shrink the fabric, when cutting the front, allow 1 extra inch all around. It can be trimmed away later after completing appliqué work.

4. Tape or pin pattern to one side of dress front, placing the motifs where they look best.

5. Follow directions on page 16 for use of carbon and tracing wheel. Trace design. Remove pattern and trace the other side in same way, reversing pattern. To do this, place carbon paper with carbon side up against pattern. Go over traced lines. You now have the pattern in reverse on back.

6. Refer to Pattern 8, steps 4 through 10, for details on how to work design.

7. When appliquéing is complete, place garment pattern over front of garment and recut, trimming away extra allowance.

8. Complete garment following pattern.

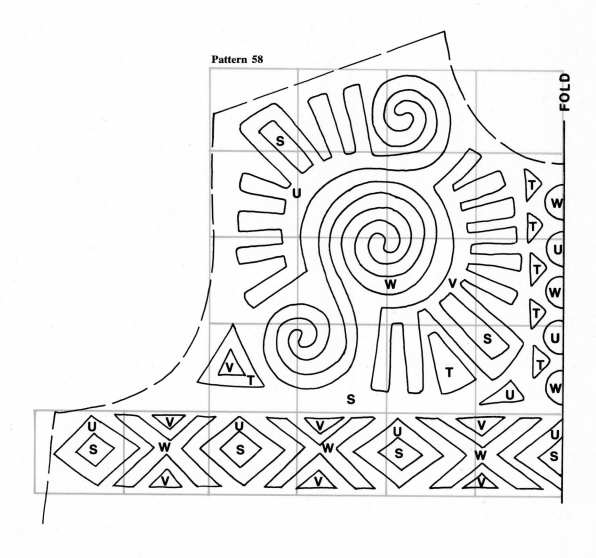

Pattern 58

219

# Mexican Motif

*(Techniques 6 and 7)*

The motifs on this skirt border combine both techniques 6 and 7 for an interesting contrast. Motif A is done in appliqué and is sewn to the background. Motif B is done in reverse appliqué and the background is sewn to it. You may prefer to use only one technique for both motifs. These motifs could be placed on garments in ways suggested in Diagram 119.

## Materials

**scraps of fabric, in any 2 desired colors or ¼ yard in each color if making skirt border**
**any garment, ready-to-wear or make-it-yourself**

**Completed size:** Motifs are 8 by 8 inches

## Instructions

1. Enlarge pattern according to instructions on page 19. Each square equals 2 inches. Each pattern should measure 8 by 8 inches.

2. Press fabric pieces.

3. Tape motif A pattern to one of the fabrics as chosen. Follow directions on page 16 for use of tracing wheel and carbon. Trace as many motifs as required.

4. Cut out motif A, leaving at least ⅛ inch all around for turning under. Do not cut completely around circles. Leave them attached to the main piece. It will be cut out later.

5. Position motif A on garment, leaving

**A**

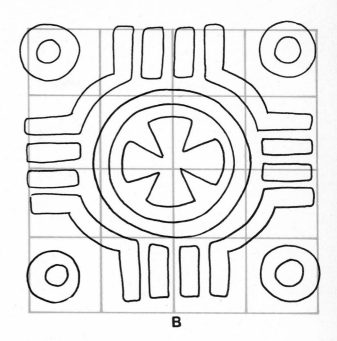

**B**

adequate space for motif B. Pin in place.

6. Position motif B pattern in proper place on garment. You may want to cut several squares of paper the size of motif B to aid in laying out the design properly. If you are making a skirt border, position both motifs the same distance from the hemline with equal space between each other.

7. Tape motif B pattern to garment in proper position. Trace.

8. Work motif A onto garment using whip stitch, as shown in Diagram 25. Slit, clip, and whip down edges of motif, as shown in Diagram 133. Continue until all motif A pieces are complete.

**Diagram 133**

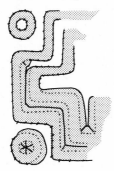

**Diagram 134**

9. Cut 9- by 9-inch squares in second color fabric for each motif B piece. Pin them underneath motif B patterns, making sure each one is completely covered from behind.

10. Work motif B, as shown in Diagram 134. Refer to Pattern 7, steps 5 through 15, and Pattern 8, steps 4 through 10, for details on slitting, clipping, and whipping down edges. This design is different from Patterns 7 and 8 in that it involves only one layer of fabric. Continue until all motif B pieces are complete. If you are making your dress from a pattern, it is easiest to complete motifs before seaming.

221

# 7

# Holiday and Seasonal Ideas

Everyone appreciates having handmade, personal decorations for the holidays. These little ornaments help make Christmas, Thanksgiving, or Easter special family traditions. Holiday decorations, made with lots of love and care, remain in one's memory for a lifetime. Families enjoy creating traditions together. It is even more fun to add a few new ornaments to the Christmas tree each year so that your tree grows as your family grows. A special Thanksgiving tablecloth becomes just as essential to the holiday spirit as your special turkey dressing does. Large banners made by a group or you alone will spread the joy of Christmas all around town.

*Pattern 60: Christmas Tree Ornaments*

# Hex Signs

*(Technique 1)*

*These colorful, Pennsylvania hex sign ornaments are fun and easy to make. Felt pieces are cut and glued to plastic lids from supermarket products. If you buy frozen puddings, dessert toppings, or salads from the dairy counter, you will easily accumulate plastic containers. These lids make excellent beginnings for the ornaments. The lip around the edge forms a frame around the design. They can also be mounted on a circle of cardboard if lids are not available.*

### Materials
**9- by 12-inch rectangles or scraps of felt, in lemon**

224

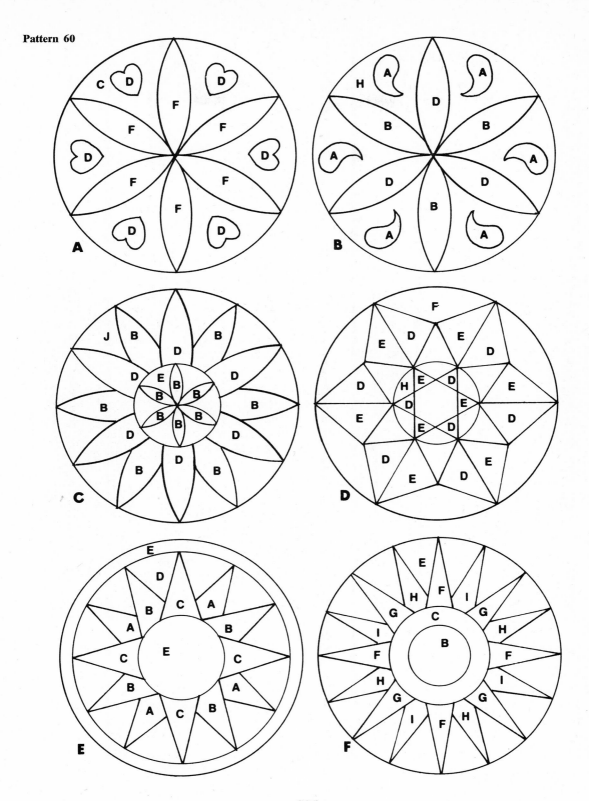

yellow, golden yellow, yellow-orange, orange, hot pink, royal blue, medium blue, turquoise, light turquoise, and green (4 or 5 ornaments can be made from one 9- by 12-inch square)

plastic lids, 4¾ inches in diameter or less, or cardboard cut into 4-inch-diameter circles

compass

white glue

nylon line or heavy thread

**Color code:** A—lemon yellow, B—golden yellow, C—yellow-orange, D—orange, E—hot pink, F—royal blue, G—medium blue, H—turquoise, I—light turquoise, J—green

### Instructions

1. Measure diameter of plastic lid excluding the lip. If you are using cardboard instead of lids, cut a 4-inch-diameter circle. To draw a circle on paper for each of the six ornaments set compass at appropriate radius. Construct the six designs. Ornaments A, B, C, D, and E are six-point divisions of the circle. See Diagram 120 and Pattern 54, step 1, for instructions on how to construct. Ornament F is divided into sixteen points. Draftsman's triangles will be helpful in constructing these designs.

2. Tape patterns to felt pieces to be used for main part of circles. Follow directions on page 16 for use of tracing wheel, pencil, and carbon. Trace outer circles, and make enough marks or points to indicate placement of design parts. Untape patterns and cut out circles.

3. Tape patterns to appropriate pieces of felt, and trace design parts. Repeated shapes need be traced only once and then used as models from which to cut the rest.

4. Glue the main circle pieces to plastic lids within the lip. If you have used cardboard circles, the edges will be flush.

5. Position shapes within each circle.

6. Starting with underlapped shapes, glue shapes in place.

7. With a large needle or point of compass, punch a hole at top of each ornament. Run nylon line or thread through hole, make a loop, and knot. Hang to Christmas tree branch.

# Sparkles

*(Technique 2)*

*These ornaments are so easy and inexpensive to make that you will be able to decorate a large tree on a small budget in no time. They are padded with Dacron quilt batting just as were the pot holders in Pattern 11 and the Mediterranean rug in Pattern 40. Make a large supply of them and try selling them for a small price at the next fund-raising event. By the way, making these ornaments is an excellent way to use leftover felt pieces.*

## Materials
**9- by 12-inch rectangles or scraps of felt, in as many bright colors as desired**
**Dacron batting, 1 layer for each shape**
**nylon line or string**
**thread in matching color or clear nylon**

**Completed size:** A—6 inches, B—7 inches, C—6 inches in length, D—5 inches in diameter

## Instructions
1. Enlarge patterns following instructions on page 19. Each square equals 1 inch. Patterns for figures A, C, and D should measure 6 by 6 inches; figure B should measure 4 by 8 inches.
2. Press felt pieces.
3. Tape pattern to felt pieces. Follow directions on page 16 for use of tracing wheel and carbon. Trace outer edges of each

ornament, and make enough marks to show placement of inner shapes. Cut out along edges. Pin each shape to another piece of felt and cut matching piece for a backing.

4. Tape felt pieces to back of pattern and trace inner shapes. Cut out.

5. Cut a piece of Dacron quilt batting slightly smaller than each ornament shape.

6. Place two felt shapes together with Dacron layer in between. Pin all three to-gether. Cut a 2-inch length of string or nylon line. Form a loop and pin it to the top of each ornament, between layers.

7. Using a medium-width zigzag stitch, set at 20 stitches to the inch, sew together around edge.

8. Position shapes on ornaments, and pin in place. Using same stitch as before, sew down.

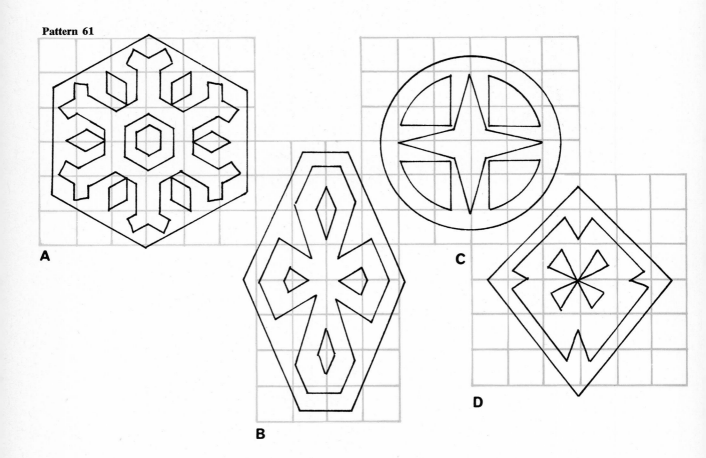

Pattern 61

A

B

C

D

# Peace and Goodwill

*(Technique 2)*

Although originally designed for a church, these banners contribute to the Christmas spirit just as well in an auditorium, community hall, club room, or even your home if you have the room for them. Why not make it a community project? The parts can be divided among several people to be appliquéd separately at home and then brought together for final assemblage. One or two persons might work on the lettering strips, and another two can work on each inner scene. One can do the cutting and positioning, while the other does the sewing. If there are two more people who do not wish to sew, they can each take a picture frame to glue at home. When these parts are completed, meet at one home. While someone pins and another quickly sews the four parts of each banner together, someone else can prepare coffee and cookies to celebrate the occasion. Then everyone can lean back, admire this joint achievement, and enjoy peace and goodwill together!

## Materials

1  yard felt, in green
1  yard felt, in turquoise
⅔ yard felt, in magenta
⅔ yard felt, in violet
⅜ yard felt, in red
⅓ yard felt, in ocher
¼ yard felt, in white

¼ yard felt, in black

¼ yard felt, in tan

¼ yard felt, in sienna

⅛ yard felt, in hot pink

⅛ yard felt, in orange

⅛ yard felt, in pink

⅝ yard fabric, in any desired color (for Joseph's robe)

⅓ yard fabric, in any desired color (for king's robe)

thread in medium brown (for facial details)

colorless nylon (for rest of design)

fabric glue

1 metallic mylar sheet, ⅛ by 1½ yards (from art-supply store) or ¼ yard silver fabric

6½ yards metallic silver edging, ⅜ inch wide

½ yard edging, ½-inch width, in ocher

four 35-inch lengths lath, ¼ by 1 inch

4 metal rings

**Completed size:** 36 by 62 inches

**Color code:** K—green, L—turquoise, M—magenta, N—violet, O—ocher, P—white, Q—red, R—black, S—hot pink, T—orange, U—tan, V—sienna, W—pink, X—chosen color, Y—metallic mylar

### Instructions

1. Enlarge patterns according to instructions on page 19. Each square equals 2 inches. Each pattern should measure 36 by 62 inches.

2. Press fabric pieces.

3. Cut all strips that contain lettering from the pattern. Tape magenta felt to the back of Peace Banner pattern and violet felt to the back of the Goodwill Banner pattern. Tape appropriate lettering strips to same pieces of felt so that upper strips have an allowance of at least 2 inches from upper edge and lower strips have 2 inches allowance from lower edge. The allowance is for slots that will accommodate lath strips at top and bottom of banners.

4. With dressmaker's carbon and tracing wheel, mark corners of inner scenes and lettering strips. Also mark the 2-inch allowance mentioned in step 3. Make enough marks to indicate placement of all figures, lettering, and details. Untape patterns. Cut strips apart from scene, leaving an allowance around each. Allowance will be trimmed away later.

5. Tape patterns to green and turquoise felts. Trace inner and outer edges of frames. Trace enough marks to show placement of decorative details. Untape patterns.

6. One by one, tape pattern to appropriate felt or fabric pieces, and trace all figures, lettering, and details. Broken lines indicate underlapped parts. Repeated shapes need be traced once and then used as models from which to cut the rest. Cut out all pieces. Cut Joseph's and Mary's lashes and shepherds' and kings' pupils from sienna, kings' and shepherds' eyes from white, and donkey's and sheep's eyes from sienna.

7. Position lettering to strips, and pin in place. Sew over facial detail lines of Mary, Joseph, and Infant, using medium-width zigzag satin stitch. Stitch curl lines on sheep's head. Position and pin down figures and details to inner scenes. Baste if you wish. Position parts of picture frame and glue in place. For an extra-fine job, sew them in place. However, if time is of the essence, gluing is adequate. Metallic mylar shapes should be glued.

8. Using a medium-width zigzag stitch, set at 20 stitches to the inch, sew all pieces in place on strips and scene. Gently press flat.

9. Retape patterns to each part and mark corners. Untape patterns. Connect corner marks with chalk, using yardstick for guide.

10. Carefully cut inner scene on chalk line. Pin inner scene over glued picture frame in position, and sew in place. Trim frame carefully on the chalk line. Sew silver metallic edging around edge of scene.

11. Trim side edges of lettering strips on

chalk line. Cut along bottom edges of upper strips, leaving a 1-inch allowance, and along top edges of lower strips, leaving same allowance. Leave the 2-inch slot allowance mentioned in step 3.

12. Fold top and bottom slot allowance over and press. Straight stitch across slot, 1¼ inches from pressed edges.

13. Pin picture frame containing scene to upper and lower strips, on top of the 1-inch allowance. Seam together. If further pressing of banners is necessary, do not let the iron touch the metallic mylar.

14. Insert lath strips through slots at top and bottom of banners. Sew up each end. Sew one ring to each upper corner.

*Pattern 63: Christmas Wreath*

# Wreath of Joy

*(Technique 3)*

*Hang this cheerful wreath on your door to greet your visitors with the joy of Christmas. You can also hang it over the fireplace, on a window, or wherever else you want to place* a unique Christmas decoration. Sewn with running stitches throughout, you will find this project easy to make.

**Pattern 63**

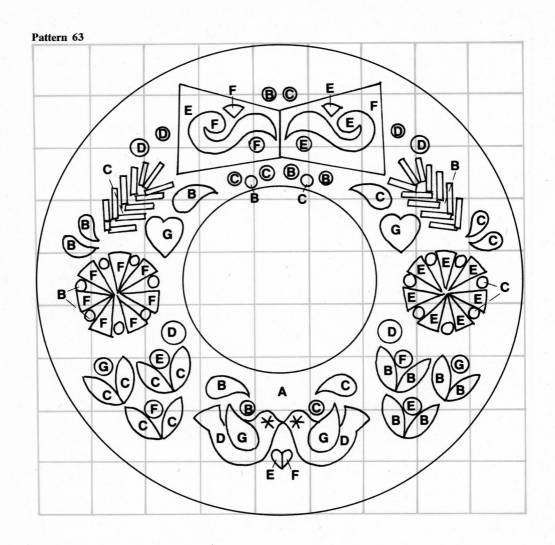

## Materials

½ yard felt, in dark green

9- by 12-inch rectangles or scraps of felt, in bright green, turquoise, white, red, orange, and magenta (If rectangles are purchased, buy 1 of each color.)

1 skein 6-strand embroidery floss, in dark green

8 inches buckram tape, 4-inch width

1 pound polyester fiberfill

thread in green

1 curtain ring

**Completed size:** 15½ inches in diameter

**Color code:** A—dark green, B—bright green, C—turquoise, D—white, E—red, F—orange, G—magenta

## Instructions

1. See Pattern 27, step 1. Substitute the 10½-inch radius with a 9-inch radius, and draw an 18-inch-diameter circle. Draw a 7-inch-diameter circle within it, using same center point.

2. Press felt pieces.

3. Tape pattern to dark green felt. Follow directions on page 16 for use of tracing wheel and carbon. Make enough marks to show placement of all shapes to be appliquéd. Trace edges of both circles. Untape pattern.

4. Tape appropriate felt pieces to back of pattern, and trace shapes. Repeated shapes need be traced only once and then used as models from which to cut the rest.

5. Position shapes on dark green circle, and pin in place. The bow at the top is attached later. Pin the inner shapes of bow to bow shape.

6. Using embroidery floss separated into 3 strands, make running stitches, as shown in Diagram 13, to stitch pieces in place. Stitch bow shapes in place on bow. Work a star stitch for dove's eye. (See Diagram 67 and description on page 110.)

7. Pin two bow shapes to same colors of felt, and cut a matching piece for each.

8. Cut another piece for each bow shape from buckram tape. Place the two matching pieces together back to back, with buckram piece in between. Sew around edges, using a medium-width zigzag stitch, set at 20 stitches to the inch. Do this for both halves of bow.

9. Position the two halves in place at top of wreath. Stitch down center with a zigzag stitch wide enough to catch both halves.

10. Pin wreath to remaining piece of dark green felt. Cut a matching piece to be used for back.

11. Pin these two together with design facing back piece. Using a straight stitch, stitch around outside about ¼ inch from edge.

12. Turn inside out. With embroidery floss, whip 4 inches of inside edge of circle together. Start to insert polyester fiberfill. Continue to sew edge, stuffing as you sew, until edge is completely closed and wreath is well stuffed.

13. Sew ring to back of wreath at top for hanging.

# Bethlehem Village

*(Technique 4)*

This group of buildings can be used as a centerpiece for your buffet or displayed on your mantel. If you are ambitious, you might want to make extra buildings to enlarge it. You could add one every year so that, eventually, it will spread out across the top of your fireplace or around the entire Christmas tree. Why not put it near a crèche and let the three kings come riding through?

## Materials

⅓ yard felt, in royal blue
¼ yard felt, in turquoise
¼ yard felt, in cerise
1 felt rectangle, 9 by 12 inches, in lavender

hard pencil
metallic mylar (in smallest amount you can buy) or aluminum cooking tins (Refer to Pattern 25, page 112.)
fabric glue
yarn needle
lightweight yarn, in 2 or 3 matching colors
1 gallon-sized milk carton (for mosque)
art knife or single-edged razor blade
light saw
2 long pins with beaded heads (for tops of domes)
3 or 4 assorted beads (for tops of domes)
1 styrofoam ball, 4 inches in diameter (for dome)
1 styrofoam ball, 5 inches in diameter (for dome)
cardboard cores from paper towels (for minarets)

236

**Pattern 64-A**

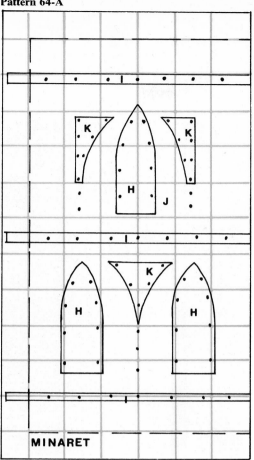

MINARET

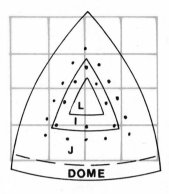

DOME

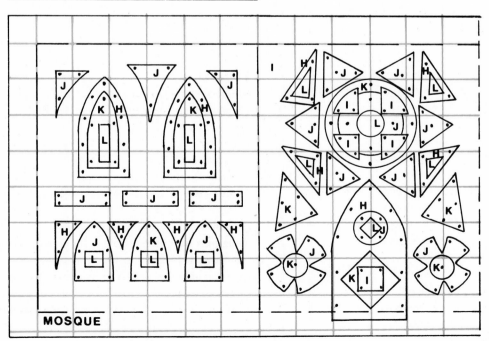

MOSQUE

**Pattern 64-B**

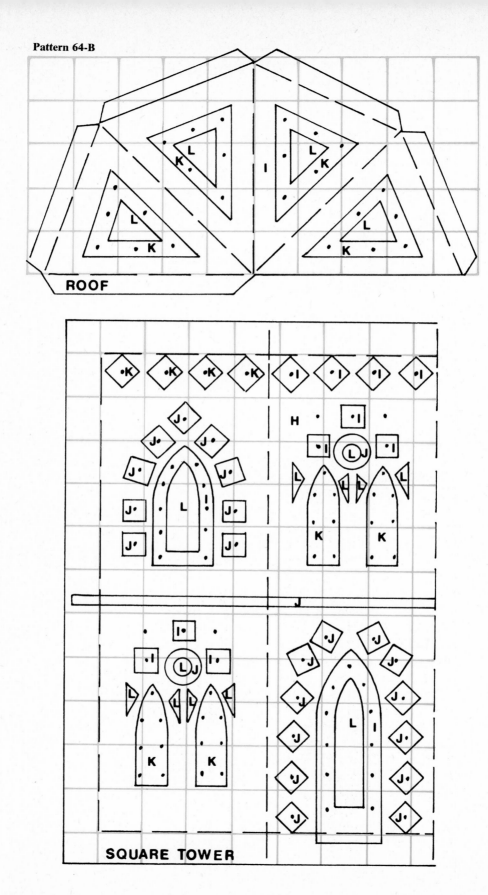

ROOF

SQUARE TOWER

2 silver deodorant or cosmetic container tops, about 1½ inches in diameter (for tops of minarets)

1 carton, 3¾ by 3¾ by 11¼ inches (for square tower) (A liquor carton will do or construct your own, using a 16- by 19-inch bristol board.)

1 decorative cosmetic bottle top, about ¾ inch in diameter (for square tower top)

salt box (for round tower)

1½ yards decorative edging, ¼ inch width, in blue

**Completed sizes:** Mosque: (including minarets) 7 by 8 by 11 inches; Square tower: 3¾ by 3¾ by 19 inches; Round tower: 4-inch diameter, 8½ inches tall

**Color code:** H—royal blue, I—turquoise, J—cerise, K—lavender, L—metallic mylar

### Instructions

1. Enlarge Patterns 64-A, 64-B, and 64-C, following instructions on page 19. Draw each pattern on a separate sheet of paper. Each square equals 1 inch.

2. Press felt pieces.

3. Tape patterns to appropriate pieces of felt. Allow enough felt on the right sides of Patterns A and B for the patterns to be traced again. Follow directions on page 16 for use of tracing wheel and carbon. Mark edges of building. (Broken lines on pattern indicate edges of building and corner folds.) Do not trace folds, but place marks on outside of broken lines to indicate folds. Make enough marks to show placement of all design pieces within. Untape patterns.

On Patterns A and B, tape the pattern to right side of fabric, placing the left broken lines of patterns on marks. Trace as before. Trace four sections for each dome and trace two minarets.

4. Working on one building section at a time, tape remaining pieces of felt to back of patterns and trace small design pieces. Repeated shapes need be traced only once and then used as models from which to cut the rest. Pieces that are smaller than 1 inch may be cut by eye. It is a good idea to position them on appropriate building parts as they are cut so that you can keep track of them.

5. Use a hard pencil to trace designs on metallic mylar or foil. Cut out and position in place.

6. Glue all metallic pieces firmly in place. Glue all design pieces in place, using a minimum amount of glue. Allow 1 hour to dry. Lift up all pieces to make sure nothing falls off. Reglue any loose pieces.

7. Following dots on pattern, make French knots with contrasting colors of yarn. See Diagram 19 and page 41 for a review on French knots.

*Finishing*
**Pattern A: Mosque**

### Instructions

1. Rinse out milk carton. With a knife or razor blade, cut off the angled top. Dry thoroughly and turn upside down. The bottom of carton will become the top of mosque.

2. Cut a square of royal blue felt to measure 7 by 7 inches. Glue this to top, and fold over edges about ½ inch. Glue overlap to sides, and clip excess felt from corners.

3. Trim off upper and right edges of building design piece on broken lines of pattern. Wrap design around carton so that corner marks on bottom edge of design line up with corners of carton. Glue in place, letting the cut right edge overlap the uncut left edge on a corner. Trim off lower edge of excess felt. Allow time to dry.

4. Cut a 5-inch foam ball in half, using a light saw. Place a pin in foam ball at top center. Glue four dome sections to it. Pin as you glue to make it conform as well as possible to the round shape. Fold over, and glue bottom edges to flat portion of foam. Allow 1 hour to dry. Remove pins, and glue edg-

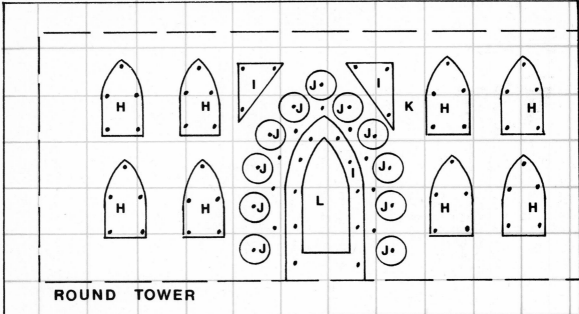

ROUND TOWER

ing over seams. Place a long pin through one or two beads, and place it into center top of foam ball. Center and glue dome to top of mosque.

5. Trim top edges from minaret pieces. Wrap each one around a paper towel core, overlapping side edges and gluing together on seam. Trim off lower edge. Glue silver domes to top of each.

6. Glue each minaret to front corners of mosque. Allow time to dry.

**Pattern B: Square Tower**

### Instructions

1. Tape tower roof pattern to cardboard, and trace outline. Cut out cardboard roof shape. With a light touch, use knife to score it on the broken lines. If proper size carton is not available, trace tower pattern to cardboard, positioning it twice, as you did when tracing felt. Draw one square 3¾ by 3¾ inches. Cut out all pieces, and score on folds. Form roof into pyramid shape, tape corner seam, and fold lower edges under. Form

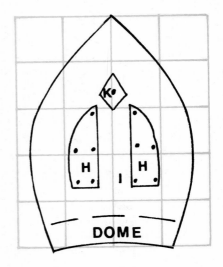

DOME

building, and tape together at corner seam. Tape square to top.

2. Wrap each tower felt piece around its proper part and glue at overlapping corner seams. Fold and glue top edge of felt to top square of building. Clip off corners and trim off lower edge of excess felt.

240

3. Glue roof to top of building, placing glue along folded under edges of roof top. Glue decorative bottle top to top point of roof. Allow time to dry.

### Pattern C: Round Tower

#### Instructions

1. Wrap felt around salt box, and glue along overlapping edge. Clip upper edge of felt allowance, making clips about ½ inch apart. Fold and glue clipped edge down to top of salt box. Trim away bottom edge of excess felt.

2. Cut a ¾-inch slice from 4-inch foam ball, and discard slice. Place a pin at center of top of ball. Glue the four sections to ball as you did in step 4 for the mosque. Glue edgings over seams, and pin beads to top.

3. Glue dome to top of round building. Allow time to dry. The three buildings can now be arranged in any way you wish.

# My Three Angels

*(Technique 5)*

*These three angels herald the joy of Christmas. The hanging was made of a silklike rayon fabric. For real luxury you may want to use silk. Lightweight cotton will do just as well. Bits of lace and edgings embellish the robes. Thin gold thread is hand- and machine-embroidered over the wispy halos and the hem motifs.*

*For this pattern, the fabric is not cut right on the edge and satin stitched, as before in technique 5. Instead, the pieces are cut with a ¼-inch allowance for turning under and then stitched with a more open zigzag stitch.*

### Materials
**½ yard silk, rayon, or cotton, in pale olive**

**Pattern 65**

½ yard silk, rayon, or cotton, in pale blue

½ yard silk, rayon, or cotton, in pale turquoise

¼ yard silk, rayon, or cotton, in pale tan

¼ yard silk, rayon, or cotton, in pale gold

¼ yard silk, rayon, or cotton, in pale white

¾ yard lightweight lining fabric

thread in matching colors and metallic gold

8 edging lengths, ¼ yard each, ½ to 1 inch width, in 5 or 6 patterns, similar colors or all in metallic gold (use leftovers if available)

embroidery floss in gold

24 inches half round molding, ½ inch width

curtain rod, extending to 26 inches

**Completed size:** 24 by 36 inches (excluding rod)

**Color code:** M—olive, N—blue, O—turquoise, P—tan, Q—gold, R—white

### Instructions

1. Enlarge pattern according to instructions on page 19. Each square equals 2 inches. Pattern should measure 24 by 36 inches.

2. Cut olive, blue, and turquoise fabric into strips, each measuring 9 by 37 inches. Seam lengths together, making ½-inch seams and following color order on pattern. Press seams open.

3. Tape pattern to this seamed piece so that vertical lines of pattern line up with seams and there is a ½-inch margin of fabric all around. Follow directions on page 16 for use of tracing wheel and carbon. Make marks to indicate placement of angels and wings. Trace halos.

4. With gold thread, use a wide zigzag stitch, set at 12 stitches to the inch, to sew around halos on traced lines. Stitch over the inner traced lines of each halo with narrow zigzag stitches. To further define them, run two strands of gold thread through machine stitches, as shown in Diagram 135.

5. Tape appropriate fabrics to back of pattern, and trace heads, hands, feet, robes, hair, and wings. Cut out all pieces, leaving about ¼-inch allowance all around. Trace lines within wings.

6. Begin with hair, wings, and feet. Crease each piece on traced outline, and press edges under. When these have been pressed on edges, position them on background. Using a medium, narrow-width zigzag stitch, set at 20 stitches to the inch, sew around edge of each piece. Change thread to match colors.

7. With tan thread and same stitch, stitch over inner lines of wings.

8. Proceed with faces, robes, hands, and headbands, pressing edges, positioning, and sewing them in place. Sew motifs of robes with metallic thread.

9. Couch on gold floss over lines of hair,

**Diagram 135**

lips, nose, and eyes, either by machine, as shown in Diagram 56, or by hand, as shown in Diagram 75.

10. Cut out the tiny pieces for eyelids and pupils, matching colors to robes. These are too small to press and sew by machine. Whip them into place by hand, creasing as you sew.

11. By machine, sew edgings in place, following broken horizontal lines on robes.

12. Make French knots, as shown in Diagram 19 and described on page 41, following dots on pattern. Make large lazy daisy stitches, as shown in Diagram 20, on circle and diamond motifs.

13. Cut lining fabric to measure 25 by 37 inches. Pin lining and hanging together, face to face. Seam together around top and sides, ½ inch from edge. Turn inside out. Gently press flat. Use pressing cloth over metallic parts.

14. Fold bottom edges to inside, ½ inch from edge, and press edges flat. Hand-stitch together.

15. Glue flat side of molding to back lower edge of hanging.

16. From remaining scraps of olive, blue, and turquoise, cut rectangles to measure 7 by 11 inches. Fold them in half to measure 5½ by 7 inches. Seam on length and one end of each, making ½-inch seams. Clip corners and turn inside out. Press.

17. Stitch closed end of blue rectangle to the upper edge of hanging, in center of blue panel, 1 inch from edge. In same way, sew olive piece to olive panel and turquoise piece to turquoise panel.

18. Fold each piece over to the back, turning the edges to the inside, ½ inch from edge. Stitch them to back edge by hand. Slip rod through loops. Use hooks that accompany rod for hanging.

# Snowflakes

*(Technique 5)*

These place mats may be saved for the Christmas holidays or used throughout winter. They are especially appropriate for a ski cabin. The snowflakes are made of a white cotton that is thin so that the underneath print shows through slightly. Several country prints were used to give them a cozy look. You may prefer using stripes or solids. As an added feature, the place mats are reversible. Use a solid fabric for the back. The outline of the stitched snowflakes that will be seen on the back is typical of the clean, graphic look of modern ski resorts.

### Materials (for 2 place mats)

½ yard light cotton, in white

½ yard light cotton, in blue or turquoise print, or turquoise print, stripe, or solid

½ yard sailcloth or any heavy cotton, in blue or turquoise (for backing)

compass

thread in white

**Completed size:** 16¼ by 18¾ inches

### Instructions

1. Using a compass, draw an 18¾-inch-diameter circle. Refer to Pattern 54, step 1, for construction of hexagon. This is your place mat pattern.

2. Draw two more 16-inch-diameter circles, and construct hexagons within. Cut out

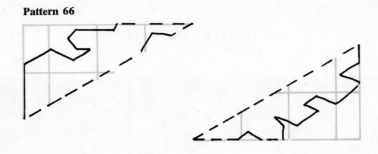

hexagon. Fold each in half and make two more folds, as shown by broken lines in Diagram 136, to form a triangle. Fold in half once more, as shown in Diagram 137.

3. Draw in squares on folded hexagons, as shown in pattern. Enlarge the patterns according to instructions on page 19. (Broken lines indicate folded edges.)

**Diagram 137**

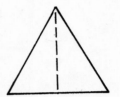

**Diagram 136**

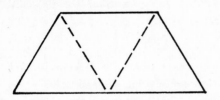

4. Cut on design lines of pattern. Unfold hexagons. These are the snowflake patterns.

5. Pin snowflake patterns to white fabric, and trace around edges of snowflakes with pencil. Remove patterns.

6. Pin place mat pattern to wrong side of place mat fabric. With ruler, draw lines parallel to edges of hexagon, leaving ½ inch from edges for seam allowance.

7. Pin this face down to backing fabric, and cut on drawn lines.

8. Seam together, around five sides, making ½-inch seams. Clip excess fabric from corners, and turn inside out. Press flat. Turn unsewn edges to inside, creasing ½ inch from edges, and press. Whip these edges down.

9. Cut out snowflakes. Center and position them to place mats. Pin in place and baste by hand or machine. Sew around edges with a medium-width zigzag satin stitch, as shown in Diagram 23-A or B. Gently press flat.

246

# Fall Colors

*(Technique 6)*

This tablecloth can be saved for the Thanks-giving feast or can be used throughout the entire fall season. It was made for a round table, but it can be made into a rectangular, oval, or square shape if desired. (See Diagram 138.)

## Materials

**5 yards cotton or synthetic blend, in medium brown**

**1¼ yards cotton or synthetic blend, in light brown**

**1 cotton or synthetic blend square, 9 by 9 inches, in gold**

**scraps of cotton broadcloth, in eggshell, gold, yellow, yellow-orange, orange, and rust**

**thread in medium brown**

**Completed size:** 97 inches in diameter

**Color code:** S—medium brown, T—egg-shell, U—gold, V—yellow, W—yellow-orange, X—orange, Y—rust

## Instructions

1. Cut medium brown fabric into four squares, each measuring 45 by 45 inches; cut light brown fabric into four equal lengths, each measuring 9 by 45 inches; and cut gold fabric into a 9- by 9-inch square.

2. Press all fabric pieces.

3. Enlarge pattern according to instructions on page 19. Each square equals 2 inches. Pattern should meausre 16 by 18 inches.

4. Angled line of pattern shows edge of fabric. Tape pattern to corner of one medium brown square. (See Diagram 139 for placement.) Follow directions on page 16 for use of tracing wheel and carbon. Trace design onto fabric. Untape pattern.

5. Tape appropriate scraps of fabric to back of pattern, and trace trunk and leaves. Cut them out, leaving an allowance of about ¼ inch all around for turning under.

6. Lay out pieces on medium brown background, and pin in place.

7. Sew all pieces in place with whip stitch, as shown in Diagram 26, turning edges under as you sew.

8. Edge each piece with a running stitch, as shown in Diagram 13, about 3/16 inch from edge.

9. Repeat steps 4 through 8 for the three remaining medium brown squares of fabric. Trace design on each one so that grain of fabric runs in same direction throughout entire tablecloth.

10. Making ¼-inch seams on wrong side, sew a length of light brown fabric between two medium brown squares, as shown in Diagram 139. Seam gold square to lengths, at center crossing, as shown in Diagram 139. Seam all three pieces together. Finish off each seam with zigzag stitch. Press each seam as it is sewn.

11. Spread tablecloth out on floor. If you

**Diagram 138**

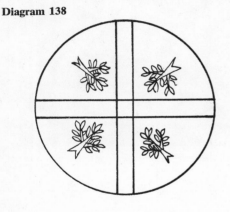

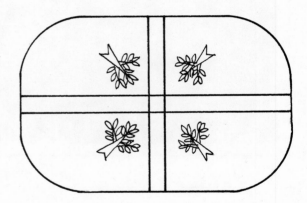

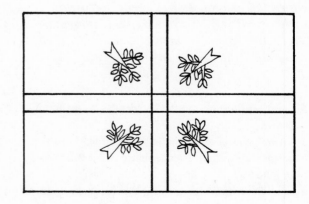

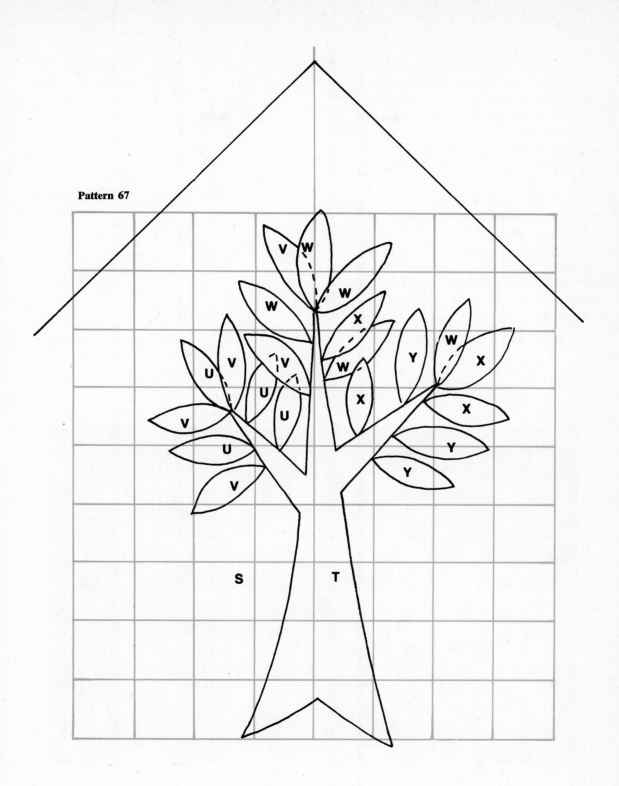

**Pattern 67**

are making a round tablecloth, find center of gold square and mark with pin. Using a tape measure, measure a radius of 49 inches from center and mark spot with chalk. Measure and mark this same point all the way around tablecloth, making marks a foot apart or less. With scissors, cut circle, linking these marks as you cut.

12. Hem edge of tablecloth by hand or machine, turning the edge under twice to cover raw edges. *Note:* If table is square, hem under edges without marking radius. If table is rectangular or oval, buy enough yardage to allow for an equal overhang all around. For an oval tablecloth, round corners to fit.

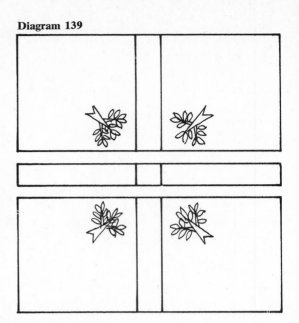

**Diagram 139**

*Pattern 68: Table Runner*

# Eastertime

*(Technique 6)*

This table runner will add color to an Easter brunch buffet after all the eggs have been hunted and counted or after sunrise services. You might want to use it to add a seasonal touch to an Easter eve supper or to the Easter dinner itself.

## Materials

1¼ yards sailcloth, Indian Head®, or linen, in lavender

¼ yard broadcloth, in pale pink

¼ yard broadcloth, in coral

⅛ yard broadcloth, in medium pink

⅛ yard broadcloth, in lime

⅛ yard broadcloth, in orchid

thread in pink and lavender

2¼ yards edging, ½ inch width, in pink (any braid or lace edging will do)

**Completed size:** 14 by 68 inches

**Color code:** A—pale pink, B—coral, C—medium pink, D—lime, E—orchid

## Instructions

1. Enlarge patterns according to instructions on page 19. Each square equals 2 inches. Patterns should measure 9 by 12 inches.

2. Press fabric pieces.

3. Tape Pattern A to pale pink fabric so that at least ¼ inch of fabric surrounds sides of egg. Follow directions on page 16 for use of tracing wheel and carbon. Make marks to

Pattern 68

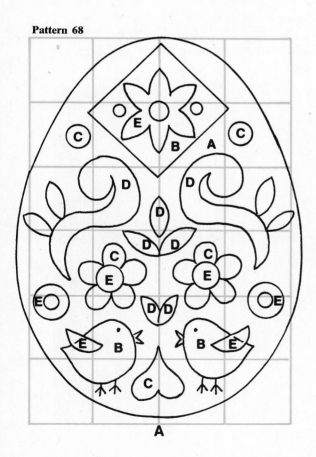

A

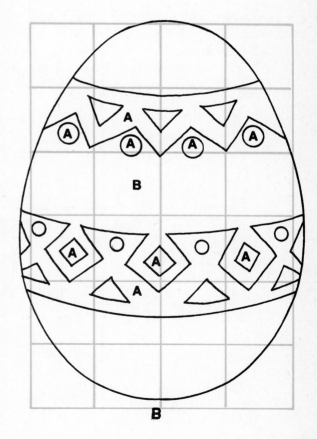

B

show placement of flowers, leaves, chicks, and all shapes. Trace a few marks to show outline of egg. Untape pattern.

4. Tape Pattern B to coral fabric in same way, and trace marks to show placement of motif and outline of egg. Repeat this on another piece of coral. Untape pattern.

5. Tape appropriate colors of fabric to back of pattern, and trace parts of design. Trace shapes of Pattern B twice. Cut out all pieces, leaving at least ⅛ inch all around for turning under.

6. Position pieces to appropriate egg shapes, and pin in place.

7. Using whip stitch, as shown in Diagram 25, sew all pieces in place, clipping when necessary and turning under edges as you sew.

8. Pierce cutout portions with tip of scissors, clip, and turn under edges. Whip in place.

9. Embroider feet and beak of chicks with straight stitches. Use French knots, as shown in Diagram 19, for eyes.

10. Cut out each egg, leaving ¼ inch all around for turning under. Put aside for now.

11. Cut lavender fabric into three strips, two measuring 14¼ by 29 inches each; and the other measuring 14¼ by 21 inches.

12. Position egg A to center of 21-inch length, as shown in Diagram 140. Place each B egg on a 29-inch length, 15 inches from each end, as shown in diagram. Whip eggs in place by hand, turning under edges.

13. Seam the three lengths together on wrong sides, finishing off seams with zigzag stitch. Gently press.

14. Sew braid or edging over these two seams. Sew two more lengths of edging to each end, placing them 3 inches from edge and 2 inches apart from each other, as shown by broken lines in Diagram 140.

15. Hem edge of runner by hand or machine, creasing under twice to cover raw edge.

**Diagram 140**

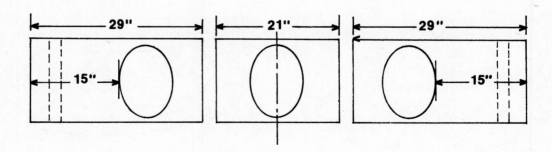

252

# Valentine

*(Techniques 7 and 8)*

*This unusual hanging will express your love for someone in a unique way. These two squares are festooned with hearts, reverse appliquéd, and stretched to hang at a window that allows light to shine through. If you prefer, you could also use the squares to make pillows for your Valentine—a gift that will show your love all year around.*

## Materials

1 KETTLE® CLOTH, broadcloth, or similar light fabric square, 18 by 18 inches, in magenta
1 KETTLE® CLOTH, broadcloth, or similar light fabric square, 16 by 16 inches, in vermilion
1 KETTLE® CLOTH, broadcloth, or similar light fabric square, 13 by 13 inches, in magenta
1 KETTLE® CLOTH, broadcloth, or similar light fabric square, 13 by 13 inches, in turquoise
scraps of KETTLE® CLOTH, broadcloth, or similar light fabric, in vermilion, pink, violet, and green
9- by 12-inch rectangles or scraps of felt in 2 or more matching colors
thread in matching colors
embroidery scissors
white glue
staples and staple gun
2 balsa wood strips, each ¼ by 1 by 16 inches
4 balsa wood strips, each ¼ by 1 by 14 inches
2 balsa wood strips, each ¼ by 1 by 12 inches
scraps of buckram or ⅔ yard buckram tape
8 grosgrain ribbon lengths, ½ yard each, in 2 or more matching colors (Braids may be used if you wish.)
1 package bias tape, 1-inch width, in red

**Completed size:** Approximately 16 by 48 inches
**Color code:** F—magenta, G—vermilion, H—turquoise, I—pink, J—violet, K—green

## Instructions

1. Enlarge patterns according to instructions on page 19. Each pattern represents half. Broken lines indicate center. Each square equals 2 inches. Pattern A should measure 7 by 14 inches, and Pattern B should measure 8 by 16 inches.

2. Press fabric pieces.

3. Place carbon paper underneath patterns, face up, and trace over lines. Pattern now appears on back, in reverse. Tape Pattern A to vermilion fabric and Pattern B to magenta fabric with an allowance of 1 inch on the left, top, and bottom edges of each. Follow directions on page 16 for use of tracing wheel, pencil, and dressmaker's carbon. Trace hearts of Pattern A and shapes of Pattern B, omitting all inner shapes. Mark the center line above and below edge of

pattern. Trace all of the word *love* on Pattern B. Untape patterns. Tape reversed patterns to right side of fabric, lining up top and bottom edges and placing center line on marks. Trace as before.

4. Baste a layer of turquoise and then one of magenta to back of design A so that all hearts are covered from behind.

5. Refer to Pattern 7, steps 5 through 15, for reverse appliqué technique. Cut through the vermilion to reveal turquoise. Whip down edges. Save half the cutaway vermilion

**Pattern 69**

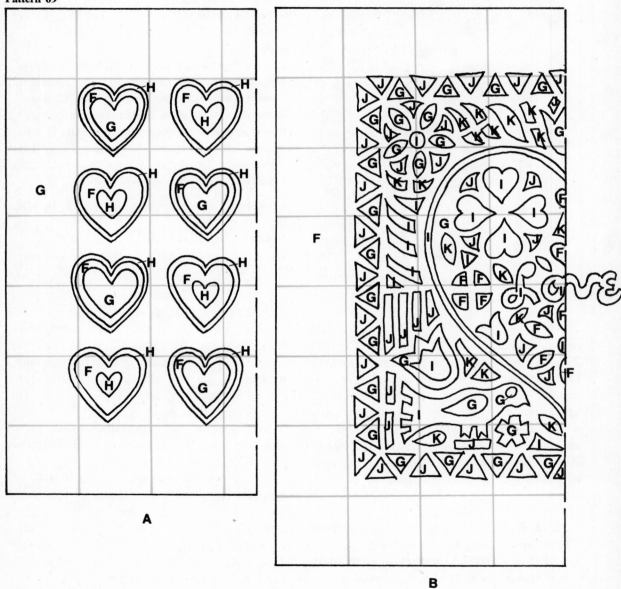

A

B

254

hearts. They will be used later.

6. With pencil, draw line within hearts on turquoise, about 3/16 inch from whipped edge. Snip out the turquoise hearts, leaving an allowance of ⅛ inch from drawn line. Save half these turquoise hearts. Whip down the turquoise edges to magenta.

7. Starting with the first heart, pin a cut vermilion heart to inside on magenta. Appliqué it in place with whip stitches. Continue this for third heart in row and second and fourth in next row. Repeat this for other two rows.

8. Starting with the second heart, pin a cut turquoise heart behind it. With pencil, draw a small heart that is about ¾ inch wide on the center of magenta. Do this for fourth heart in row and first and third in next row. Repeat this for other two rows.

9. Snip away center of drawn heart on magenta, leaving an allowance of ⅛ inch. Whip the edges to turquoise beneath. Design A is ready to be stretched.

10. Before starting design B, refer to Pattern 8, steps 4 through 10, for technique details. Work design B, pinning each piece one at a time. When completed, it is ready to be stretched.

11. Glue and staple tips of 12-inch balsa strips to edges of 14-inch strips, as shown in Diagram 141, to form a frame. Do same with 14-inch strips and 16-inch strips. Allow time for thorough drying.

12. Stretch and staple each design to appropriate balsa frame, stapling on reverse side and folding corners neatly. Refer to page 22 for tips on stretching.

13. Cut hearts from felt scraps. Vary the sizes from 2- to 3½-inches in width. Sew smaller hearts to larger hearts by hand or machine, or leave some or all plain. Make eight of these hearts.

14. Cut duplicate heart for each of the eight completed ones. Trace around each of eight hearts on buckram. Cut buckram hearts so that they are a tiny bit smaller than felt hearts.

15. Place each matching heart together with a buckram heart sandwiched in between. Sew edges together on sewing machine. Before sewing top of heart, place an end of ribbon or braid between layers at top of each heart. Continue to sew, making sure ribbon is secured.

16. Cut the ribbons to lengths varying from 8 to 13 inches. Staple upper ends to back of lower balsa edge of design B.

17. Cut five 3-inch lengths of ribbon or braid. Staple three of these to lower edge of design A and upper edge of design B to secure them together. The middle one should be at center and the other two equally distanced from corners. Form loops with the other two, and staple them to upper corners of design A.

18. Cut bias tape into four 14-inch lengths and four 16-inch lengths. Glue these to back of balsa frames, all around, to hide staples. The Love Token is now ready to hang by a window. Use nylon line or heavy thread to hang from upper window frame.

**Diagram 141**

# Getting
# Ideas for
# Appliqué

Where do ideas come from? This is a question that people often ask and every designer probably has a different answer for. Everyone has his own source of inspiration. I will try to give some idea of where I get my ideas.

## Environment

It is helpful, indeed, if you are fortunate enough to live in an area that provides inspiration. Some people find that a large city with good museums, libraries, and shops gives them the kind of stimulation they need. Others prefer to examine and explore nature—to study the textures of the landscape, the way leaves form patterns against the sky, or the network of veins within a single leaf. Close examination of the wildflowers in an alpine meadow may instill an exciting desire to try to depict a simplified version of nature. Trees whose barks have formed gnarled patterns from constant exposure to winds and storms and the cactuslike plants of the desert may be the source of inspiration for many abstract patterns.

It is always a good idea to carry a camera with you. No matter what it is that inspires you, it is helpful to take a picture of it. This way you'll be sure not to forget it.

Traveling abroad or anywhere else is always a stimulating experience for a designer. Instead of reserving your camera for photographing landscapes, buildings, and the usual landmarks that are seen, spend some of your time photographing interesting items in shop windows and markets. Most tourists love to shop, but since you couldn't possibly buy everything you admire, try to take pictures of the merchandise that inspires ideas.

## Fabric

Traveling is also a wonderful opportunity for fabric collectors. The street markets and bazaars of Mexico, Central and South America, and the Middle East offer huge supplies of fascinating fabrics. Europe also features many interesting fabric shops that are hard to resist. What sewing enthusiast can walk through the streets of an Austrian city without buying a few yards of dirndl fabric? European fabric shops have textiles you just can't find back home.

Even if your traveling is limited to a visit back to your home town, don't miss revisiting the fabric shops. Chances are that a few new ones have popped up in your absence. Every shop offers something you can't find in your own town. Fabric can certainly be a chief source of inspiration for appliqué.

You never know where you might find exciting fabrics. I dropped into a Navajo trading post in Shiprock, New Mexico, one day and was delighted to find a vivid array of calico prints that would have been the answer to a quilt maker's prayer. I had never before seen such an assortment of colors in so many small prints.

Be sure to make the rounds continually at your local shops. People often ask me, "Where do you buy your fabrics?" hoping I will name the one store that surpasses all others for one-stop shopping. But it is not that easy. Fabric shopping requires constant searching. Large shops will have dazzling displays, but sometimes a real gem is found in a very tiny shop. Remember that the fabric you use in your work can make it outstanding or just another mediocre needlecraft design.

Sometimes you may be inspired by things in the fabric shops other than fabric, such as trimmings. I am fortunate enough to live near an elaborate shop that sells nothing but a huge variety of trims, braids, and edgings. Just to enter the shop is immediate inspiration.

Fruits of Life developed as a result of a shopping event. Some bright-colored dotted Swiss and striped organdy were displayed near each other. I bought a bit of each with the idea in mind that I would do an overlapping floral pattern. Years later, when I finally got around to it, I created a fruit design, since the colors of the fabric were actually fruit colors. You may want to make it, too.

*Pattern 70: Wall Hanging*

# Fruits of Life

*(Technique 6)*

*This see-through hanging is for a window or translucent room divider. The dotted Swiss and striped organdy accent the texture of the fruit, but plain voile or organdy can be substituted for a similar effect. The nylon net background almost disappears so that the fruits appear to be floating in air. If you will be placing the hanging against clear glass, you may want to substitute white organdy for the net. This will obscure those objects on the other side of the glass that might interfere with the design.*

## Materials

1  nylon net rectangle, ¾ by 2 yards, in white, or
  2 yards organdy, in white
½ yard voile or organdy, in white
½ yard voile or organdy, in lemon yellow
½ yard voile or organdy, in orange
½ yard voile or organdy, in lime
½ yard voile or organdy, in cherry red
27 inches embroidery floss, in brown
thread in white
fabric glue
2 curtain sashes, extending to 24 inches, in white
1½ yards nylon line

**Completed size:** 24 by 68 inches
**Color code:** L—white net or organdy, M—white, N—lemon yellow, O—orange, P—lime, Q—cherry red

## Instructions

1. Enlarge pattern according to instructions on page 19. Each square equals 4 inches. Pattern should measure 24 by 68 inches.

2. Press all fabric pieces.

3. Tape fruit fabrics on top of pattern. Since fabrics are transparent, it is not necessary to use dressmaker's carbon. With pencil, lightly trace pieces. Cut out all pieces, allowing about 3/16 inch all around for turning under.

4. Tape net or organdy over pattern so that at least 1 inch of fabric surrounds edge of pattern. Position fruit shapes over it. Pin or baste shapes in place. You may find it easiest to position only a few pieces at a

time, working in six stages. Start with the underneath pieces first—white pineapple shape and green stalk. Now move on to yellow squares of pineapple, solid orange, and lemon; then solid lime, white circles of orange, and lemon cross sections; then segments of orange and lemon; then white circle of lime cross section, grapes, and banana; and last segments of lime, strawberries, and cherries.

5. Using whip stitches, as shown in Diagram 25, and turning under all edges, appliqué all fruits in place. Include side edges of those that touch edge of hanging.

6. Couch brown floss in place, as shown in Diagram 75, to form stems of cherries. Tape design over pattern for positioning of couched floss.

7. While design is still taped to pattern, trim at side edges on edge of pattern. Leave 1 inch on top and bottom edges. Be especially careful along the edges where the fruits touch so that no stitches are cut. If using organdy, trim 1 inch from edge all around.

8. Remove design from pattern and turn it over. Because the edges of the fruits along the edge of net hanging will be loose, they must be glued. Using fabric glue very sparingly, glue these turned-under edges to the net edge. If using organdy, hem under the side edges, creasing edge twice for a ½-inch hem.

9. Fold top and bottom edges under 1 inch, and press. On sewing machine, sew a slot about ⅜ inch from folded edges or whatever size is necessary to allow the sash rods to slide through with a snug fit.

10. Slip rods through slots. On top corners, tie a loop of nylon line through the two holes on ends of rods. Adjust length of line as desired for hanging.

## Files

All would-be designers should keep files of

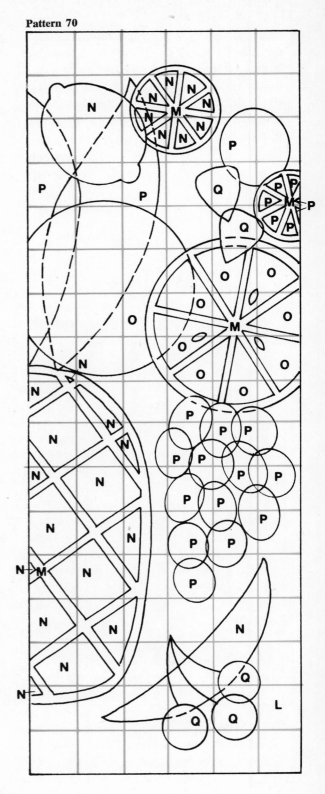

260

clippings they have come across. Magazines offer many ideas. Instead of limiting your clipping to recipes and coupons, snip out anything from a magazine that inspires you —a certain color scheme, a pattern-against-pattern interior, or any craft idea article. Keep them in a box until you have enough to start a filing system. Use a filing cabinet or an accordian file, and start separating your clippings into categories. Whenever you want an idea, thumb through your clip file and you will probably find something that will spark your imagination. I usually find that the simple act of clipping and filing leaves a residual image in my mind, which stays there until I have time to adapt it.

Don't forget to add other things to your files, such as those greeting cards you receive that are too nice to throw away. In fact, when you are card shopping for a friend, buy yourself a card that catches your eye and put it in your file. When you are wrapping a gift or if you have received one with exceptionally nice wrapping paper, cut a scrap of it for the file. Occasionally, even "junk mail" will reveal a nice design that can be snipped out and saved. Get into the habit of really seeing, and don't ignore anything that catches your eye. When you have a favorite print fabric, place a piece of it in your file along with the paper clippings.

Merchandise packages sometimes offer inspiring designs. When a product in the supermarket attracts your eye, don't ignore it. It might be the fresh start to a wonderful, new design.

## Books
Books are wonderful sources for ideas. If you can't afford to buy many of them, browse through the bookshops and look over the craft and applied art section. Books on many subjects other than needlework often provide stimulation for appliqué ideas.

Books on batik, fabric printing, paper cutting, poster art, folk art, architecture, Americana, and stained glass are just some examples of the kinds of books that can spark ideas. Make frequent trips to the library to look for inspiring books. If you don't want to take the book out, take advantage of the copy machine or make a sketch of it while you are there.

## Personal Interests
Some of your personal interests, and those of your family's, such as cooking and sports, may start influencing your designs. Make your son a quilt depicting his favorite toys and pastimes. Make your daughter a pillow or a wall hanging design of her favorite doll and clothes, pet, or a story.

At a needlework fair for which I was serving as a judge, I awarded a lovely piece of reverse appliqué that had been made as a joint effort by one family. The mother had done the needlework, but the father and children had designed it. The family was greatly interested in sailing. One member had designed the boat, another, the water, and another, the sky with clouds and sun. It was a charming representation of a whole family having fun together.

## Occasions
There are many occasions in life that warrant special celebrations—anniversaries, birthdays, weddings, just to name a few. Such occasions can be reasons for making special banners. A twenty-fifth wedding anniversary banner can be designed to depict events in the lives of the honored two. If it is made with special care, they will cherish it for the next twenty-five years to come. You might also want to make one quickly, just to add a festive atmosphere to the celebration.

Whether your wedding takes place in a church, under a tree in the park, or in your garden, think of the joy that can by emphasized by an array of colorful banners. Large or small, they become especially meaningful to the joined couple.

You may want to make a large banner to hang near your front door so that party guests will have no trouble finding the right house. Use banners to decorate your house or garden for the party.

If you are planning a community fund-raising event, get a bunch of workers in the organization to glue together some colorful banners. These will surely attract passers-by. They won't be able to resist coming in to see what is being offered.

Such banners do not have to be permanent works of art. Sometimes just the array of color is enough to add the right festive touch. They can be disposed of right after the event. They can also be made to use over and over again.

Today, many churches are encouraging their congregations to participate more in the liturgy. What better way is there for a group of needle enthusiasts to participate than to make special church adornments? Many churches are reviving the medieval custom of adorning the church with colorful banners. You might prefer to make a set of vestments or perhaps an altar frontal or altar cloth. Your particular religion will probably suggest its own symbols that can be used to adorn your place of worship.

## Encouraging Children

Something really delightful happens when children are given a bag of scraps, felt squares, leftover yarns, glue, thread, needles, and scissors. Two of the banners here were made by children. The patches for the Noah's Ark Banner were planned ahead to fit together, and the children were each as-

signed specific animals to make. They were allowed to design their own panel as they wished. Why not plan to do this banner with a class or any other group of children who like to keep their hands busy.

The Love-Peace-Joy Banner was not planned ahead of time. Thirty squares of felt were given to the children, and they chose the word they wanted to depict. This is an example of true freedom achieved through appliqué.

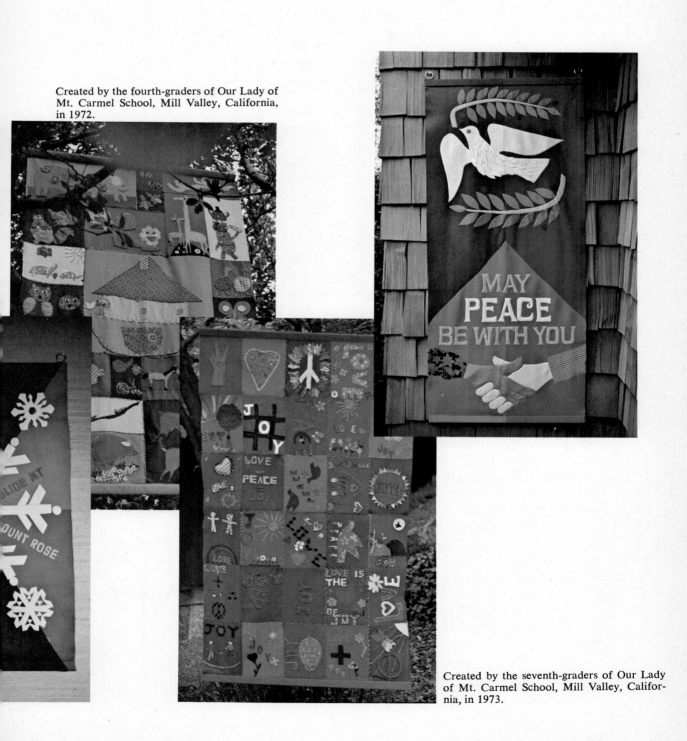

Created by the fourth-graders of Our Lady of Mt. Carmel School, Mill Valley, California, in 1972.

Created by the seventh-graders of Our Lady of Mt. Carmel School, Mill Valley, California, in 1973.

# Bibliography

Bacon, Lenice Ingram. *American Patchwork Quilts*. New York: William Morrow & Co., Inc., 1973.

Bauhof, Ellwood, and Chapin, Robert C., Jr. *Handmade Picture Frames from Simple Moldings*. Philadelphia: Countryside Press, 1971.

Bossert, Helmut Th. *Folk Art of Asia, Africa, and the Americas*. New York: Praeger Publishers, Inc., 1964.

————*Folk Art of Europe*. New York: Praeger Publishers, Inc., 1953.

Dean, Beryl. *Creative Appliqué*. New York: Watson-Guptill Publications, 1970.

————*Ideas for Church Embroidery*. Newton Centre, Mass.: Charles T. Branford Co., 1968.

Enciso, Jorge. *Design Motifs of Ancient Mexico*. New York: Dover Publications, Inc., 1947.

Gink, Karoly, and Kiss, Ivor Sander. *Folk Art and Folk Artists in Hungary*. New York: Hastings House, Publishers, Inc., 1972.

Hansen, H. J. *European Folk Art*. New York: McGraw-Hill Book Company, 1968.

Laliberte, Norman, and McIlhany, Sterling. *Banners and Hangings: Design and Construction*. New York: Van Nostrand Reinhold Co., 1966.

Laury, Jean Ray. *Appliqué Stitchery*. New York: Van Nostrand Rheinhold Co., 1966.

————*Quilts and Coverlets*. New York: Van Nostrand Reinhold Co., 1970.

Laury, Jean Ray, and Aikens, Joyce. *Handmade Rugs from Practically Anything*. Garden City, N.Y.: Doubleday and Co., Inc., 1972.

Leman, Bonnie. *Quick and Easy Quilting*. Great Neck, N.Y.: Hearthside Press, 1972.

Lewis, Alfred Allan. *The Mountain Artisans Quilting Book*. New York: Macmillan Publishing Co., 1973.

Lichten, Frances. *The Folk Art of Rural Pennsylvania*. New York: Charles Scribner's Sons, 1963.

Meilach, Dona Z., and Snow, L. Erlin. *Creative Stitchery*. Chicago: Reilly and Lee, 1970.

Rainey, Sarita R. *Wallhangings: Designing with Fabric and Thread*. Worcester, Mass.: Davis Publications, Inc., 1971.

Russell, Pat. *Lettering for Embroidery*. New York: Van Nostrand Reinhold Co., 1966.

Safford, Carleton, and Bishop, Robert. *America's Quilts and Coverlets*. New York: E. P. Dutton & Co., 1972.

Shears, Evangeline, and Fielding, Diantha. *Appliqué*. New York: Watson-Guptill Publications, 1972.

Svennas, Elsie. *Patchcraft: Design, Materials, Technique*. New York: Van Nostrand Reinhold Co., Inc., 1972.

Timmins, Alice. *Making Fabric Wall Hangings*. Newton Centre, Mass.: Charles T. Branford Co., 1970.

Vanderbilt, Gloria, and Lewis, Alfred A. *Gloria Vanderbilt Book of Collage*. New York: Van Nostrand Reinhold Co., 1970.

Wilson, Erica. *Erica Wilson's Embroidery Book*. New York: Charles Scribner's Sons, 1973.

Wood, Jane. *Selling What You Make*. Baltimore, Md.: Penguin Books Inc., 1973.